ROUTLEDGE LIBRARY EDITIONS: WELFARE AND THE STATE

Volume 4

I0130841

SOCIAL SECURITY: BEVERIDGE AND AFTER

SOCIAL SECURITY: BEVERIDGE AND AFTER

VICTOR GEORGE

R Routledge
Taylor & Francis Group

LONDON AND NEW YORK

First published in 1968 by Routledge and Kegan Paul Ltd
Reprinted in 1998 by Routledge

This edition first published in 2019
by Routledge
2 Park Square, Milton Park, Abingdon, Oxon OX14 4RN

and by Routledge
711 Third Avenue, New York, NY 10017

*Routledge is an imprint of the Taylor & Francis Group, an informa
business*

Trademark notice: Product or corporate names may be trademarks or
registered trademarks, and are used only for identification and
explanation without intent to infringe.

British Library Cataloguing in Publication Data
A catalogue record for this book is available from the British Library

ISBN: 978-1-138-61373-7 (Set)
ISBN: 978-0-429-45813-2 (Set) (ebk)
ISBN: 978-1-138-60119-2 (Volume 4) (hbk)
ISBN: 978-1-138-60121-5 (Volume 4) (pbk)
ISBN: 978-0-429-47026-4 (Volume 4) (ebk)

Publisher's Note
The publisher has gone to great lengths to ensure the quality of this
reprint but points out that some imperfections in the original copies
may be apparent.

Disclaimer
The publisher has made every effort to trace copyright holders and
would welcome correspondence from those they have been unable to
trace.

SOCIAL SECURITY:
BEVERIDGE AND AFTER

by

V. GEORGE

ROUTLEDGE

First published in 1968 by
Routledge and Kegan Paul Ltd

Reprinted in 1998 by
Routledge
11 New Fetter Lane, London EC4P 4EE

Printed and bound in Great Britain

© 1968 V. George

The publishers have made every effort to contact authors/copyright holders
of the works reprinted in *The International Library of Sociology*.
This has not been possible in every case, however, and we would
welcome correspondence from those individuals/companies
we have been unable to trace.

British Library Cataloguing in Publication Data
A CIP catalogue record for this book
is available from the British Library

Social Security
ISBN 0-415-17723-5
Public Policy, Welfare and Social Work: 18 Volumes
ISBN 0-415-17831-2
The International Library of Sociology: 274 Volumes
ISBN 0-415-17838-X

FOREWORD

SOME years ago I expressed the view that the Welfare State in Britain had become a hotchpotch of administrative units, a tangle of legislative complexity and a jungle of vested interests. I regret to say that I still hold this view, and it seems to me that we are in great danger of making our social services so complicated as to be unintelligible even to well-educated citizens. Social security, which is one of our major social services, is now so elaborate and complex that not many of us can fully understand the benefits it provides and the obligations and duties it imposes on us. I am, therefore, delighted that Mr. Victor George has undertaken the task of analysing and describing the system of social security in this country in such an interesting and readable manner.

One of the main problems facing anyone who attempts to write about social security is where to begin. Most writers have adopted an historical approach tracing the evolution of social security through the hundreds of years since the Poor Law was first enacted. Much as I approve of the view that to understand the present we need to know the past, the explosion in the growth of knowledge in modern times requires specialisation of topics within fields of study. I am glad therefore that Mr. George has concentrated on the development of social security in this country since the publication of the Beveridge report.

Now that our system of Social Security has been administratively unified within the Ministry of Social Security it is appropriate that an examination should be made of the extent to which the original proposals of Lord Beveridge have been modified over time. There are many ways in which such an examination could have been made and the results recorded. For example, each new act or regulation could have been dissected in great detail and the results laboriously and drearily recorded for us to read. Mr. George has avoided this pitfall and instead has adopted an interesting functional approach which brings out clearly and concisely the essential principles and elements in this complicated field of social provision.

Foreword

I am sure that students and the general reader will find this book to be of real value, and despite the fact that social legislation changes so rapidly these days, it will continue to provide a firm foundation for an understanding of social security for some time ahead.

DAVID C. MARSH

INTRODUCTION

THIS book is concerned with the development of social security in this country from the Beveridge Report onwards and it is aimed mainly at social science students and social work students. References to the 1930's and earlier or to social security provisions in other countries are made with the sole intention of illuminating the events that make up the central theme of the book. Broadly, the book examines first the recommendations of the Beveridge Report and how and why they were or were not implemented in the immediate post-war years; second the development of social security during the 20-year period covered by the book; and third it attempts briefly to look at some of the possible changes in social security in the future. The general problems affecting all social security benefits, e.g. their scope as regards persons, risks and level of benefits, the administrative machinery and the financial considerations, are discussed in the first four chapters. Individual social security benefits are discussed in chapters five to twelve. An attempt is made to discuss these benefits in relation to other related social services and to occupational fringe benefits. Inevitably I had to look at the details of social security legislation and at the extent to which benefits have been used by the general public. This necessitated some detailed discussion and the presentation of statistical information which some readers may find rather heavy going. The final chapter examines briefly the current discussion on the role of the state in social security provision.

I am indebted to Professor D. C. Marsh who encouraged me to write the book and who read the manuscript and made valuable suggestions; to Mr B. Hughes, of the Ministry of Social Security, who also read the manuscript and helped me with some of the recent changes in social security legislation; and to my wife, Enid George, who typed the manuscript and whose forbearance and constant criticism have been invaluable to me.

V. GEORGE

The University, Nottingham, September, 1967

vii

CONTENTS

ix

Contents

LIST OF TABLES

List of Tables

List of Tables

Chapter One

SOCIAL SECURITY

SOCIAL security is a new concept and it represents society's current answer to the problem of economic insecurity. It has evolved out of previous methods used to deal with the same problem. A number of textbooks have been written charting this slow evolution and it is not the aim of this work to repeat these events.[1] The story will instead be taken up from the 1930's because this period is most important in the evolution of social security.

Social security as an evolutionary stage in man's attempts to deal with economic insecurity was born out of the economic depression of the early 1930's. It was in fact an outcome of the realisation that government social policies in all the advanced societies, let alone the underdeveloped, were inadequate in guaranteeing to all citizens a decent standard of living. The existing methods of national insurance and public assistance had failed to cope with the problem because firstly they were sectional in scope and shallow in depth and secondly because they were dealing with the effect rather than the cause of the malaise. Social services providing financial benefits of one form or another can only be meaningful if the benefits they provide are adequate in amount for what is currently considered a decent standard of living; if they cover the whole population and all the economic risks of the industrial system; and if they are backed by other social services which aim at preventing and curing large scale distress. None of these conditions existed in any country in the early 1930's. Payment of insurance and assistance allowances was erroneously considered as an alternative to social and economic planning in the fields of employment and health.

Leaving out underdeveloped countries, the reaction of govern-

[1] W. Robson (Ed.) *Social Security*, 3rd Ed., Allen & Unwin, 1948. D. C. Marsh, *National Insurance and Assistance in Gt. Britain*, Pitman, 1950. B. G. Gilbert, *The Evolution of National Insurance in Great Britain*, Michael Joseph, 1966.

ments to this new realisation varied depending, *inter alia*, upon the particular political situation existing in the country and the country's economic development. It is true that all democratically elected governments are under constant pressure from the electorate to extend the scope of their social services but the response of governments can vary according to their political philosophy. It is interesting that the countries which took the first hesitant steps towards social security at this time were under left wing governments. The Social Reform Act, 1933, of the Social Democratic Government in Denmark codified, simplified and extended previous social insurance and assistance legislation. The Social Security Act, 1935, passed by the Roosevelt administration in the U.S.A. was the first official use of the term social security though the provisions of the Act were limited. The Labour Government's social security Act, 1938, in New Zealand provided the most comprehensive interpretation of social security at that time.[1]

It is difficult to imagine what progress or what course this new movement would have taken had it not been for the intervention of the Second World War. It is generally accepted that the war provided the best conditions for the extension of government services. People were more willing to accept government intervention, they were less likely to oppose the raising of more state revenue and they were more prepared to forget their social class differences. In many of the advanced countries fighting against Nazism, the desire for social security became identified in the minds of the people with the better world they were fighting for. National and international official pronouncements encouraged this belief. Article V of the Atlantic Charter, 1940, declared that the objectives of post-war economic policies of member governments of the United Nations should be to assist each other to secure 'for all, improved labour standards, economic advancement and social security'. President Roosevelt's speech of 4 January 1941, promised a post-war world 'founded upon four essential freedoms' had a great impact not only in the United States but in Europe as well.

Government preparations for social security schemes started early in the war. In June 1941, the coalition government of this

[1] For a discussion on the relationship between political structure and social security, see 'Political Structure, Economic Development, and National Social Security Programs', Phillips Cutright, *American Journal of Sociology,* Vol. LXX No. 5, March 1965.

country appointed an inter-departmental committee under the chairmanship of Sir William Beveridge 'To undertake, with special reference to the interrelation of the schemes, a survey of the existing national schemes of national insurance and allied services, including workmen's compensation, and to make recommendations'. In July of the same year the Menzies government in Australia appointed a Commonwealth Joint Parliamentary Committee on Social Security. The Beveridge report was published a year later,[1] the same year as Dr L. Marsh's equally important report for social security reform in Canada, and one year before the publication in the United States of the National Resources Planning Board Plan. The impact of the war on the reforming spirit of these reports is shown in the tone of the last paragraph of the Beveridge report. 'The Plan for social security in this Report is submitted by one who believes that in this supreme crisis the British people will not be found wanting, of courage and faith and national unity, of material and spiritual power to play their part in achieving both social security and the victory of justice among nations upon which security depends.'

The war not only stepped up the tempo of the developments for social security but it also affected the very nature of the concept of social security. Whereas before the war plans were put forward piecemeal to deal with individual problems such as sickness, unemployment or old age, the trend now was to plan comprehensively in depth and breadth. Social security plans (Beveridge, Marsh plan, etc.) were designed to provide adequate protection to the entire population for the whole range of risks of the economic system. In addition, social security was only one of the many social services that were deemed necessary to stimulate national prosperity. In this way social security was 'conceived in positive and creative terms rather than as merely fending off misery or destitution by money payments'.[2]

This trend towards comprehensive social security planning found expression in two international events. The 26th Session of the International Labour Conference in Philadelphia in 1944 adopted two recommendations dealing with social security: Income Security and Medical Care. 'The Income Security Recommendation has had a marked impact since it was the first

---

[1] 'Social Insurance and Allied Services' Cmd. 6404, 1942.
[2] Evidence of the Fabian Society to the Beveridge Committee.

major international instrument to view social security as an integral whole made up of various programmes formerly treated separately.'[1] The Declaration of Philadelphia included 'the extension of social security measures to provide a basic income to all in need of such protection and comprehensive medical care.' The second event, though of not the same importance but equally indicative, was the change in 1947 of the name of the International Social Insurance Conference to the International Social Security Association.

The war also affected the motivation behind social security legislation. This was a reflection of the emerging philosophy concerning the role in general of social policy. The traditional view was that social policy should deal with problems of minority groups, i.e., education and housing for the poor, social insurance for the low income groups, public assistance for the worthy needy, etc. It was a negative role which was considered bad business for the state. The less time and money the state spent on these services the better. Excessive government intervention would only undermine the independence (whatever this term may mean) of the people. This view of social policy has not altogether vanished yet as Professor Titmuss reminds us, 'There are today those at one end of the political spectrum who see social policy as a transitory minimum activity of minimum government for a minimum number of poor people.'[2] The new concept of social policy envisaged the provision of social services, universal and non-discriminatory in character. The ultimate aim of social policy should be to enable the maximum self-fulfilment of the maximum number of citizens. Social policy in this sense is a necessary prerequisite to national growth and prosperity. We know today that the claims made for universality and non-discrimination were over-optimistic. The fact that social services are equally accessible to all sections of the community does not mean that they will make equal use of them or, when they do, they will benefit equally from them.

The general agreement on the desirability of social security that was evident during the last war and which still prevails today has not been matched by a corresponding agreement on the definition

[1] R. Myers and W. Yoffee, 'Social Security Issues: Fiftieth International Labor Conference', *Social Security Bulletin*, Vol. 29 No. 11, November 1966.
[2] Prof. R. M. Titmuss, 'The Role of Redistribution in Social Policy', *S.S. Bulletin*, Vol. 28, No. 6, June 1965. See also Chapter XII.

of social security. The International Labour Organisation which has done very valuable work in this field had to declare in 1949 that 'there does not yet exist an internationally accepted definition of social security'[1] and in 1961 that 'the concept of social security varies greatly from country to country'.[2] This is understandable in a way because of the differential social and economic development of societies in different parts of the world. The need for economic protection is universal but the risks against which protection is deemed necessary and the methods adopted to protect against these risks are far from uniform. 'Social legislation by definition can conceive of the basic universal needs of the individual only in the form of the specific needs of the society of which he is part, with the result that a national social security scheme becomes a specific instrument catering for specific needs of a particular society and reflecting its socio-economic situation.'[3] On the other hand these differences must not be exaggerated. Admittedly there are differences among the legislatures of various countries but there are also similarities which outweigh the differences in a large number of cases. The situation is not as hopeless as it appears at first sight and there is every reason to believe that this concensus of opinion will grow as more nations become industrialised and as the standards for social security laid down by the I.L.O. gain international acceptance.

The numerous definitions of social security can be grouped under two broad headings: the specific and the philosophic. One of the best known exponents of the specific approach is the Beveridge Report. 'The term social security is used here to denote the securing of an income to take the place of earnings when they are interrupted by unemployment, sickness or accident, to provide for retirement through age, to provide against loss of support by the death of another person, and to meet exceptional expenditures, such as those concerned with birth, death and marriage.'[4] Defined in this way, social security is equivalent to income maintenance, i.e., to provide cash benefits to meet certain specified contingencies. Qualified support for this view comes from an American expert who considers the central function of social

---

[1] 'Systems of Social Security, New Zealand', I.L.O. p. iii, 1949.
[2] 'The Cost of Social Security, 1949–1957', I.L.O. p. 2., 1961.
[3] Vladimir Rys, 'Comparative Studies of Social Security', *Bulletin of I.S.S.A.*, Vol. XIX, No. 7–8, p. 249, July–August 1966.
[4] Ibid., p. 120.

security to be 'the provision of a cash income to individuals and families in designated sectors of the population under specified conditions'.[1] This rightly implies that though different countries have added other benefits to this list, it is universally accepted that it covers either all or some of the benefits of social security. No known definition has excluded the benefits listed by the Beveridge Report. A close look at the benefits suggested in that Report, however, reveals some interesting inconsistencies. Family allowances for children were not considered part of social security but one of the three basic services – the other two being Health and Full Employment – which were a necessary prerequisite to social security. Child tax allowances which exceed the cost of family allowances were not considered at all. This was partly explained by administrative reasons – family allowances were to be provided by the Ministry of Social Security while child tax allowances were not. It was also due to the traditional view that benefits whose provision depended partly on achievement were not considered part of the social services. This remnant of the poor law philosophy still exists today and tends to exaggerate the benefits which the poorer sections of the community receive from the social services and vice-versa underestimates the benefits of the wealthier section. It is very important to bear this in mind when the redistributive role of social security and the social services is discussed.

Britain is unique in restricting social security to income maintenance. All other countries include at least medical care. The definitions used by I.L.O. fall in this category. 'Social security measures include those which in virtue of legislation provide: a basic income in case of inability to work (including old age), inability to obtain remunerative work or the death of a bread-winner; assistance for dependent children and comprehensive medical care.'[2] The majority of American and Canadian definitions also fall in this group. Dr Marsh's report on Canadian social security gave three contingencies to be covered by social security. '1. Interruptions of earnings, due to unemployment, sickness, permanent disability, old age, premature death; 2. Occasions requiring expenditure which strains the family budget, such as

[1] Ida C. Merriam "The Relations of Social Security and Social Welfare Services' *Bulletin of I.S.S.A.* Vol. XV, Nos. 3–4, March–April, pp. 5–6, 1962.
[2] *Systems of Social Security, New Zealand*, p. v.

medical care and funeral costs; 3. Insufficiency of income to meet the cost of child maintenance.'[1] The obvious reason for including medical care within social security is that, with the exception of Britain, medical care is partly or wholly linked with social insurance. There is nothing unique about medical care which distinguishes it from education, for example, and thus qualifies it to be part of social security. This extension complicates the issue because all the other benefits are in cash while medical care is a benefit in kind. It opens the door first to many other social services, unrelated to social insurance, which provide benefits of a kind that have a 'welfare' connotation, i.e., services for minority groups, and secondly to general government services concerned with economic development. In the end social security becomes another grandiose term for social and economic policy.

Beveridge's definition has been criticised in this country and abroad as being too narrow. 'Social security to me has meant not merely a system of preventing people from dying of starvation, but a system which will assure people a full life; a system which will embrace health, education, leisure and culture – all those things, as well as what we have always fought for, food, shelter and a medical service.'[2] Beveridge replied to these criticisms by pointing out that his plan was only 'part of a general programme of social policy. It is one part only of an attack upon five giant evils: upon the physical Want with which it is directly concerned, upon Disease which often causes that Want and brings many other troubles in its train, upon Ignorance which no democracy can afford among its citizens, upon the Squalor which arises mainly through haphazard distribution of industry and population, and upon the Idleness which destroys wealth and corrupts men, whether they are well or not, when they are idle.'[3] Obviously Beveridge used the term social policy where others used social security. This is made quite clear by one of the exponents of the philosophic approach to social security. 'Social security is a social objective – a social ideal. It envisages a structure of society in which each member enjoys the highest material well-being compatible with potential productive resources. Pathological

[1] 'Social Security in Canada', *International Labour Review*, Vol. 47, No. 5, May 1943.
[2] Mrs Ridleagh, 2nd Reading of National Insurance Bill, House of Commons, 6 February, 1946.
[3] Beveridge Report, p. 170.

social conditions – continuous mass unemployment, unnecessary ill health, and accidents – cannot be reconciled with social security. Social security is an ephemeral myth until such cancers are removed. The mere palliative provision of cash benefits is not enough. Consequently, social security is a positive concept, and this view of social security must be considered the basic and ultimate approach when more specific and limited aspects of social security are discussed.'[1] Fundamentally there is complete agreement between the two seemingly opposing views. The difference between them is a matter of semantics and not of substance.

The main exponent of the Philosophic approach is Pierre Laroque, President of the National Social Security Fund in France. He regards the increasing acceptance of social security today as 'a stage in general social development'. Legislation on social security today is going through a 'transitional' phase between the old forms of assistance and insurance and the modern forms of social security. What does social security stand for? 'It represents a guarantee by the whole community to all its members of the maintenance of their standard of living or at least of tolerable living conditions, by means of a redistribution of incomes based upon national solidarity.'[2] No one can argue against these sentiments. They are accepted by all the writers on social security. But what really is social security? It is a combination of three separate trends. 'It is, first of all, an economic policy aimed at full employment. Secondly, it is a medical policy, one of equipment and organisation for the struggle against disease, including both preventive action and the best possible treatment; as a natural counterpart of this it is also a technical policy for the prevention of industrial accidents and occupational diseases. Social security is, thirdly, a policy of income distribution aimed at modifying the results of the blind interplay of economic forces and at adapting the income of each individual and each family to that individual's or family's needs, having regard to all the circumstances which may affect such income in the future.'[3] The specific approach will accept only the third component of

[1] S. Eckler 'Modern Social Security Plans and Unemployment', *International Labour Review*. Vol. 48, No. 5, November, 1943.

[2] P. Laroque 'Social Security and Social Development', *Bulletin of I.S.S.A.* Vol. XIX, Nos. 3–4, March–April, 1966.

[3] P. Laroque, 'From Social Insurance to Social Security', *International Labour Review*, Vol. 57, No. 6, June 1948.

Laroque's definition as part of social security and will consider the other two as necessary prerequisite conditions. An even broader approach to social security is shown in the statistical reports of the Nordic countries.[1] Social security expenditure covers seven broad areas of government activity. I. Health, i.e., sickness insurance cash benefits, public health, and medical treatment. II. Occupational injuries and workers' protection. III. Old age and disability, i.e., cash benefits, rehabilitation services and housing. IV. Expenditure on employment and unemployment services. V. Family welfare, i.e., ante-natal and post-natal care for mothers, day nurseries and nursery schools, child family and child tax allowances, child protection, school meals, school health services, home-help service, marriage loans, rent subsidies to families with children, and holidays for housewives and children. VI. Public assistance and VII. Relief to military or war casualties. Such a diverse array of services renders the concept of social security too unwieldy for meaningful discussion.

This lack of agreement has led Mr Altmeyer to make a special plea for the use of the term in a 'restricted' rather than an 'expansive' sense.[2] Similarly the I.L.O., having given up the idea of a definition that would be internationally acceptable, formulated three criteria that had to be satisfied before a scheme or service could be considered part of the national social security system. These were: '1. The objective of the system must be to grant curative or preventive medical care, or to maintain income in case of involuntary loss of earnings or of an important part of earnings, or to grant supplementary incomes to persons having family responsibilities. 2. The system must have been set up by legislation which attributes specified individual rights to, or which impose specified obligations on, a public, semi-public or autonomous body. 3. The system should be administered by a public, semi-public or autonomous body.'[3] The third criterion is not always necessary as the I.L.O. itself concedes. Certainly it would exclude contracted-out wage-related retirement pensions in this country and other schemes in the U.S.A.[4]

---

[1] 'Social Security in the Nordic Countries', Oslo, 1965.
[2] A. J. Altmeyer, *The Formative Years of Social Security*, p. 6, University of Wisconsin Press, 1966.
[3] *The Cost of Social Security*, p. 2, I.L.O. ibid.
[4] 'Social Security Programs Throughout the World 1967' *U.S. Dept. of Health, Education & Welfare*, New York, 1967.

Social Security is used here in the specific sense of income maintenance discussed in the Beveridge Report with one slight modification. Family allowances are considered part of social security and not a basic assumption of it. The only possible reason for excluding it from the collective social security benefits is that it is a non-contributory benefit granted to all without reference to insurance. This argument, however, betrays a confusion between social security and national insurance. Social security is the objective while national insurance is the means of achieving that objective. Other countries have employed different means with equal success in achieving the same objective. For the same reason national assistance and redundancy payments are part of social security even if they are financed by the state and the employers respectively.

The use of the term social security in the specific sense in no way belittles the importance of the other social and economic services closely related to it. As mentioned several times so far, social security can only function in advanced societies where a comprehensive system of social and economic services are also in existence. This condition, however, is of primary importance to social security but it is not in any way limited to it. A system of compulsory and free primary and secondary education together with free higher education cannot function properly in a society with large-scale chronic unemployment and underemployment. Similarly, a comprehensive free health service will not be attempted, let alone succeed, in societies with extensive illiteracy. All social and economic services depend on one another and they tend to go forward as integral parts of social policy and not as isolated and unrelated services. Some of these services, however, are basic and others are ancillary.

The aim of social security in this country has altered since the Beveridge Report. Its aim then was to offer universal protection against poverty, to ensure that no one fell in destitution. Today it is proceeding beyond that stage. It still retains that aim but it also aims at providing a safeguard against the loss of an acquired standard of living. It does not content itself with providing uniform benefits adequate for a basic standard of living but extends further to provide differentiated allowances which reflect the wage-structure and at the same time attempt to safeguard it. In spite of considerable progress social security in this and other countries is still bedevilled by excessive emphasis on 'insurance' and the 'ninepence for four pence' mentality.[1] The statement made 25 years ago that social security could only prosper when all citizens are 'convinced that they may have to pay ninepence but only get fourpence in some circumstances, while in other circumstances they may pay twopence and get a shilling' is as true today as it was then.[2]

---

[1] Under the National Insurance Act, 1911, the weekly contribution of 9d was made up of 4d paid by the employee, 3d by the employer and 2d by the State. The supporters of the scheme contended that the insured would get 'ninepence for fourpence',

[2] *Planning* P.E.P., No. 190, 14, July 1942.

Chapter Two

THE SCOPE OF SOCIAL SECURITY

SOCIAL security schemes of industrialised societies, whether capitalist or socialist, tend to be comprehensive both as regards the people covered and the risks against which protection is provided. As it was shown in the last chapter, social security must be comprehensive if it is to be of any real meaning to the people. This completeness and indivisibility of social security is indicative of the changes in political philosophy that have taken place during the last sixty years regarding the role of the state vis-à-vis the well-being of its citizens. In this country, it is now accepted dogma that the state must offer economic protection to all its members irrespective of sex, age, class, religion, race or other minority traits. This chapter examines the historical development from partial to complete coverage, the groups of people covered by social security and the various risks against which protection is afforded.

History

The poor law system provided by poor law authorities was in one sense comprehensive: Relief was granted to all who were deemed to be in need. In real practice, however, the method of selection of those in need was so cruel and capricious that more people were excluded than included. The benefits provided were either so inadequate or so degrading that even those who had to be assisted enjoyed nothing like full or decent economic protection. In essence the aim of public assistance was to repel rather than relieve people from distress. Poverty was tantamount to crime and legislation for combating crime was often similar to legislation dealing with poverty. Finally this assistance was provided to a person by his more prosperous neighbours, at first those who lived in the same parish and as from 1834 by those living in the same union. It was not a national but a local system. The relief of distress through local relief schemes was so discredited that the use of national schemes and especially of insurance was received with universal acclaim as the only decent, respectable methods of state protection against economic insecurity.[1]

The first national scheme was the provision of old age pensions. The 1908 Old Age Pensions Act provided state non-contributory pensions to people over the age of 70 who satisfied certain conditions: Their annual income should not exceed a certain maximum; those with incomes below a fixed minimum were paid the full pension while those whose incomes fell between the fixed minimum and maximum received proportions of the pension. There were also certain moral clauses regarding the conduct of the recipients which were designed to allay the fears of those who saw in universal pensions an undermining of individual responsibility. It was a compromise Act – a venture into a new form of state provision for economic insecurity with a number of peace formulae to appease the traditional exponents of laissez-faire. The full pension of 5s. which the Act provided was not adequate for the necessary weekly expenditure, even excluding rent, to keep people above the primary poverty line as set out in Rowntree's survey in York. During its first years in operation the Act covered two-thirds of people over the age of 70 and gradually it was extended to most of the others until a contributory scheme was introduced under the Widows' Orphans' and Old Age Contributory Pensions Act, 1925. This Act provided contributory pensions for almost all widows, orphans and old people.

It was, however, the National Insurance Act, 1911, that set the precedent for future legislation in this field in this country. Unlike the 1908 Act it provided contributory benefits for sickness and unemployment and it was completely divorced from any moral conditions. It was an insurance Act in the sense that employed persons paid contributions together with their employers and the state and in return they received benefits when they were off work on account of illness or unemployment provided they satisfied certain insurance conditions. The element of eligibility was still

---

[1] 'If I had my way I would write the word "Insure" over the door of every cottage, and upon the blotting book of every public man, because I am convinced that by sacrifices which are inconceivably small, which are all within the power of the very poorest man in regular work, families can be secured against catastrophes which would otherwise smash them up for ever.' W. S. Churchill, *Liberalism and the Social Problem*, pp. 315–316.

present but its main criterion was insurance record rather than morality. It introduced what was considered at the time a revolutionary contractual relationship between the individual, his employer and the state. All three were equal partners in the scheme and each had to fulfil its contractual obligations for the smooth running of the scheme. At the same time the prominence given to the insurance principle, understandable though it was, created the myth which still persists today that beneficiaries have paid for their benefits. It has also overshadowed the fact that insurance benefits can be too high for some individuals or too low for others as they do not take account of the individual's financial position.

The number of people insured by the Act against sickness was far greater than those insured against unemployment. Sickness insurance covered all manual workers whatever their income and those non-manual workers whose annual income did not exceed a certain amount. Initially sickness insurance covered only three-quarters of all persons engaged in some form of work. Unemployment insurance covered manual workers in seven selected trades which were most susceptible to unemployment. The high rate of unemployment and underemployment that prevailed in many occupations made unemployment insurance almost impossible for them. The scope of unemployment insurance was gradually extended so that by 1938 it covered almost as many persons as sickness insurance. Briefly, it is true to say that by 1938 the coverage of social insurance schemes was almost complete as regards persons and fairly extensive with regard to risks.

TABLE I

NUMBER OF PERSONS INSURED IN GREAT BRITAIN

Year	Unemployment	Sickness	Widows, Orphans and Old Age
1914	2,500,000	13,689,000	—
1921	11,081,000	15,165,000	—
1926	11,774,000	16,375,000	17,089
1931	12,500,000	17,353,000	18,513
1936	14,580,000	18,081,000	19,651
1938	15,395,000	19,706,000	20,678

Source: Beveridge Report, p. 213.

The Beveridge Report, the White Paper of the Coalition

Government on Social Insurance[1] and the National Insurance Act (1946) of the Labour Government were in complete agreement that the gaps in the scope of social insurance should be filled and the groups of people excluded because they were covered by occupational schemes should be brought into the state scheme. In the words of the White Paper comprehensiveness, one of Beveridge's six basic principles of social insurance, was an expression of 'the solidarity and unity of the nation, which in war have been its bulwark against aggression and in peace will be its guarantee of success in the fight against individual want and mischance.' (p. 6). The unifying influence of the war on social policies is unmistakable. Mr James Griffiths, the Minister of National Insurance, considered clause 1 of the National Insurance Bill that defined its comprehensiveness 'an epoch-making document'.[2] To those who demanded special exemption because they were protected by occupational schemes superior to those proposed in the National Insurance Bill, he replied that 'There will be no adjustment in our Bill; it is one Bill for everybody in the country.'[2] There was complete agreement among M.P.s of all parties on this.

This unanimous acceptance of universality was defended on ethical, practical and actuarial grounds, succinctly expressed in the White Paper. Firstly, 'in a matter so fundamental it is right for all citizens to stand in together, without exclusions based upon difference of status, function or wealth'. This is a far cry from the 19th century doctrines which regarded poverty as the fault of the individual, completely divorced from the faults of the economic system. 'Secondly, that there are many people at present outside the scope of national insurance whose need of its benefits is at least as great as that of many of the insured population.' Mr Griffiths stated in the debate on the second reading of the National Insurance Bill that one-third of the letters received at his Ministry on social insurance were complaints from people left out of insurance schemes. The National Insurance Act, 1946, extended the scope of insurance schemes to five more population groups. The non-manual workers whose income was above the limit – £420 p.a. in 1942 – required for inclusion in the sickness and

[1] 'Social Insurance', Part I, Cmd. 6550, September, 1944.
[2] 2nd Reading of the National Insurance Bill, House of Commons, 6 February, 1946.

unemployment insurance schemes. The rather privileged groups – civil servants, local government officers and similar employees – who were substantially free from some of the risks covered by the National Insurance Act and who enjoyed better benefits from their own occupational insurance schemes. The small groups of people, such as domestic servants, who though exposed to the risks were not covered. All the early social insurance schemes in all countries excluded the self-employed and the non-employed. They were now brought within the scope of the Act. It is doubtful whether the first two groups and many of the self-employed and non-employed benefited very much, if anything at all, from their drafting into the state scheme. Nevertheless, Mr Griffiths felt that it was right that 'sectional interests are abolished in order to serve the general interests'.[1] 'Thirdly, that without universality it is not possible adequately to maintain the cover needed during various normal changes from insurance class to class.'[2] The White Paper here expressed one of the fundamentals of insurance schemes, i.e., the pooling of risks which is essential to the success of such insurance schemes. In Churchill's words insurance's great asset is 'bringing the magic of averages nearer to the rescue of the millions'.[3]

The Family Allowances scheme introduced under the Family Allowances Act, 1945, was also universal in scope. It provided a weekly allowance for every child in the family, excepting the first, under school age. The possibility of a scheme restricted to certain income groups was considered and rejected. It was generally felt that the amount saved would have been so negligible by any reasonable income limit that it was not worth serious consideration. Moreover as family allowances were taxable, the Exchequer would get back a portion of them from wealthy parents.

The Insured Population

Though the entire population was to be covered in one way or another it was to be treated differently for contributions and benefits purposes. The Beveridge Report classified the population into six groups to take into account 'the different ways of life of

[1] 2nd Reading of the National Insurance Bill, House of Commons, 6 February, 1946.
[2] 'Social Insurance', p. 11.
[3] W. S. Churchill, *The Second World War*, Cassell, Vol. IV, p. 862.

different sections of the Community' (p. 122). This classification was accepted by the White Paper and the National Insurance Act, 1946. Groups V and VI were those below and above working age respectively. The first would be covered by contributions paid by their parents while the latter would be insured by contributions which they made during working age. We need only examine in detail here the four other population groups, i.e. those of working age. Class I, the employees, i.e., those who depend for their livelihood on the remuneration they receive under contract with an employer. They constitute the largest group and they are entitled to the whole range of benefits provided by the Act. Their weekly contributions are supplemented by an equal amount from their employers. All three insurance classes receive subsidies from the state. Class II, others gainfully employed, i.e., the self-employed. They were treated differently from Class I in two ways: firstly, they had to bear the contribution cost themselves as they had no employer to share it with and secondly they were not entitled to unemployment benefit. Initially the Labour Government laid down stiffer conditions for their entitlement to sickness benefit. Public pressure, from Labour M.P.s in particular, during the debates on the National Insurance Bill, forced the Government to change its mind and to allow the self-employed sickness benefit on the same conditions as the employed. Their exclusion from unemployment benefit was widely accepted as necessary because it was thought that it would be difficult to ascertain when they were unemployed as their income was not related directly to particular days of work. 'The income of a farmer, a shopkeeper or a business manager may come at any time; how busy or how active he is on a particular day is largely within his own control'.[1] Ironically it was the Liberal Leader who argued strongly in the second reading of the National Insurance Bill (6 August, 1946) that there should be no distinction between the employed and the self-employed. Mr Butler, for the Conservatives, had also mild misgivings but they were of a different kind. He was sceptical whether in many cases the provisions of the Bill would be 'worthwhile' for them. In spite of the general belief that the self-employed would benefit from the new arrangements, they were not over-anxious to join the scheme. By May 1948 only 354,000[2]

[1] Beveridge Report, p. 54.
[2] *The Economist* 15 May, 1948.

applications for National Insurance cards were received at the Ministry from self-employed and non-employed persons which was only a small proportion of their actual numbers. Self-employed contributions made up 6·3% of the total number of contributions in 1950 and 5·7% in 1965. The decline was completely in women self-employed persons.

This differential treatment of self-employed persons has never been questioned seriously and it was accepted also by the 1959 National Insurance Act which provided graduated retirement pensions. An editorial of the *Manchester Guardian* (25 October, 1958) argued strongly that the National Insurance Act 1959 should include the self-employed in spite of the practical difficulties involved. For technical and administrative reasons the data of the Inland Revenue would not be adequate for insurance purposes without a great deal of extra work and expense. Because of these practical difficulties involved in assessing the annual income of the self-employed accurately and speedily the suggestion was to allow the self-employed to contribute at a level decided by them. As Mr Macleod, the Conservative Minister of Labour and National Service, pointed out 'this option would be exercised by those who could obtain the most pension for the least contributions and I cannot see any Chancellor of the Exchequer agreeing to this proposition'.[1] Equally important was the simple fact that there was no demand from the self-employed people themselves as many of them could get a better pension bargain with the same expense in the open market particularly as a result of the Finance Act, 1956. Similar views were later expressed by the Labour Joint Parliamentary Secretary to the Ministry of Pensions and National Insurance, Mr N. Pentland, regarding earnings-related sickness, unemployment and industrial injuries.[2] He argued that the earnings of the self-employed fluctuate so much that it would be difficult to calculate in good time the amount of their contributions and of their benefits. Moreover, as they have no employer to share the contribution cost, some may find the burden too heavy.

Class III, non-employed persons, i.e., people not at work living on private incomes. Their numbers were more than halved

[1] 2nd Reading of National Insurance Bill, 27 January, 1959.
[2] 2nd Reading of National Insurance Bill, House of Commons, 7 February, 1966.

between 1948–1965. The reduction in numbers was higher in the case of women than men particularly single women whose numbers were cut to one-third. This is due mainly to the overall reduction of single women with independent means. Non-employed married women who pay contributions are mainly in the older age-groups, 45–59, because of the transitional conditions mentioned earlier.

TABLE 2

ESTIMATED NUMBER OF CONTRIBUTORS[a]

GREAT BRITAIN – THOUSANDS

	Employed[b]	*Self-employed*	*Non-employed*	*Total*
1950				
Men	14,500	1,300	170	15,970
Married Women	2,650	30	80	2,760
Other women	4,050	130	310	4,490
Total	21,200	1,460	560	23,220
1954				
Men	14,620 (240)[c]	1,290	200	16,110
Married Women	3,040 (1,760)	30	70	3,140
Other Women	3,860 (170)	120	300	4,280
Total	21,520 (2,770)	1,440	570	23,530
1958				
Men	14,940 (270)	1,250	120	16,310
Married Women	3,650 (2,450)	30	50	3,730
Other Women	3,820 (290)	100	160	4,080
Total	22,410 (2,910)	1,380	330	24,120
1965				
Men	15,180 (190)	1,320	110	16,610
Married Women	4,440 (3,300)	20	30	4,490
Other Women	3,680 (340)	80	100	3,860
Total	23,300 (7,830)	1,420	240	24,960

Source: Reports by Government Actuary on first, second and third Quinquennial Reviews of National Insurance Acts.

(a) Includes cases where contributions were excused because of unemployment, maternity or incapacity for work.

(b) 'Employed' includes those for whom only the employer's contribution is payable.

(c) Numbers in brackets refer to insured persons where there were employers' contribution only. They are included in the overall numbers.

Married women of working age in paid employment were to be

given preferential treatment. They could choose whether to pay full contributions in Class I or II, as the case might be, or not to pay any contributions at all apart from the small portion of Class I contribution for industrial injuries benefits. This preferential treatment to married women was justified for three main reasons. Firstly, they have a legal right to maintenance by their husbands who are all compulsorily insured and who draw the social security benefits not only for themselves but for their wives and children. For this reason married women in employment are not on the whole in the same need of their earnings as single women. Consequently interruptions to their earnings do not involve the same hardship as they do for single women. Secondly, as married women, whether at work or not, they 'have a vital work to do in ensuring the adequate continuance of the British race and of British ideals in the world.[1] Husbands' contributions are not adequate in themselves actuarially to provide benefits for themselves and their families. The benefits which wives and children receive are a reflection of society's recognition of the value of the family and the mother's important role to its prosperity. Thirdly, compared with single women and men, married women are more liable to interruptions at work, due to child-births with the result that their ability to maintain good contribution records which are necessary to the receipt of benefits suffers a great deal.

The proportion of married women at work increased tremendously during the last thirty years. In 1931 married women constituted 16% of all women at work while in 1961 the proportion was 51·4%. Looked at from a different angle the proportion of married women occupied was 13% in 1931 and 30% in 1961. This tremendous change in the employment situation of women is due to four main reasons: Firstly the change in social attitudes towards the employment of women, secondly the rise in marriage rates, thirdly the reduction in family size which has allowed married women more time to go out to work and fourthly the scarcity of labour which has prevailed since the end of the last war. It is generally accepted that the proportion of married women at work will continue to rise in the future though it is difficult to predict what this increase will be exactly. The rise in educational standards, the automation of more industrial processes, the continuing demand for labour and the adjustment of husbands to

[1] Beveridge Report, p. 53.

the employed status of their wives will encourage the employment of women, to a greater degree than most predictions allow. On the other hand two factors tend to slow down the growth of female labour. There is some concern about the detrimental effects the absence of the mother from home has on her children. Research findings have been inconclusive on this point and it is generally agreed among social scientists that much more needs to be done before any definite correlation can be said to exist between working mothers and child deprivation or delinquency. It is not even known how many mothers of young children are in full or part-time employment. The second factor is the lack of adequate nursery facilities for the children of working mothers. In general, society's attitude is very ambivalent. On the one hand, it recognises that female labour is indispensable to economic growth and prosperity while on the other, for theoretical and financial reasons, it does very little to encourage the employment of women.[1]

The number of married women who pay full contributions has declined and there is no reason to believe that this trend will be reversed in the future. Women who married before 1948 are subject to certain contribution conditions for the award of pensions with the result that a relatively high proportion of older married women pay contributions. This will decline in the years to come. Any changes in the pattern of child-bearing will also affect the number of women who pay full contributions since married women have little to gain from full contributions once they have completed their families. On the whole the increased number of women at work will not affect seriously the amount of contributions paid since this increase will be mainly in favour of married women and at the expense of single women. Increased employers' contributions are likely to cancel out any losses in contributions from married women.

Employed married women lost their privileged position in the National Insurance Act, 1959 for graduated retirement pensions and in the National Insurance Act, 1966 for wage-related sickness, unemployment and industrial injuries benefits. They were

[1] For a good discussion on employment problems of married women see: Pearl Jephcott, *Married Women Working*, Allen & Unwin, London, 1962. S. Yudkin and Anthea Holme, *Working Mothers and Their Children*, Michael Joseph, London, 1963, Viola Klein, *Britain's Married Women Workers*, Routledge & Kegan Paul, London, 1965.

expected to pay full contributions like all other employed persons. The reason for this was that 'In any scheme providing for an element of graduation in the retirement pension, it is clearly right that women should qualify for it strictly on their own graduated contributions, and that it should be the same for married and single women'.[1] These benefits are designed to provide a standard of living above the bare minimum and it is presumably 'right' that married women should pay full contributions for them to reduce the cost that would otherwise fall on the state, employers and the other contributors.

The principle of universality with regard to persons covered by state insurance schemes has been adhered to so far with one major and one minor modification introduced by the National Insurance Act, 1959 and the Redundancy Payments Act, 1965, respectively. The National Insurance Act made compulsory provisions for wage-related retirement pensions for all employed persons but it allowed employers to contract their employees out of the state scheme under certain conditions. The two main parties were agreed in principle that contracting out should be allowed though they disagreed on the mechanics of the operation. The Labour Party's proposals for half-pay on retirement in 1957 permitted[2] individual employees who were members of occupational pension schemes that were as good as those proposed to be provided by the state to contract out of the state scheme. The decision was left to the individual workers while employers were allowed to decide whether to continue running their scheme if they found it impossible on account of too many defections to the state scheme. The Labour Party had been in close consultation with the TUC during the preparatory stage of its superannuation proposals and must have known of the electoral dangers involved in forcing employees to abandon good occupational schemes for the uncertain fruits of a state scheme. The Conservative Government's hasty White Paper on graduated retirement pensions placed the responsibility for the decision to contract out squarely on the employer. This was softened up by the requirement that employers must give notice to their employees of their intention to contract out and it is up to the latter to make representations, if they wish, to the authorities. Mr Boyd-Carpenter, Minister of

---

[1] 'Provisions for Old Age', Cmd. 538, p. 11, October 1958.
[2] 'National Superannuation', *Labour Party*, London, 1957.

22

Pensions and National Insurance, feared that employers might be 'left with the worst insurance risks'[1] if employees could themselves contract out. This of course could be put right by the Labour Party's proposal for employers to wind up their scheme if they found them impossible to run. Mr Boyd-Carpenter also pointed out the real administrative difficulties and uncertainties involved in granting complete freedom of choice to employees. Mr Crossman for the Opposition acknowledged that there must be some limitations to individual choice. 'There certainly must be a limit to the right of the individual to play hanky-panky with the scheme.'[1] It would have to be a once-for-all individual decision whether to contract in or out. Employees would not be allowed to move freely from one scheme to another. He did not, however, make it clear in the debate whether he favoured individual decisions or majority decisions. Would individual workers have complete freedom to decide or would they have to abide by the majority decision of their fellow workers in the firm? It seemed that the Labour Party had shifted its position since 1957 though when in power it passed the National Insurance Act, 1966 for wage-related benefits, no contracting out was allowed. Contracting-out is a modern term but an old idea. Both the National Insurance Act, 1911 and the Widows' Orphans' and Old Age Contributory Pensions Act, 1925 authorised the Minister to grant 'exception' certificates to persons in certain occupations which provided insurance schemes at least as good as those of the state.

The number contracted out has exceeded the government's initial expectations of $2\frac{1}{2}$ million. This has to some extent been due to the fact that the benefits provided by the Act were so ridiculously low compared with the contributions paid. By the end of 1966, there were about $4\frac{3}{4}$ million contracted out, seven-eighths of whom were men. Over $1\frac{1}{2}$ million of the contracted out were employed in the public services and another million in nationalised industries. As the table below shows the great majority were contracted out before April 1961 when the Act came into operation. After that date certificates for contracting out concerned mostly small groups of employees. A number of the large industries contracted out their employees at the earliest opportunity.

[1] 2nd Reading of National Insurance Bill, House of Commons, 27 January, 1959.

TABLE 3

CONTRACTING OUT DECEMBER 1959–31 MARCH, 1966

GREAT BRITAIN

	No. of Certificates Issued	No. of Employees Covered
December 1959–1 April, 1961	27,854	4,292,500
3 April, 1961–31 March, 1962	9,046	145,250
2 April, 1962–31 March, 1963	3,033	66,743
1 April, 1963–31 March, 1964	2,746	90,244
1 April, 1964–31 March, 1965	3,068	74,193
1 April, 1965–31 March, 1966	3,420	57,133
1 April, 1966–31 December, 1966	2,622	101,295

Source: Annual Reports of Ministry of Pensions & National Insurance.

What safeguards are there for contracted out employees? Firstly, the benefits which private pension schemes offer to contracted out employees must be equal at least to what the state scheme provides. This means that even if an employee's income is below £18 per week – the maximum income taken into account by the Act for pension purposes – he will still receive the same pension as that provided by the state scheme for those earning £18 per week, i.e., he will receive the maximum possible pension provided under the state scheme. Secondly, the scheme guarantees employees who leave contracted out employment for contracted in employment the maximum pension they would have earned under the state scheme as already explained. Thirdly, contracting out schemes must be approved by the Registrar of Non-participating employments – a specially set up body by the Ministry of Pensions and National Insurance. Employers, having first notified their employees of their intention to contract out of the state scheme, must submit their plans to the Registrar for approval. If he is satisfied with the financial and other provisions of the scheme he will grant a certificate of non-participation. If he is not satisfied he will ask the employer for necessary adjustments before granting the certificate. Employees or their representatives have the right to apply to the Registrar for a deferment or variation of a certificate that concerns them. Not very much use has been made of this provision. From the beginning of the scheme to the end of March 1966, 106 such representations from employees were made all but one of which were rejected by the Registrar. In one case the Registrar postponed the issue of the certificate for a month to allow for further discussions between the employees and the employer. Some of the representations from the employees were asking the Registrar to vary the certificate so that they could also be contracted out. On the whole, employees have not shown any active opposition to contracting out. 'Comparatively few of the representations (from employees) showed any objection to contracting out itself.'[1] The largest number of certificates varied by the Registrar follows the application of the employer himself. This happened in cases where the nature of the employment had changed or ceased. In a small number of cases, however, the Registrar had varied or cancelled certificates without the employers' consent where he had established that the scheme did not comply with the relevant requirements. These cases concerned small employers. Apart from the granting and variation of certificates, the Registrar is also responsible for ensuring that when employees leave contracted out employment their employers make the necessary payments for the pension rights they had earned.

The employer's decision whether to contract out employees is fairly complicated depending on many factors such as the degree of labour turnover in the firm, the proportion of women employees, the amount of weekly wages of various groups within the firm and so on. Though employers can not contract out individual employees, they can do so in terms of specific groups of workers.

Apart from the administrative problem, the main drawback of contracted out schemes is the risk involved – however small this may be – that some firms or insurance companies may become insolvent and therefore unable to pay out pensions. Pension rights can accumulate over as long as a forty year period that could entail an element of uncertainty in the fortunes of firms or insurance societies. Very much related to this risk is the fear that some firms may find it impossible to meet unknown pension sums in the future if the state decides to increase the amount of the pension because of inflation, or political or other reasons. In fact this was exactly what happened to those persons 'excepted' from the pre-war state insurance schemes.

The present system of contracting out is an uneasy compromise and it is almost certain to be abolished in the near future in favour

[1] Annual Report, Ministry of Pensions and National Insurance for 1960, p. 38.

of either complete state responsibility or complete employers' responsibility for the provision of wage-related pensions. It does not serve any useful purpose now and it satisfies neither the exponents of state universal provision nor the supporters of private enterprise. It was recognised from the start that the 1959 Act was a 'holding operation, designed to last until it is seen down which road national provision for the old is mostly likely to go'.[1] Both the main political parties have come out openly for the abolition of contracting out. The Labour Party are anxious to replace it with a comprehensive state scheme. The Conservatives feel that now that it has achieved its original purpose of saving the National Insurance Fund from going into the red, it ought ot be replaced by occupational schemes under government control. The state should pull out except from supervising the occupational schemes.[2]

The Redundancy Payments Act 1965 was comprehensive in the general sense that it covered all men and women employees of working age irrespective of their occupational status. It excluded, however, employees with less than 2 years continuous service with the same employer; part-time employees who work less than 21 hours a week, employees who are husbands or wives of their employer and a few other small groups of the employed population. It is difficult yet to estimate the proportion of the employed population excluded but the Government Social Survey's findings shown in Table 4 indicate that just over half of men and women employees change employers in less than a two-year period. There are substantial occupational variations with manual workers changing jobs more often than non-manual workers. Thus the proportion of the professional and administrative group who change their employer in less than two years was 37%. The proportions for the skilled manual and unskilled groups were 46% and 69% respectively. It should be stressed that only 14·6% of all employees changed employers because they had been made redundant. The risk of redundancy is also related to occupational status. The proportions of the professional and managerial group, the skilled manual and the unskilled that were made redundant during the whole ten-year period were 6%, 19% and 20% respectively.

[1] *The Economist,* 18 October, 1958.
[2] See Chapter XII.

The Scope of Social Security

TABLE 4

CHANGES OF EMPLOYERS 1953–63 (EXCLUDES CURRENT EMPLOYER)

GREAT BRITAIN

Length of employment	Men %	Women %	Both Sexes %
Under 6 months	21·6	22·7	22·1
6 months but under 1 year	14·6	15·6	15·0
1 year	15·3	17·0	16·0
2 years	12·6	11·0	11·9
3–5 years	15·2	16·1	15·6
6–9 years	7·2	9·8	7·5
10–19 years	6·4	6·6	6·5
20–29 years	2·4	1·2	1·9
30 years or more	4·7	2·0	3·5
Total	100·0	100·0	100·0

Source: A Harrison. 'Labour Mobility in Great Britain, 1953–63.' and R. Clausen. Government Social Survey, 1966.

Social Security Benefits

The Beveridge Report received generous universal acclaim.[1] As the *Economist* pointed out the Beveridge plan was one of the 'most remarkable state documents', but it was not 'revolutionary'. Its distinctive feature was that it fused existing schemes and methods of national insurance and produced 'a new amalgam – the National Minimum'.[2] Lord Beveridge considered National Insurance legislation after the last war as 'no more than a completion of what was begun in Britain in 1911: the battle of Social Insurance for cash benefits and for medical treatment was fought and won in principle thirty-six years ago'.[3] The Report and the National Insurance Act of 1946, extended the scope of state national insurance to some sections of the middle and upper classes who did not need state protection and to some sections

[1] One discordant note which, because of the very nature of its source, added to the stature of the Report. 'What Beveridge has produced is a bastard which has the shortcomings of all existing social insurance systems, and which is without a single constructive idea. The realisation of this plan would reduce the British people to the level of persons living on charity'. (Dr Ley of the German Propaganda Dept., see House of Commons Debate 16 February, 1943, Mr Graham White's speech, M.P. for Birkenhead East.)
[2] Editorial, *The Economist*, 5 December, 1942.
[3] Eleanor Rathbone, *Family Allowances*, 1949 edition, p. 269, Allen & Unwin.

27

of the working class who were in urgent need of it. What changes did the Report recommend in the types of insurance benefits?

The range of benefits which the Report recommended were all in existence with the exception of family allowances, marriage allowances and death grants. The Report also suggested marriage grants but as it did not consider them vital to the total scheme, they were not implemented by the National Insurance Act, 1946. End of marriage allowances were not implemented because they were fraught with complications – both legal and moral. It also made radical improvements to the system of benefits for industrial injuries, for maternity and for widows. The new system of benefits recommended by the Report and provided by the National Insurance Act, 1946, was superior to the existing one in two respects. Firstly, it streamlined and simplified the procedure for the finance and the award of benefits; and secondly it provided more comprehensive coverage by increasing the number of beneficiaries and benefits, by extending the periods for which certain benefits were paid, by providing more generous benefit allowances and by widening the 'density' of sickness insurance to provide benefits not only for the insured person but for his family as well. There was general agreement then that the new system would assure people of the security they deserved as members of a state which survived the perils of the war vastly damaged but with its honour intact.

It is important to realise that the aim of the Beveridge proposals as well as the National Insurance Act was not to abolish inequality but rather to provide a national standard of living below which no one should be allowed to fall. It was generally accepted then and it is today that though economic equality is theoretically a worthwhile ideal, in practice inequality is not only unavoidable but in some ways a desirable evil. Economic equality, it is argued, would discourage hard work, thrift and efficiency and thus, in the long run, harm even those whom it intended to benefit. In fact in spite of the modest aims of social security, there were still those few, and they still exist today, who saw the new benefits as yet another effect of and another cause to national decline. As *The Economist* pointed out these fears were groundless. 'The stock-brokers who write to *The Times* about Sir William's threat to individual initiative and enterprise need not worry. The last-ditch supporter of the rights earned by work and effort is the man in the

street.'[1] As we shall see later a number of conditions were
attached to the receipt of the various benefits in order to safeguard, even at the expense occasionally of genuine cases, against
'droning' and abuse of benefits.

The three insurance classes are entitled to different benefits as
Table 5 shows. Married women receive benefits according to
their insurance class, if they choose to pay full contributions. The

TABLE 5

NATIONAL INSURANCE BENEFITS

Class I   Family Allowances,ª sickness benefit, unemployment benefit,
industrial injury benefits, maternity benefits, retirement pension, widows' benefits, guardians' allowance and death grant.

Class II   As Class I except unemployment benefit and industrial injurie
benefits.

Class III As Class II except sickness benefit and part of maternity benefits.

(a) For the sake of comprehensiveness, Family Allowances are included in
the table in spite of the fact that they are not an insurance benefit.

only two additions to the battery of insurance benefits provided
by the immediate post-war legislation are redundancy benefits and
child's special allowances. The Beveridge Report was written
against the background of the pre-war trade recession, in the
midst of austerity, and any recommendation for redundancy
benefits would have appeared irresponsible and too costly. The
scheme had to wait until 1965 when unemployment rates were
low and when it became generally accepted that a worker had a
moral and a legal right to his job. Child's special allowances were
introduced in 1957 and are paid for children whose parents are
separated and whose father is dead. Redundancy benefits are
limited to Class I while child's special allowances are payable to
all insurance classes. It is also worth mentioning that though
holidays with pay have not been included in state national
insurance nor have they been made the legal responsibility of
employers, they are provided to almost all workers under
agreements between trade unions and employers.

One of the fundamental questions any society has to answer is
which risks should be covered by the state and which should be

[1] Editorial, *The Economist*, 16 January, 1943.

left to private provision. The basic principle was that 'any risk so general or so uniform' should be covered by national insurance. Such risks were the province of national insurance and not of' assistance or voluntary insurance because 'national assistance involves a means test which may discourage voluntary insurance or personal saving. And voluntary insurance can never be sure of covering the ground'.[1] National assistance and its relationship to national insurance will be discussed later. Reliance on private insurance will certainly leave gaps which will include persons who can afford to do without insurance but also persons who can least afford to be left uninsured. As it was shown earlier in the chapter, the climate of opinion during the last war was most definitely in favour of universal state protection irrespective of liability of risks. Even in the more affluent days of the 1960's and 1970's the state cannot afford to leave insurance to the discretion of the individual for there are still those who cannot afford unaided to insure privately and those who will not bother to insure until it is too late. State compulsion is unavoidable in societies where the welfare of individual citizens is accepted to be the concern of the state. State intervention, however, can take the form of state administered schemes or compulsion to insure privately under approved conditions. There is almost universal agreement in this country that state administered schemes are best for the provision of subsistence benefits but opinion is divided between state administered schemes and state approved schemes for the provision of wage-related benefits that cater for needs above subsistence.

The dividing line between national insurance and voluntary insurance has always been a bone of contention. Friendly and industrial societies were openly hostile to the Beveridge proposals because they feared, and with good reason, that their business would suffer. They did not take kindly to the general opinion that there was still a great deal for them to do 'in ministering to requirements above the statutory minima'.[2] In fact this has happened, partly due to the rise in national prosperity which contrasted with the much slower growth of state insurance benefits and partly as a result of government encouragement in the form of improved tax allowances for contributions to private

[1] Beveridge Report, p. 122.
[2] *The Economist*, 26 August, 1944.

life insurance policies and for expenditure of firms on occupational pensions and benefits. Tax relief for payments on life insurance policies has a very long tradition in this country. It was granted in 1799 the very first year of the establishment of income tax and though it was later discontinued for a brief period it was resumed in 1853 and was expanded gradually to other forms of insurance policies and to occupational schemes for various types of benefits. Following the recommendations of the Tucker committee,[1] the Finance Act of 1956 extended similar tax reliefs for the self-employed as well as to other groups. The amount of tax relief varies according to the various types of occupational pensions and benefits included in the scheme.

This clash between state action and private enterprise is unavoidable because private effort has preceded state action in many important aspects in the field of social security. The National Insurance Act, 1911, was preceded by a long experience of private insurance. Seven million workers, comprising mainly the healthier, better paid and more regularly employed section of the working class, had insured privately against sickness with insurance companies and another 1½ million had insured against unemployment with Trade Unions. It was not surprising then that insurance societies opposed state intervention partly to protect their vested interests. The outcome was a compromise enabling the insurance societies to act as administrative agents for state action. In 1946 they lost this role and they had to content themselves with insurance schemes outside the state field. A similar situation occurred again in 1959. The National Insurance Act of that year was preceded by an extensive network of occupational schemes mostly wage-related both in the private sector of industry and in the public services. Thus in 1958 about 8,750,000 persons were covered by occupational schemes, of whom five million were in the private sector of industry and the remaining in public services and nationalised industries.[2] The conflict was not as sharp this time since both political parties were willing to allow freedom of choice between the state and the private schemes. The Labour Party, however, felt that insurance societies had been

[1] 'Report of the Committee on the Taxation Treatment of Provisions for Retirement.' Cmd. 9063, 1954.
[2] 'Occupational Pension Schemes, A Survey of the Government Actuary,' 1958.

unduly condemning of state insurance in order to further their own interests. 'It is a most short-sighted attitude on the part of the insurance companies to say that they want a mean, miserable national scheme because that discredits insurance'.[1] Occupational sick pay schemes also preceded the National Insurance Act, 1966, to an even greater extent. In 1961, 13 million workers out of a total of 22½ million workers were covered by occupational sick pay schemes of one type or another but largely wage-related. In this case, even unskilled men to the ratio of two for every five were covered while the proportion was naturally higher among professional people – nine out of ten.[2] In this case and the case of redundancy there was no compromise. It is noticeable that Labour Governments tend to place the whole responsibility – administrative, financial and otherwise – in the hands of state organisations. The state scheme of family allowances had also been preceded by limited occupational schemes in the professions. Methodist Ministers were entitled from the first half of the 19th century to a basic child allowance and an additional educational allowance for every child. University teachers were first granted family allowances at the London School of Economics in 1926 under the directorship of William Beveridge. Also officers in H.M. Forces were paid allowances for their children. Finally, the Redundancy Payments Act 1965 was also forced on the Government by the extensive privately negotiated redundancy agreements for some sort of lump sum compensation involving almost five million workers. Perhaps the perfect example of legislation ratifying current practice is in the field of holidays with pay. At present all professional people are covered and 97% of the workers enjoy two weeks' holidays exclusive of public holidays under privately arranged agreements.[3] Any legislation in this field would only legalise existing practice. The role of private effort as the initiator of new ideas is its everlasting source of strength. In this country, however, it has so far been accepted that when private enterprise has proved the worth of a service, it must give way to state action if that service is needed for the whole community. Private effort can not expect to deal with

[1] R. Crossman, House of Commons 2nd Reading of National Insurance Bill, 27 January, 1959.
[2] Report on an Inquiry into the Incidence of Incapacity for Work, Part I, M.P.N.I., 1964.
[3] Ministry of Labour Gazette, October 1962.

universal needs in the field of social services whether this may be health, social security, education, etc.

Level of Benefits

The first and fourth fundamental principles of social insurance according to the Beveridge Report were the provision of flat-rate benefits adequate for subsistence 'irrespective of the amount of the earnings which have been interrupted'.[1] The responsibility of the state did not extend to the provision of benefits above subsistence. It was up to the individual to make use, if he wished, of the services of voluntary insurance. Flat-rate benefits were to be granted as of right to all those who satisfied specified contribution requirements. Lord Beveridge considered the subsistence principle the central idea of his report. 'This central idea was that which caught the public imagination; without this the report would have been no more than a rationalisation of existing powers.'[2] The term subsistence benefits is of course misleading. Flat-rate benefits can be of subsistence level at the very most for the average wage-earner only. They can not deal with individual need. The difficulties involved in deciding what is an adequate subsistence benefit for people living in different parts of the country paying different rents and accustomed to different standards of living were fully discussed in the Beveridge Report and in the national debate in and out of Parliament that followed its publication. For reasons of principle and of administrative practice it was generally agreed, with a few voices of dissent, that benefits for the insured person and his dependants should be flat rates, realising that some kind of supplementation from national assistance would be necessary in exceptional cases.

For a sound basis of benefit rates Mr James Griffiths, Minister of National Insurance, suggested two essential requirements. First 'the leading rates must be fixed initially at figures which can be justified broadly in relation to the present cost of living'.[3] The Beveridge Report estimated the cost of necessities necessary for subsistence, at 1938 prices and added 25% to that figure for the

[1] Beveridge Report, p. 121.
[2] Lord Beveridge, 'Social Security Under Review', *The Times,* 9 November, 1953.
[3] 2nd Reading, National Insurance Bill, House of Commons, 6 February, 1946.

rise in the cost of living up to 1944. The Labour Government using the same basis but adding a more generous rise to the cost of living arrived at the sum of 26s. per week for an adult single beneficiary and £2 2s. od. for a married couple. These figures were incorporated in the National Insurance Act, 1946. Secondly, 'definite arrangements should be made for a review of the rates from this point of view at periodic intervals'.[1] Section 40 of the National Insurance Act provided for quinquennial reviews of rates of benefits to follow the quinquennial reports by the Government Actuary. This proviso proved totally ineffective, for benefits had to be raised much more often than every five years.

The Labour Government had given some thought to the notion of pegging benefits to a definite cost of living with automatic upward and downward adjustments but rejected it rather too easily because of past experience. The idea was tried at the end of World War I for war pensions but broke down soon after. The Government was 'convinced, after examination, that it will break down again'.[2] This has been accepted by successive governments and it was rejected again by the Conservative government during the debates on the National Insurance Act, 1959. Mr Macleod, Minister of Labour and National Service, went even further to suggest that an automatic adjustment of benefits to the cost of living index might act to the detriment of those it was supposed to benefit. 'I am not sure that the pensioners would in fact benefit . . . from such a provision. It would be tempting to leave them where they are on an automatic review and not to give them the increase in real standards which we want to see, and which has happened over the years'.[3]

There are two other arguments, equally unconvincing, for not linking benefits to the cost of living. Firstly, it is argued that though beneficiaries will welcome rises in benefits when the cost of living rises, they will resent any reductions when the cost of living drops. Experience since the last war in this and other European countries has shown that the cost of living is unlikely to drop. Even supposing that the cost of living ever drops, is it true

[1] 2nd Reading, National Insurance Bill, House of Commons, 6 February, 1946.
[2] Mr Griffiths, 2nd Reading, National Insurance Bill, House of Commons, 6 February, 1946.
[3] 2nd Reading, National Insurance Bill, House of Commons, 27 January, 1959.

that in an educated democracy people will fail to see the justice and fairness of having their benefits reduced accordingly? Secondly, automatic rises in benefits will exert an inflationary pressure on the national economy. This may be true up to a point but what social justice is there in a society which expects its weakest members to act as a buttress against inflation? This refusal to apply automatic adjustment of benefits to the cost of living index has meant that benefits were allowed to lag behind the cost of living and the wages indices for a number of years; and that rises in benefits have tended to be tied to the date of general elections.[1] It is also 'morally a breach of contract'[2] because people pay insurance contributions believing that they will get paid benefits of a certain standard of adequacy. Automatic adjustment of benefits to cost of living index, however, can only prevent benefits lagging behind if it is done at short intervals. How many points should the cost of living index change before benefits are adjusted is a matter that needs careful consideration. The experience of many European countries where this has been standard practice for a number of years should be useful. Automatic rises or reductions in benefits, however, will have to be accompanied by corresponding adjustments of contributions. It must never be assumed in social insurance that the state can offer 'nine pence for four pence' without having to find the extra five pence from somewhere.

Opinion within the Labour Party, however, in the 1950's was shifting gradually towards index-related benefits. The Labour Party Conference in October 1953 and the Party's Election Manifesto 'Forward with Labour' in April 1955 both suggested annual reviews of benefits. The Party's Superannuation Scheme in 1957 also suggested linking benefits to a special cost of living index. Linking benefits to the cost of living, however, does not ensure the beneficiaries their fair share of the national cake if wages rise faster than prices. They benefit, however, if prices rise faster than wages which is a rare phenomenon in countries with strong trade unions. The alternative of linking benefits to wages rather than prices has not received so much atention as it is considered to be more inflationary. Yet this is the only real

---

[1] See pp. 183–186.
[2] J. H. Richardson, *Economic and Financial Aspects of Social Security*, p. 223, Allen & Unwin, 1960.

method of ensuring that those not at work benefit equally with those at work from rising national prosperity.[1]

The demand for equal benefits for all may have suited the war period when the nation was under the same physical dangers to life and property and the immediate post-war conditions of rationing and austerity but it soon wore thin in the more affluent fifties and sixties. With the rise and diversification of wages, the steady demand for labour that gave hope to the working man for a continuing rise in his standard of living, there came a diversification in the way people spent their earnings. This was eventually followed by a demand for diversified social insurance benefits. If men were unequal during most of their life there was no good reason why they should be forced into a deceiving state of equality at times when their earnings ceased or were interrupted. Occupational schemes for sickness and retirement were increasingly offering wage-related benefits. Sociologists also began to question seriously the traditional concept of poverty. They argued that poverty was not a static but a relative concept. What constituted poverty in the 19th century is different from what poverty is today. Similarly poverty has a different meaning to a man earning £30 per week and to another earning £10. They have created for themselves different standards of living to which they have grown accustomed and consequently their obligations and expectations during times of interruptions of earnings are different. Benefits can only be meaningful to them if they bear some relationship to their earnings. Labour politicians began to point to the 'two nations' one earning wage related occupational benefits and the other still relying on Beveridge's flat-rate benefits. 'What we had hoped would become a milestone in our history has become a millstone round the necks of many old people' said Mr Norman Mackenzie addressing the Labour Party Conference in October 1957.[2] Trade Union thinking was divided between those who approved because they considered wage-related benefits as a form of deferred payment which workers had earned during their working life, and those who disapproved as they considered such benefits an extension of the amount of inequality existing in society. Mr Crossman in his address to the Labour

[1] Prof Elizabeth Liefmann-Kiel, 'Index Based Adjustments for Social Security Benefits', *I.L.O. Review*, Vol. 79, No. 5, May 1959.
[2] Report in *The Times*, 2 October, 1957.

Party Conference in October 1957 had the latter group in mind when he pointed out that it was up to the Trade Unions to achieve equality in wages if they considered it desirable. He certainly felt that it was tough to impose equality on retirement pensioners or other social insurance beneficiaries. Occupational schemes offering wage-related benefits were on the increase and the state could either remain a passive observer to this trend or actively encourage it or discourage it, Socialists, he thought, should support the extension of wage-related benefits to all because 'levelling up is genuine Socialism. The proper Socialist attitude to privilege is not to destroy it but to transfer privileges of the minority into the rights of the majority'.[1] This is exactly what the Labour Party's policy statement of that year on wage-related benefits recommended. 'Wage-related pensions satisfy the social requirements of the second half of the twentieth century just as flat-rate pensions suited the first half.'[2] The Conservatives approved of wage-related benefits – though not necessarily provided by the state – because it was in line with the basic principles of a capitalist society with its emphasis on rewards for free enterprise and hard work.

The aims of the Labour Party's proposals were to guarantee the flat rate retirement pension to all at a level equal to $\frac{1}{4}$ of the current average wage and to add to it a wage-related sum amounting to about another $\frac{1}{4}$ of each individual's wage. In other words the average wage earner would receive a retirement pension (flat-rate and wage-related) equal to one-half his pay on retirement, the below average wage earner would receive more than half pay on retirement and the above average wage earner, less than half. Contributions, on the other hand, would be completely wage-related thus making for a fair amount of vertical income redistribution. The plan was criticised by Conservatives and others as inflationary because employers' contributions being too high would be passed on to the consumers in higher prices. Moreover since the amount of pension would be related to the man's wages at retirement it might act as an extra incentive for claims for higher wages.

The Conservative Government's answer to the Labour proposals was the publication of the White Paper 'Provision for Old

[1] Report in *The Times*, 2 October, 1957.
[2] 'National Superannuation', *The Labour Party*, p. 17, London, 1957.

Age'[1] which led to the National Insurance Act, 1959. There is no doubt that the Conservative Government passed the Act 'prompted mainly one cannot help feeling, by the activity of the Labour Party in opposition'.[2] The Act was a stop gap based on a series of compromises. Its provisions for contracting out have already been discussed and the contributions and benefits it involved will be discussed later. It initiated for the first time a state insurance scheme which was financed by wage-related contributions and which provided wage-related benefits, inadequate though they may have been. The Act was opposed strongly by the Labour Opposition because while it took the wind out of the sails of the Labour Party proposals it satisfied none of their aspirations. There was general agreement that this was a shrewd political move of the Macmillan administration. One pension expert rightly suspected that wage-related pensions 'were proposed mainly because it had been felt politically necessary to include them, and because their promise would to some extent sweeten the pill of higher contributions'.[3]

The National Insurance Act of the Labour Government in 1966 extended the principle of wage relation to benefits for sickness, unemployment, industrial injuries and widows' allowances. It involved no innovations in principles and there was no political controversy about it. As Sir Keith Joseph, for the Conservative Opposition, said, the main principle of the Bill for earnings related benefits 'is accepted by both sides of the House'.[4] In fact it was acceptable to all sides of the House as well as to the Trade Unions and Employers. The N.E.D.C. had recommended earnings-related benefits as far back as April 1963 and the Conservatives would have introduced such a scheme had they been returned to power in 1964.

Thus the Beveridge revolution spent itself with the rise in national prosperity. Social insurance benefits must not only guarantee a minimum subsistence living but a decent standard of living above the minimum. The three main political parties are agreed on the desirability of the dual system of flat-rate and wage-

[1] Cmd. 538, 1958.
[2] Pilch and Wood, *Pension Schemes,* p. 143, Hutchinson, 1960.
[3] Conference of Actuaries on the Government's White Paper. Report in *Journal of the Institute of Actuaries,* Vol. 85, p. 16, 1959.
[4] 2nd Reading of National Insurance Bill, House of Commons, 7 February, 1966.

related benefits which together can guarantee people a decent standard of life. They are clearly divided, however, on whether the state or private enterprise should be made responsible for wage-related benefits. We shall return to this question in the last chapter.

Chapter Three

THE COST OF SOCIAL SECURITY

SOCIAL security is a complex system of vertical and horizontal income redistribution. It involves the collection of large sums of money from the general population and the allocation of these sums to groups of beneficiaries. This chapter examines the financial aspects of social security, i.e. what taxes are being paid for social security and by whom, how these taxes are collected and managed, and the overall cost of social security to the community.

Social Security Taxes

There are three main methods of financing modern social security programmes: First, all the necessary moneys can be provided by the central government out of general taxation; secondly, the population is divided into certain insurance classes who are required to pay flat rate contributions for social security; thirdly, the contributions paid by the insured may not be flat rate but related to their earnings. The first method provides non-contributory benefits while the second and third are supposed to provide contributory benefits. These three methods are not exclusive of one another and in fact they are all used to finance different aspects of the social security system of this country and of many other advanced countries. It is certainly common practice to use concurrently the first and one or both of the other two methods of social security finance.

The Beveridge Report came down very heavily in favour of the second method though it accepted the first method for the finance of two social security benefits – assistance and family allowances. For obvious reasons, state national assistance has to be financed out of the Exchequer. Family allowances, however, could be financed in one of three ways – by the employers, through taxation or through national insurance contributions. The Family Endowment Society which initiated in 1917 and subsequently championed the cause for family allowances considered only the first two alternatives.[1] It rejected the employer-financed scheme as paternalistic and unsatisfactory as it did not provide cover for the whole community. The contributory scheme for family allowances, first put forward in 1926 divided the cost between the three parties who were interested in the welfare of children:[2] The State as its future citizens, employers as their future workers, and actual or potential parents. The scheme did not cover self-employed people and it was generally criticised on the grounds that the contributions involved were too high when added to those already paid by employees for other benefits. The Beveridge Report commented that in principle it was possible to argue equally in favour of both the non-contributory and the contributory state scheme. 'It can be said, on the one hand, that children's allowances should be regarded as an expression of the community's direct interest in children; it can be argued on the other hand that children are a contingency for which all men should prepare by contributions to an insurance fund.'[3] On practical considerations, however, the non-contributory scheme seemed preferable because firstly, contributions were high enough for the other benefits without any extra addition and secondly allowances for children included benefits in kind which could be more easily adjusted from time to time to a non-contributory cash benefit. This view was readily accepted by the government and was incorporated in the Family Allowances Act, 1945. The Report of the Royal Commission on Population endorsed these views. On the other hand, it observed that family allowances had been neglected and that 'their limitations and inadequacies are mainly due to the desire to keep the cost to the Exchequer within reasonable bounds'.[4]

The flat-rate contributory principle was preferred for the other benefits for three reasons:

'(i) The insured persons themselves can pay and like to pay, and would rather pay than not to do so. It is felt and rightly felt that contributions irrespective of means is the strongest ground for repudiating a means test.

'(ii) It is desirable to keep the Social Insurance Fund self-contained with defined responsibilities and defined sources of

[1] Eleanor Rathbone, *The Disinherited Family*, 1924.
[2] J. L. Cohen, *Family Income Insurance*, King & Son, 1926.
[3] The Beveridge Report, p. 155.
[4] Royal Commission on Population, p. 166. Cmd. 7695, 1949.

income. The citizens as insured persons should realise that they can not get more than certain benefits for certain contributions, should have a motive to support measures for economic administration, should not be taught to regard the State as the dispenser of gifts of which no one needs to pay.

'(iii) To require contribution on an insurance document for each individual has administrative convenience, particularly for a scheme which, while it covers all citizens, takes account of their different ways of livelihood, and classifies them, giving different benefits according to their needs. Contribution provides automatically the record by which the insured person's claim to be qualified for any particular benefit can be tested.'[1]

The second and third reasons are arguments against the use of general taxation for social security financing. They do not apply to the earnings related contributory method for it involves specific taxes for social security like the flat-rate method. It involves the creation of a special insurance fund for the accumulation of contributions as well as a system of record keeping for the administration of benefits. The essential difference between the two types of contributions is that earnings related are a progressive form of taxation while flat rate are regressive. Only part of the first reason applies to earnings related contributions. The Report felt that flat-rate contributions were preferable to earnings related contributions because they did not involve a break with tradition and as such they were familiar to the general public and they were supported by the various interested pressure groups – the trade unions, the friendly societies, etc. A close look at the national debate within and outside Parliament after the publication of the Beveridge Report bears out the contention that public opinion as well as expert opinion were in favour of flat-rate contributions for flat-rate benefits. There was no opposition in the House of Commons to the Minister's statement in the debate on social insurance that the government had accepted the flat-rate contributory principle because first, 'it is well known to our people' and second, 'it has been a central feature of every government scheme since 1911 and our people are therefore well versed in the idea of a system whereby they get benefit as of right. . . .'[2]

[1] Beveridge Report, p. 108.
[2] Sir William Jowitt, Minister of Social Insurance (designate) House of Commons, debate on White Paper on Social Insurance, 2 November, 1944.

Similarly the supporters of earnings related contributions were very few in the debate on the National Insurance Bill, 1946. Only isolated M.P.s voiced support for Mr Arthur Lewis' argument that a 'contribution on the basis of a percentage of the total income'[1] would be more equitable than flat-rate contributions. Outside Parliament supporters of the earnings related contributions were equally in the minority. The *Economist*, for example, declared that 'though there are arguments of tradition and custom' against the use of earnings related contributions, they were 'undoubtedly the only equitable' method.[2] Beveridge himself also acknowledged elsewhere that 'a compulsory insurance contribution can be described as a poll-tax raised without reference to capacity to pay, and on that ground can be criticised as bad in principle'.[3] As he pointed out in his Report, however, the wealthier section of the community pay more in taxation which provides some of the money for social security benefits. Once it was decided to provide flat-rate benefits, the nature of the contributions was settled. The idea that people should pay contributions varying in amount but receive benefits which are equal has never been popular in this or in any other country. Earnings related contributions have always been linked with earnings related benefits. The mood of the nation was expressed perfectly by one writer who declared: 'Besides being intolerably complex, such systems are out of place in a scheme designed to establish a national minimum standard of living below which no one should fall. If the higher paid workers wish to receive higher benefits, they can arrange it by voluntary insurance, for which ample facilities exist in this country; surely nobody suggests that the state should subsidise benefits above the necessary minimum. It is soundly democratic to have flat rates paid by everybody and payable to everybody on an equal footing.'[4]

Both the earnings related and the flat-rate contributory method involve the insurance principle and the payment of benefits to all as of right. The financing of social security from general taxation can have no relation to the insurance principle and in practice it has always been associated with the payment of benefits after a

[1] 2nd Reading, National Insurance Bill, House of Commons, 6 February, 1946.
[2] *The Economist*, 30 September, 1944.
[3] Wm. Beveridge, *Pillars of Security*, p. 123–24, Allen & Unwin, 1943.
[4] W. A. Robson, *Social Security*, p. 291.

means test. The Beveridge Report, the Government, all the political parties and public opinion were firmly opposed to any scheme which related benefits to a means test. Even the most cursory examination of the history of the poor law in this country will justify this unanimous opposition to the means test in a social security scheme drafted in the early 1940's. There is no good reason, however, why such a scheme should not be considered equally effective in countries with a different historical background. There is also evidence that the trade unions and certain sections of the Labour Party favoured non-contributory benefits provided they were paid to all as of right without the application of the means test.

During the debates preceding the Widows', Orphans' and Old Age Contributory Pensions Act, 1925, the trade unions wanted the existing non-contributory old age pension to be paid to all as of right instead of being subject to a means test. It was with reluctance that they agreed to the payment of a small contribution as a means of achieving that right. They insisted that the flat-rate contribution should be low so as to allow as much as possible of the cost of pensions to fall on the wealthier section of the community. What the trade unions were after was not the contributory principle but the securing of the payment of the pension to all as of right. By the very nature of their political philosophies the Conservative and the Liberal Party favour the payment of specific social security taxes. There is no ideological objection, however, to the use of general taxation for the financing of universal social security benefits in the political philosophy of the Labour Party. This is not to say that there are not historical, social or electoral considerations against the adoption of this particular method of finance by the Labour Party. Mr Bevan's suggestion at the Labour Party Conference in October 1955 that the national insurance scheme 'should be removed from its present actuarial basis and should be financed wholly through the Exchequer'[1] received little support for purely tactical, not ideological, reasons. Mr Bevan had in mind flat-rate universal benefits without a means test. He based his arguments on the fact that the Insurance Fund was 'an actuarial fiction'; he could also have mentioned that all the social services which provided benefits in kind – education, health, employment exchanges, etc. – were wholly or largely financed

[1] See report of conference proceedings in *The Times*, 14 October, 1955.

from general taxation. Mr Crossman, the Party's official spokesman on social security, referred to this suggestion at the Party's
conferences of the following two years. He rejected it in 1956
because such a change would have meant a rise of two or three
shillings in the standard rates of income tax, a measure which was
not practical politics.[1] This argument assumes that people are
more willing to pay specific contributions for specific benefits
instead of higher income tax in order to receive the same benefits.
Though there is no evidence to support or refute this, it has been
voiced several times in diverse quarters in this and others countries. *The Times* stated in support of the National Insurance stamp
that 'Psychologically and socially the stamp . . . is accepted as
different in kind from taxation.'[2] On the other hand, one can
equally argue that if social security contributions were incorporated in the income tax, people would be more willing to pay
income tax as they could visualise direct cash benefits they could
receive when in need. A year later, Mr Crossman rejected Mr
Bevan's suggestion again but for a different reason. 'You cannot
trust a Tory Chancellor with that power over every old age
pension or sickness and unemployment benefit. If you are going to
protect these benefits against governments, then you must have an
insurance system and fund and definitely be able to say "Here is
something you cannot touch because it is ours by right".'[3] It is
difficult to visualise such a situation arising in this country
irrespective of the political beliefs of the Chancellor.

The use of the insurance technique for the financing of social
security benefits so strongly recommended by the Beveridge
Report can be explained on historical and social physchological
reasons but it has no actuarial foundation. Social insurance as used
in state social security schemes must not be confused with private
insurance. The contributions of individual persons are not
accumulated separately to provide for their benefits but are paid
out as benefits to the sick, the unemployed, the retired, etc. The
amount of contributions is not calculated according to the risks of
individual insured persons as it is the case in private insurance but
they are the same flat-rate amounts for all. Finally, no retirement
pensioner, even if he entered the scheme at the age of 16, would

---

[1] See report of conference proceedings in *The Times*, 6 October, 1956.
[2] 'The Future of Pensions', *The Times*, 2 March, 1955.
[3] See report on conference proceedings in *The Times*, 2 October, 1957.

contribute enough for his pension. It is estimated that the average man retiring at the age of 65 in 1965 paid only one-fifth in contributions of the married man's pension he would be entitled to. This does not mean that other people necessarily paid for the remaining four-fifths of his pension. He may well have paid the whole cost himself in direct and in indirect taxation. This point is often overlooked because of the excessive emphasis placed on the 'insurance' aspect of benefits. Beveridge's argument that 'the insured persons themselves can pay and like to pay and would rather pay than not do so' is misleading. It is inevitable that they will pay in one form or another, either in direct or in indirect taxation or both. Whether the contributory or non-contributory method is used, the fact still remains that the social security benefits of the retiring generation are financed to some extent by the rising generation.

The Beveridge Report and the National Insurance Acts, 1946 accepted the established tripartite method of social security finance. There were the few who considered employers' contributions either undesirable or inadvisable or both. The Beveridge Report gave four reasons why employers should pay contributions for their employees: First, employers could be held partly responsible for occupational diseases and accidents. This is not of course true in all cases and the cause of industrial accidents is a far more complicated matter than mere neglect on the employer's part. Nevertheless this is a widely held belief and employers are responsible for the finance of industrial injury schemes in the majority of industrial countries. In some countries employers' contributions are even related to the degree of hazard involved in the particular employment. It is argued that such a method of finance spurs employers to improve their safety precautions. This may have been true in the days of small businesses when the owner had to pay directly compensation to his workers but it is of doubtful validity today with the practice of commercial insurance and the evolution of complex industrial organisations. There were the advocates of complete employer liability in this country, too. As the Beveridge Report pointed out, however, apart from the above misgivings, if employers were made responsible for the finance of the industrial injury scheme they would also be entrusted with its administration. Such a step would destroy the comprehensiveness of the state social security plans. Secondly, there was the paternalistic argument that employers are morally responsible for the welfare of their workers. 'It is equally desirable, that employers should feel concerned for the lives of those who work under their control, should think of them not as instruments in production, but as human beings.'[1] Thirdly, there were purely good business considerations. It pays employers to have a healthy, contented labour force especially in a period of labour shortages and of the increased importance given to staff-management consultation. Fourthly, if employers wanted to have a say in the administration of social security then they should earn this status by paying contributions for their employees. Employers are affected by a social security scheme because it involves the collection and payment of large sums of money. Such a large scale economic operation necessarily involves the economy of the country and of individual employers. For all these reasons employers were to pay flat-rate contributions for their employees, irrespective of their ability to pay, of any private insurance scheme they may be running, or any other considerations.

Beveridge had some doubts, however, on the desirability of employers' contributions. These centred round the question whether employers bear the extra cost of contributions themselves or whether they pass it on in higher prices to the consumers or by resisting wage rises to their employees. Economists are agreed that employers are bound to pass on part of the extra cost but they are not agreed on the extent that this takes place. There are those who maintain that employers can not afford to translate all the extra cost in higher prices because of the adverse effect this would have on their overseas markets. It is difficult to see why this should be so since employers are expected to contribute towards social security in all industrialised countries. This could only apply to employers in countries where they are expected to pay an excessive share of the social security cost. It is incidentally worth noting that in this respect underdeveloped countries subsidise the social security systems of advanced countries by buying manufactured goods from them. The second point on which economists are agreed is that employers are more likely to pass on the extra cost when wages are rising fast and consumer demand is high. In so far as employers contributions are passed on to the con-

[1] Beveridge Report, p. 109.

sumers, they are a regressive form of taxation since higher prices hurt most the lower income groups. These economic considerations do not seem to have had much impact on government policy because they are so involved and ambiguous. Referring to a round of contribution rises, one Minister of Pensions and National Insurance said: 'Because of the burden of the weekly contribution on the lower-wage earner the Government decided that this time the employer should pay a larger share of the increase.'[1] Suggestions have also been made for employers' contributions to be based on profits. This would take into account the employers' ability to pay and it would be more likely to lead to more vertical redistribution of wealth. Apart from misgivings as to whether taxation on profits would encourage vertical redistribution of wealth, there are also fears that this may penalise efficiency and vice-versa encourage inefficiency. Leaving aside all these arguments for and against employers' contributions, governments in all countries have made wide use of them because they are an easy source of social security revenue.

In addition to the insured person's and employer's contribution, there is also the state subsidy. This is the only part of the contribution that involves clearly an element of vertical income redistribution. Government revenue consists of direct taxation which is a progressive form of taxation and indirect taxation which is a mixture of progressive and regressive taxation depending on the type of goods consumed, and by whom. In addition to the contribution portion, the state was required under the National Insurance Act, 1946, to pay a block grant of £36m. per annum rising by annual increments of £4m. until it reached £60m. in 1955. The purpose of the block grant was to meet the extra cost of allowing people to enter the insurance scheme at ages above 16 years which was the age on which the actuarial contributions was calculated.

The National Insurance Act, 1946, required all persons of working age to pay contributions according to their insurance class, their age and sex. Working age for men was the ages of 15 to 70 excluding those over the age of 65 who retired from regular employment. For women, working age was between the ages of 15 and 65 not including those over the age of 60 who

[1] Miss Herbison, 2nd Reading of National Insurance Bill, House of Commons, 25 November, 1964.

retired from regular employment. Boys and girls below the age of 18 paid a smaller contribution. Men also paid higher contributions than women to cover benefits for their dependants. The actual amount paid by employed persons themselves was less than that paid by the non-employed who in turn paid less than the self-employed. On the other hand, the employed persons' contribution was supplemented by an almost equal amount from their employers with the result that their total contribution was the highest of the three. Finally the state subsidy was one-quarter, one-sixth and one-seventh of the contribution of the employed person and his employer, the self-employed and the non-employed respectively. Higher contributions by the employed persons entitled them to more benefits than the other two classes and higher contributions by the self-employed entitled them to more benefits than the non-employed.

Certain groups of people were excepted from paying contributions. These were: (a) full time students and unpaid apprentices; (b) the special position of married women has already been discussed. They can elect whether or not they will pay contributions irrespective of the insurance class they belong to. (c) Contributions are not payable by employed persons during periods of unemployment, nor by employed and self-employed during incapacity for work due to sickness or injury. (d) Self-employed and non-employed persons with small incomes. The Beveridge Report suggested that the annual income for such exemption should be less than £75. During the passage of the National Insurance Bill through Parliament this was considered too low and it was raised to £104. Today it stands at £312 a year having been raised in 1955, 1962, 1965 and 1967. The number qualifying for exemption stood at 130,000 at the end of 1949 but by the end of 1950 it rose to 200,000, it remained at that figure until 1956, then dropped to 180,000 in 1957, remained stable till 1962 when it dropped to 166,000, again continued at that figure until 1965 when it dropped to 153,000 where it stands today. These fluctuations are mostly due to the raising of the annual income level qualifying for exemption rather than to any real improvement in income. The Report of the National Insurance Advisory Committee in 1955 estimated that about 90% of those exempted were non-employed persons and 75% were women. A sample analysis indicated that 'about 28% of certificate holders are engaged in household duties for parents or relatives, about 23% are invalids living with relatives, about 10% are widows with 10s. pensions, and about 10% are members of religious communities'.[1] This picture has been very constant during the whole period from 1949 onwards. The position is different for employed persons with low incomes. The Act required employed persons with weekly earnings below 30s. to pay reduced contributions but also required their employers to pay increased contributions to make up for the loss. The sum of 30s. per week was raised in 1955 to 60s., in 1962 to 80s. and in 1967 to £6 per week. Suggestions that employed persons should be given the same treatment as self-employed and non-employed on this point were considered and rejected on general principles by the National Insurance Advisory Committee.

The actual amount of the contribution was a matter of considerable discussion during the passage of the National Insurance Bill, 1946, through Parliament. A number of M.P.s complained that it was too heavy for the lower-paid workers, for the small employers with one or two employees and for the self-employed person with a business of meagre returns. For the Government, Mr Griffiths commented that taking into account all the benefits, their level and their duration, he had 'no hesitation in saying that this scheme is the best and cheapest insurance policy ever offered to the British people, or to any people any where'.[2] In fact some people paid more under previous insurance schemes in 'bobs' and 'tanners'.

The rates of contribution were based on an 'actuarial contribution'. This was an almost meaningless term introduced by the National Insurance Act, 1911, implying that the rate of contribution should be sufficient in amount to pay for the benefits to which the insured person was entitled provided that, first all insured persons enter the scheme at the age of 16 and second that no increases in benefits are made. People who enter the scheme later than the age of 16 naturally pay less for the benefits they are likely to receive depending on the age at which they enter the scheme. Similarly whenever there is an increase in benefits the Exchequer has to find part of the increased cost of benefits for

[1] 'Liability for Contributions of Persons with Small Incomes' Report of the N.I.A.C. Cmd. 9432, April, 1955.
[2] 2nd Reading National Insurance Bill, House of Commons, 6 February, 1946.

those aged over 16 when the increase occurs. Bearing in mind that benefits are being constantly increased, this involves a constant subsidy from the Exchequer. For this reason the Phillips Report suggested that when increases in benefits are made, contributions should be increased not as if the entire insured population was aged 16 but beyond that to take account of the fact that the great majority of contributors are above that age. They rejected the idea of varying contributions according to age because of the complexity and the intolerable burden it would place on the older generation.[1]

Contributions were raised eleven times between 1948 and the end of 1967 with the result that rates rose by about four times for all three insurances classes. In the case of employed persons, employers' contributions also rose equally though during the period 1957–1965 they were allowed to drag behind the contributions paid by their employees. The State supplement was reduced in 1951 but was restored to its original strength later. Similarly block grants were abolished in 1952 but were restored later when the national insurance scheme began to show signs of running into deficits.

The National Insurance Act, 1946, authorised the Treasury to make statutory orders to reduce or increase national insurance contributions 'for such periods as may be specified' in periods of recession or 'with a view to maintaining a stable level of employment'. These powers have never been used by any Chancellor so far.

The principle of flat-rate contributions was inseparably linked with the principle of flat-rate benefits. Beveridge, the Coalition Government and the Labour Government underestimated the rise in the standard of living that was to follow after the war was over. The upward trend in wages, prices and the standard of living that took place soon made it obvious that flat-rate contributions could not provide adequate benefits for all. To provide benefits that were considered adequate by the highest paid workers would mean raising contributions to a level beyond the ability of the lowest paid workers. 'The speed of the convoy is that of the slowest ship.'[2] As early as 1948, Mr Griffiths realised the limitations of flat-rate contributions in a world of inflation when he said 'we have about reached the limit of what can be done by

[1] Phillips Report, p. 46.
[2] Provision for Old Age, p. 9.

means of flat-rate contributions and in future we shall have . . . to see whether some method of financing the insurance scheme other than by flat-rate contributions can be found.'[1]

As it was pointed out in the previous chapter, the 1950's witnessed a number of changes in favour of earnings-related benefits which could only be financed through earnings-related contributions. No society can justify on actuarial or ethical grounds the financing of earnings-related benefits by means of flat-rate contributions or through the Exchequer. The National Insurance Act, 1959, introduced into the state scheme for the first time earnings-related contributions that were far in excess of the earnings-related benefits the Act provided. Earnings-related contributions were used for two purposes: To place on a sounder footing the finances of the flat-rate national insurance scheme and to provide earnings-related benefits. The National Insurance Fund was for the first time £14m. in the red in 1958 and it was estimated that 'within the next decade this deficiency will reach £260 millions a year and in about 20 years' time will exceed £400 millions a year'.[2] It was felt that to secure such sums through flat-rate contributions would have meant rises which would be excessive for lower income groups. Meeting the extra cost through larger Exchequer grants was not considered advisable for, among other things, the scheme would have lost the last pretence of an insurance scheme. Wage-related contributions which would provide wage-related benefits and at the same time solve the financial crises of the National Insurance Fund were also electorally attractive. Mr Crossman understandably described the scheme as a swindle, 'a deliberate attempt to persuade the people that some improvement in pensions is being carried out and that, for instance wage-related pensions are being introduced, when . . . the whole aim and object of the Bill is a fiscal arrangement to reduce the Exchquer liability and to redistribute the burden of pensions so that it falls predominantly on the middle range wage-earners'.[3] Prof Lafitte, too, was definite that the Act introduced 'graduated additional contributions – not benefits – so as to cut down the mounting charge on the Exchequer which the National

[1] House of Commons debates on National Assistance and National Insurance Scales as reported in *The Economist*, 26 June, 1948.
[2] Provision for Old Age, p. 7.
[3] Second Reading, National Insurance Bill, House of Commons, 27 January, 1959.

Insurance scheme was piling up'.[1] *The Times* also agreed that the Act essentially 'reforms not pensions but pension financing'.[2] Similarly the relief with which the business world greeted the government's plans indicated that the criticisms levied against the Act were substantially true. The Association of British Chambers of Commerce in a circular to their members described the government plan as 'an honest attempt to check the rising burden on the taxpayers which is inevitable unless the existing insurance scheme is altered'.[3] A spokesman of the Life Officers Association and the Associated Scottish Life Officers welcomed the fact that the government plan had been 'poised at a moderate level'.[4] Mr Macleod for the government did not try to hide the fact that the Act was intended to help the finances of the flat-rate insurance scheme and to provide a modest wage related scheme. He summarised the criticisms against the Conservative and Labour schemes thus: The Conservative scheme 'although it puts right the finances of the old scheme it then goes on to take far too small and far too timid a step forward'. Put more bluntly, 'it is a little mouse of a scheme'. On the other hand the Labour scheme would prove disastrous because its 'contributions would prove to be so heavy as to be insupportable' and the scheme would thus 'turn out to be a signpost to inflation'.[5]

The Labour proposals envisaged a scheme in which the employee paid 3% of his weekly earnings in contributions, the employer paid 5% and the state 2%, making total of 10% of the employee's weekly earnings. Contributions would be levied on all employees earning up to four times the national average earnings. Both the Labour proposals and the National Insurance Act provided for the earnings related contributions to be in addition to the flat-rate contributions. The National Insurance Act provided that employed persons, including married women, should pay contributions at the rate of $4\frac{1}{4}$% on a band of earnings between £9 and £15 per week. Their employers would pay an equal amount but there would be no state subsidy. The average

[1] Professor Fr. Lafitte, 'The Future of Social Security', in *Social and Economic Administration*, Vol. I, No. 1, January, 1967.
[2] *The Times*, 20 April, 1959.
[3] *The Times*, 16 October, 1958.
[4] *The Times*, 15 October, 1958.
[5] Second Reading, National Insurance Bill, House of Commons, 27 January, 1959.

weekly industrial earnings in 1959 were £12 13s. 2d. and consequently the £9 to £15 bracket was chosen because it 'straddles that figure fairly comfortably'.[1] The government's reasons for deciding to limit contributions to the average bracket of earnings were first that it felt that it would not be right for the government 'to force everyone to contribute more through a state scheme than would be needed for a reasonable provision for old age'. The benefits which the Act provided, however, were so incredulously low that it is impossible to describe them as 'reasonable provision' even taking into account the flat-rate benefits. The government's second reason was that 'an excessive extension of the state pension scheme by way of graduation could do grave damage to the existing occupational pension schemes and future development in this field'.[2] The outcome of this concentration of contributions within the wage band £9–£15 is that the low and high wage earners benefit. The low wage earners receive a subsidy in flat-rate pensions because part of the wage related contribution goes towards the cost of flat-rate benefits of which retirement pensions is the main expense. The high wage earners benefit because they pay contributions for only part of their wages.

As wages rise it is natural that the wage band for contribution purposes will have to be adjusted. Thus the upper limit was raised to £18 in 1963 but the lower income was not altered because that would have meant that 'we would in some measure at any rate be taking away from people the prospect of benefiting from the graduated pension scheme. In any case, we would be very greatly reducing the contribution to the general National Insurance Fund'.[3] There will come a time, however, when the lower limit will have to be raised otherwise it would mean that 'an increasing burden will be laid on the lower paid worker'[4] for the financing of the scheme. The Labour Government has not made any changes to the earnings band or to other aspects of the National Insurance Act, 1959, because it is more keen to abolish the whole scheme rather than reform it. Employees who are contracted out of the scheme do not pay graduated contributions for retirement pensions but they have to pay higher flat-rate

[1] Mr Boyd-Carpenter, M.P.N.I. Standing Committee debate on N.I. Bill, House of Commons, 19 February, 1959.
[2] Provision for Old Age, p. 10.
[3] Mr Macpherson, M.P.N.I. House of Commons, 28 January, 1963.
[4] T. Lynes 'Pension Rights and Wrongs', p. 14, Fabian publication, 1963.

contributions in order to meet the extra cost of flat-rate insurance benefits.

The National Insurance Act, 1966 permitted no contracting out, required graduated contributions from all employed persons and their employers and involved no state subsidy. Employed persons pay $\frac{1}{2}\%$ of a band of earnings between £9 and £30 a week and their employers pay an equal amount. This is in addition to the $4\frac{1}{2}\%$ paid by employees and employers under the 1959 Act. It differs from the National Insurance Act 1959 only in that it is more comprehensive with regards to persons and their earnings. Both Acts departed from the Lloyd George–Beveridge principle of tripartite flat-rate contributions and flat-rate benefits.

The Redundancy Payments Act, 1965, introduced another departure from the Beveridge principle of flat-rate tripartite contribution. It established a Redundancy Fund whose only source of income was the contributions paid by employers in respect of their employees – fivepence for men and twopence for women. It is difficult to see why in principle an employer is solely responsible financially for redundancy in his firm but not for accidents. Redundancy is of two main types: It is deliberately planned by the employer to bring about a better rearrangement and distribution of his labour force or it is forced on the employer because of slackening off of the demand for the firm's goods because of bad management or for reasons beyond the employer's control. In the second case, the employer can hardly be said to be financially in a position to bear the cost in spite of the collective insurance arrangements made by the Act. In the first case, the employer is rearranging his labour force not only for increased profits but also for the common good of his employees. In fact it may be that unless he rearranges his labour he may be forced into the position where he will have to apply redundancy of the second kind. Labour mobility and efficient use of manpower are essential to the economic progress and prosperity of a nation. There are therefore good reasons to argue that redundancy should be financed by the nation as a whole – the tripartite system of contributions – rather than by the employers. One need not overlabour this point because as employers do not always absorb the extra cost of contributions but pass it on wholly or in part to consumers and to workers, the whole nation bears the cost of redundancy.

The Act made elaborate arrangements to ensure a fair distribution of the cost of redundancy between the individual employer and the industry as a whole. The employer pays the redundant worker a lump sum and claims from the Redundancy Fund part of the sum paid. In this way the employer is not faced with bills which he may find impossible to meet unaided. At the same time, by having to pay part of the lump sum himself, he is discouraged from indulging in unnecessary redundancies. On the other hand, it can be argued that by having to meet part of the cost directly apart from his contributions to the Fund, an employer may tend to hold on to his labour force hoping for an improvement in his trade. The amount of the rebate given to the employer from the Redundancy Fund varies according to the age-group of the redundant employee. If he is under forty-one, his employer will get a rebate of two-thirds of the redundancy payment; if he is forty-one or over, his employer will get back seven-ninths of the redundancy payment. Bearing in mind the fact that older workers' scales for redundancy payment are higher, the rebate for them is intended to cover the two-thirds of the normal rebate and the whole of the extra cost. The Government was anxious that higher rebates should be paid for older workers in order to 'prevent the higher scale (of redundancy payments) for older workers from acting as a deterrent to employers in engaging such older workers'.[1]

The Management of Social Security Finance

One of the administrative improvements recommended by the Beveridge Report and implemented by the National Insurance Act, 1946, was the combination of the separate insurance contributions for sickness, unemployment and retirement pensions into one to cover all the benefits provided under the Act. This composite contribution also included portions for benefits provided by other Acts. The portion for industrial injury benefits was compulsory for all the employed persons, including married women, and their employers, and the income derived is transferred to the Industrial Injuries Fund. Another portion for the National Health Service was compulsory for all the employed

[1] Mr Gunter, Minister of Labour, 2nd Reading, Redundancy Payments Bill, House of Commons, 24 April, 1965.

persons and their employers, the self-employed and the non-employed. The income is transferred to the Exchequer and meets only a very small part of the cost of the National Health Service – one-tenth in 1954 and one-seventh in 1966. Finally the flat-rate contribution includes, since the end of 1965, a part for redundancy paid by employers which is transferred to the Redundancy Fund managed and controlled by the Minister of Labour. In the early 1950's the great majority of flat-rate contributions were collected in the traditional method of fixing adhesive stamps on insurance cards. By 1966 rather less than half of the contributions were collected in this way; 11·6% were collected in the form of impressed stamps, 33·4% were paid by cheque by employers and the remaining were the contributions of civil servants and H.M. Forces. Graduated contributions are collected together with income tax under the P.A.Y.E. system of the Inland Revenue.

The recommendation of the Beveridge Report for the setting up of Funds for the collection of contributions and the payment of benefits was implemented by the National Insurance Act and National Insurance (Industrial Injuries) Act, 1946. Each Act set up two Funds – an Insurance and a Reserve Fund and an Industrial Injuries and a Reserve Fund. Discussion will be limited mostly to the Funds of the National Insurance Act because they are more important and in order to avoid repetition since many of the arguments for and against the existence of such Funds are applicable to all types of similar insurance funds. The National Insurance Fund is a current account of the national insurance scheme. Its income comprises contributions paid by all the parties concerned, occasional annual government block grants and interest gained from the investment of the monies of the Reserve Fund. The expenses of the Fund consist of the administrative costs of the national insurance scheme and the payment of national insurance benefits. It is 'like a bath with no bathplug'.[1] If there are any surpluses they are transferred to the Reserve Fund at the end of the year or they may be left in the Fund itself. In years of deficits, money can be transferred to it from the Reserve Fund but only after a special House of Commons resolution. This has not happened so far. The Reserve Fund started off with the comfortable sum of £783m. representing the balance of the previous insurance funds which were wound up when the

[1] 'The Growing Cost of Social Security', *The Times*, 8 February, 1967.

National Insurance Act came into force in July 1948. Today the assets of the Reserve Fund stand at £1,168m.

The intention of the Beveridge Report was to provide a strong Reserve Fund which would enable the insurance scheme to function as far as possible as a 'save-in-advance' scheme. The government were in principle in agreement but found it difficult to accept all the consequences of a funded pay-in-advance scheme. The main issue was the payment of retirement pensions to old people who had not been in the scheme long enough to qualify. The Beveridge Report envisaged that they would have to rely on national assistance during the transition period while the government found such a proposal unacceptable both morally and electorally. The result was that retirement pensions were paid out from the very start of the scheme thus reducing any hopes it may have had to function as a funded scheme. Money paid into the Fund is paid out almost immediately. It is in effect more of a pay-as-you-go system rather than a saving-in-advance scheme in spite of the existence of the Reserve Fund. The National Insurance Act, 1959 gave up the idea of a Reserve Fund for earnings-related retirement pensions. It makes no attempt to accumulate reserve funds and relies completely on a pay-as-you-go procedure.

Actuaries and economists are not agreed as to whether a completely funded saving-in-advance scheme run by the state is possible or desirable It is argued that collection of vast sums of money and their investment at commercial rates of interest, which is one of the main sources of income of a privately funded scheme, is difficult in a state scheme not only for reasons of safety but also because of its probable inflationary effects on the national economy. The abolition of government block grants and the reduction of the government's share of the contribution in 1952 was considered necessary in order to eliminate the accumulating surpluses of the Insurance Fund. The government did not consider that this made any difference to the amount of money which the government had to pay towards the expenditure of the scheme. 'It is really no more than a book keeping matter and makes no difference one way or the other to the gap which has to be covered by taxation.'[1] It is also difficult to see how the govern-

[1] H. Gaitskell, Chancellor of the Exchequer, Budget Speech, House of Commons, 10 April, 1951.

ment can insulate the vast sums of a funded insurance scheme from the other government activities. The popular impression that the Reserve Fund holds money which is always available to be used if necessary is false. 'The National Insurance Reserve Fund is a fiction, but at times a convenient one' commented one expert,[1] an opinion which was shared by Aneurin Bevan as already mentioned. The government uses the balances of the Funds to finance its many other activities with the result that the accumulated reserve funds of the insurance scheme exist in the form of paper receipts only. There is nothing improper in this but it saves a great deal of misunderstanding on the actuarial merits of an 'insurance' scheme if the position is understood properly.

Apart from their actuarial merits or demerits, Insurance Funds are supposed to have a sobering effect on extravagant claims for higher benefits. There are strong doubts about the effectiveness of this restraining influence. The financing of all the various benefits by one combined contribution makes it difficult for the various groups of beneficiaries to know whether they are actuarially entitled to a rise in benefits. Moreover beneficiaries and contributors are not always one and the same group with the result that demands for higher benefits are made irrespective of the financial condition of the Funds. In fact, the financing of state insurance schemes is so complex that, apart from the experts, people are apt to make claims for higher benefits when they know that payments into, exceed payments out of, the Fund without realising that a large part of the reserves comes from the contributions of future beneficiaries. This happened during the House of Commons debates on the National Insurance Bill, 1951, when the Insurance Fund's reserves were mounting up. Recently, too, a number of references have been made to the meagre expenditure on earnings related retirement pensions compared with the revenues of the scheme in support of demands for higher pensions. In 1963–64 the revenue of the schemes was £229m. while only £½m. was paid out in graduated retirement pensions.

Table 6 shows that from the beginning of the scheme in 1948 up to 1958, income exceeded expenditure every year to the total of £630m. for the whole period This excess was due to two main factors. Unemployment was much lower than what had been

---

[1] A. Peacock, *The Economics of National Insurance,* p. 50, Hodge & Co., 1952.

The Cost of Social Security

TABLE 6

THE FINANCIAL POSITION OF THE INSURANCE FUND AND THE RESERVE
FUND[a] GREAT BRITAIN — £ MILLIONS

Year ended 31st March	Income	Expenditure	Balance for year ended 31st March		
			Total	Insurance Fund	Reserve Fund
At 5.7.1948	—	—	892	109	783
1948–49	358	273	977	194	783
1949–50	522	386	1113	330	783
1950–51	531	387	1257	474	783
1951–52	512	411	1358	575	783
1952–53	495	487	1366	297	1069
1953–54	553	514	1404	335	1069
1954–55	572	527	1449	380	1069
1955–56	669	634	1484	316	1168
1956–57	693	658	1519	351	1168
1957–58	723	721	1521	353	1168
1958–59	910	926	1505	337	1168
1959–60	931	963	1473	305	1168
1960–61	937	978	1432	264	1168
1961–62	1148	1135	1445	277	1168
1962–63	1194	1206	1433	265	1168
1963–64	1367	1416	1384	216	1168
1964–65	1454	1475	1363	195	1168
1965–66	1816	1791	1385	220	1168

(a) Contributions for the National Health Service are excluded from above figures.

Source: Annual Reports of M.P.N.I. and Annual Abstract of Statistics.

provided for in contributions. The average unemployment rate during this period was 2% while the Beveridge Report and the estimates of the Government Actuary which determined the amount of contributions, allowed for an unemployment rate of 8½%. The second factor was the comparatively small number of retirement pensioners which always goes with the first few years of a new social security scheme. In fact the surplus would have been higher had the government not reduced its contributions and abolished the block grants to the scheme in 1952. The financial position of the Insurance Fund changed for the worse during the period 1958–1965 when expenditure exceeded income by a total of £158m. for the whole period, due to the rising cost of retirement pensions. The deficit was kept down to relatively small sums as a result of the contribution changes introduced by the 1959 Act.

Countries differ a great deal in the way they distribute the cost of social security between employees, employers and the state. It is true to say that statistically, though not necessarily in actual fact, employers in this country bear little of the social security cost compared with a number of European countries.[1] On the other hand, other countries place even less burden on employers but a great deal more on the state. Table 7 shows clearly that in this country insured persons' contributions together with the employers' share for employed persons have been the main source of income of the Insurance Fund, varying from 67·7% of total income in 1950 to 82·3% in 1964. The contribution of the state to the Insurance Fund has not increased over the years. In fact taking state supplements and annual grants together, the contribution of the state was at its highest during the first four years of the scheme. Contribution to the Fund's income is not identical with contribution to its expenditure since income and expenditure are not equal. The government's real contribution to the Insurance Fund is not what it pays into the Fund but rather what sums of money it has to meet to make up the difference between the contributions of the employees and employers and the income derived from investment on the one hand and the expenditure of the Fund on the other. Contributions from employees and employers have accounted for the overwhelming share of the expenditure of the Fund: The State's share of the expenditure of the Fund was at its lowest – 6% – in 1950 and at its highest – 20% – in 1960. Bearing in mind that the state reaps the benefits of the Reserve Fund at low interest rates, the state's share of expenditure is not very high. This may help to bolster the insurance image of the scheme but it certainly limits the amount of vertical redistribution of income achieved through social security operations.

The National Insurance Act, 1946, required the Government Actuary to review the financial condition of the insurance scheme every five years and if necessary to provide interim reports every year. Similar arrangements were made in the National Insurance (Industrial Injuries) Act, 1946. The Reports of the Government Actuary have attempted to make both short-term and long-term

[1] *The Cost of Social Security, 1958–1960*, I.L.O., Geneva, 1964.

The Cost of Social Security

TABLE 7

SOURCES OF INCOME OF THE NATIONAL INSURANCE FUND[a]

GREAT BRITAIN – PER CENT

Year ended 31st March	Exchequer Supplements to Contributions	Payments Additional Sums	Contribu- tion from Insured Persons and Employers	Interest from N.I. Funds	Expenditure of Fund borne by contributions from Ins. Persons and Employers
5.7.1948–31.3.1949	18·3	7·4	69·1	5·2	90·6
1949–1950	18·3	7·6	68·7	5·4	92·6
1950–1951	18·0	8·3	67·7	6·0	93·1
1951–1952	15·5	4·6	72·5	7·4	90·0
1952–1953	12·7	—	79·2	8·1	80·4
1953–1954	12·7	—	79·4	7·9	85·5
1954–1955	12·4	—	78·6	9·0	85·3
1955–1956	13·8	—	79·1	7·1	83·4
1956–1957	13·9	—	78·9	7·2	83·1
1957–1958	14·0	—	78·9	7·1	79·1
1958–1959	13·7	4·3	76·3	5·7	75·0
1959–1960	13·2	5·0	76·1	5·7	73·6
1960–1961	13·5	4·7	76·1	5·7	72·9
1961–1962	16·3	—	79·7	4·0	80·6
1962–1963	15·8	—	79·7	4·5	78·0
1963–1964	15·5	—	81·0	3·5	78·2
1964–1965	15·0	—	82·3	2·7	81·2
1965–1966	15·5	—	81·2	3·3	82·4

(a) Contributions for the National Health Service are excluded from above figures.

Source: Annual Reports of M.P.N.I. and Annual Abstract of Statistics.

forecasts on the future resources and expenditure of the Insurance Fund with little accuracy so far. Table 8 is a summary of the forecasts and of what actually happened. The discrepancies between the two were not due entirely to forecasting errors but to intervening events which were beyond the work of the Actuary. Predictions of the various factors which affect the financial position of the scheme are extremely difficult. They involve changes in the population structure, variations in sickness and unemployment rates, the growth of the national economy and a host of other factors not to mention political considerations which are not within the scope of the work of the Actuary and yet affect

62

The Cost of Social Security

the scheme so much. In spite of the difficulties involved in predictions, they are a necessary part of social security planning as they foster a more responsible attitude on the part of governments. Social security is a very live political issue and an examination of the costs involved can have a salutory effect on the plans put forward by political parties.

TABLE 8

COMPARISON BETWEEN ESTIMATES AND ACTUAL FINANCIAL POSITION OF THE INSURANCE FUND GREAT BRITAIN – £ MILLIONS

	5.7.1948–31.3.1954			1.4.1954–31.3.1959			1.4.1959–31.3.1964		
	Actual	*Estim.*	*Actual minus Estim.*	*Actual*	*Estim.*	*Actual minus Estim.*	*Actual*	*Estim.*	*Actual minus Estim.*
Income	3004	2726	+278	3525	3192	+333	5574	4979	+595
Outgo	2491	2725	−234	3463	3354	+109	5696	5002	+694
Income Less Outgo	+513	+1	+512	+62	−162	+224	−122	−23	−99

Source: Reports by the Government Actuary on the Quinquennial Reviews.

The financial position of the Industrial Injuries Fund has been very sound so far. Annual income from all sources has always exceeded expenditure of all kinds. Contributions from insured persons and employers exceeded income every year during the period 1948–1962. Since 1962, however, income from this source alone was not enough but taken together with the interest from investment it was adequate up to 1964. If one takes the whole period 1948–1966 then income from the insured persons and employers exceeded all expenditure by about £29m. The only possible conclusion from this is that the Exchequer has benefited handsomely not only because it did not have to bear any cost but also because it used the reserve funds of the scheme at low interests. The reserve funds stood at £333 million on 31 March, 1966.

The Redundancy Fund soon ran into financial troubles owing to the government's economic policies for the redeployment of labour which made heavy demands on the Fund. For this reason the contributions were increased to 10d. for men and 5d. for women.

63

The Cost of Social Security

The cost of public services and particularly of the social services has been rising constantly during the last century.[1] Taking the period since the end of World War I, the cost of public services has risen by about a half while that of the social services has trebled. Expenditure on social security during the same period has doubled though the increase in the last ten years has been higher than that in the social services as a whole. It is more than likely that social security expenditure will continue to increase in the future firstly because the number of retirement pensioners will continue to rise; secondly, because of increased use of supplementary benefits as the stigma of national assistance disappears; and thirdly as the standard of benefits improves with the emergence of earnings-related benefits. Future political decisions, however, may reverse the trend towards increased expenditure on social security through the state scheme but it is most unlikely that they will reverse the trend as regards social security expenditure in general. The demand for better social security benefits is bound to continue whether they are provided by the state or by employer-employee schemes supervised by the state.

TABLE 9

EXPENDITURE ON PUBLIC AND SOCIAL SERVICES AS % OF G.N.P.

UNITED KINGDOM

Year	Public Services	Social Services[a]	Social Security
1920	26·2	6·8	3·5
1938	30·0	11·3	5·5
1955	35·4	16·3	5·8
1965	38·5	20·7	7·8

(a) Social Services = Education, Child Care, Health, Welfare, Housing and Social Security.

Source: Annual Abstract of Statistics. Figures for 1920 and 1938 from 'The Growth of Public Expenditure in the U.K.', Peacock A., and Wiseman J., National Bureau of Economic Research, 1961.

The increase in social security expenditure has not been even through the whole period since 1948 nor has it been uniform for all social security benefits. National Insurance benefits took two-

[1] See Appendix I for a full analysis of public expenditure.

thirds of social security expenditure during the first nine years and since 1958 the proportion has increased to about three-quarters.

TABLE 10

EXPENDITURE ON SOCIAL SECURITY BENEFITS, UNITED KINGDOM

Year	Total Ex-penditure £ millions	Total Ex-penditure as % G.N.P.	Benefits as % of Total Expenditure on Social Security				
			National Ins.	National Ass.	Non-Contr. Pensions	Family Allws.	War Pensions
1949–50	652·6	5·86	63·35	10·09	4·43	10·02	12·10
1950–51	665·4	5·66	62·62	11·89	4·03	9·99	11·47
1951–52	704·9	5·44	62·79	13·14	3·62	9·62	10·84
1952–53	847·5	6·0	61·92	14·31	2·87	11·02	9·91
1953–54	895·6	5·95	61·92	14·10	2·43	12·32	9·31
1954–55	920·9	5·78	61·55	15·04	2·28	12·49	9·72
1955–56	1029·1	6·1	66·29	12·22	1·84	11·06	8·59
1956–57	1077·2	5·84	65·94	12·89	1·57	11·30	8·31
1957–58	1163·3	5·96	66·66	12·92	1·35	11·24	7·82
1958–59	1387·1	6·80	71·86	9·74	1·07	9·72	7·60
1959–60	1458·2	6·80	71·17	11·40	0·90	9·37	7·16
1960–61	1498·9	6·58	70·45	12·66	0·79	9·38	6·72
1961–62	1674·4	6·87	73·26	11·06	0·60	8·61	6·47
1962–63	1776·4	6·91	73·09	12·23	0·48	8·20	5·99
1963–64	2037·9	7·61	74·84	11·76	0·36	7·41	5·63
1964–65	2125·0	7·49	74·85	11·74	0·32	7·36	5·53
1965–66	2494·2	8·07	77·34	10·98	0·21	6·36	5·10

Source: Annual Abstracts of Statistics.

The proportion taken up by national assistance has not shown any consistent trend. It rose or fell depending on the state of the national insurance benefits. Expenditure on non-contributory pensions, war pensions and family allowances has decreased during the whole period. In the case of the first two benefits, this was due to a fall in demand but in the case of family allowances the decrease was due to a fall in the value of the allowances.

A further analysis of expenditure on national insurance benefits shows that retirement pensions are the main expenditure item. They made up two-thirds of the expenditure on national insurance benefits and showed only a slight upward trend between 1954 and 1964. Expenditure on widows' benefits and industrial injuries benefits has also risen, expenditure on unemployment benefit has remained constant while expenditure on sickness benefits has declined.

TABLE 11

ANALYSIS OF EXPENDITURE ON NATIONAL INSURANCE BENEFITS

UNITED KINGDOM

Benefit	1954–55 %	1964–65 %
Unemployment	3·35	3·28
Sickness	16·36	13·69
Maternity	2·50	2·14
Widows' Pensions	6·13	7·30
Guardian's Allowance	0·06	0·03
Child's Special Allowance	—	0·002
Flat-rate Retirement Pensions	66·16	67·94
Graduated Retirement Pensions	—	0·06
Death Grants	0·57	0·49
Industrial Injuries	4·84	5·17

Source: Annual Abstracts of Statistics.

The present contributory system means that benefits are paid only when certain contribution conditions are satisfied. Yet the people who do not satisfy the required contribution conditions are said to be the very same people who qualify for supplementary benefits. It is generally felt that people who are refused insurance benefits usually apply for and are granted a supplementary benefit which is at a higher rate as it includes an allowance for rent. Research is needed to establish how widespread this practice is. If it happens on a very large scale, the contributory principle loses a great deal of its force and the suggestion that flat-rate social security benefits should be financed out of taxation and provided as of right should be examined again.

Chapter Four

ADMINISTRATION OF
SOCIAL SECURITY

THE varied systems of social security administration adopted by different countries are a reflection of the manifold influences that bear on the decision to use one system as against another. Whatever the reasons may have been for the adoption of a particular administrative system, it must attempt to meet at least three aims. Economic efficiency is obviously the first of these aims. As a large business, it is important to beneficiaries and taxpayers that social security uses the least costly administrative system. Money saved on administration can be used for higher benefits. Economic considerations, however, are rarely the deciding factor. In the first place it is not always possible to demonstrate that one system is more economical than another. The use of an 'insurance' system which pays benefits to all who satisfy certain insurance conditions without any investigation into the beneficiaries' personal circumstances is less costly to administer than an 'assistance' system which pays benefits only after a full personal investigation of each and every claim. On the other hand the 'insurance' system is more wasteful than the 'assistance' system since it pays benefits to a number of people who do not need them. On purely financial considerations it is not possible to decide which is the better of these two systems. In the second place there are usually strong historical and political reasons which favour one particular system irrespective of costs. The resentment of the means test in the U.K., the fear of disturbing the balance of power between federal and state authorities in the U.S.A., the wish to maintain active participation of members in the affairs of the insurance funds in Denmark, are illustrations of the influence of historical, political and other factors. Whether the 'insurance' or the 'assistance' system or a combination of both is adopted, administrative efficiency is still one of the top priorities.

The second aim of the administrative system is how to enlist public interest and participation where possible in the work of the social security department. Where this is achieved, it ensures that the work of the department adapts itself to the changing needs and demands of the public. Vice-versa it enables the public to be informed on the work of the department so that it can criticise it intelligently. Legislators of social security systems have attempted to achieve this in different ways depending on the particular configuration of factors present at any one time. The administration of social security by popularly elected members of local authorities or by insurance society committees elected by members, achieve the maximum public participation. Social security systems which are administered by central government departments try to stimulate public interest by the use of appointed local advisory or appeals committees representing the different sections of the public.

Social security administration must also be alive to the human problems of the people it tries to help. A large number of beneficiaries face not only financial but emotional and psychological problems. The widowed mother, the older worker who is made redundant, the person who has a serious accident, all suffer from emotionally traumatic experiences. They have to come to terms with a new situation which involves financial as well as emotional adjustments. Any investigations into the beneficiaries' life should be made with understanding by trained staff; enquiries should be answered courteously and efficiently; payment of benefits should be prompt; and social security offices should be easily accessible.

Economic efficiency, public participation and humane administration are not always compatible. Easy accessibility of social security offices to the public may be contrary to economic efficiency. Public participation may work against humane administration if examination of individual claims is guided by an excessive zeal to reduce the financial burden on the local community as was the case under the poor law system.

Centralisation

The U.N.O. enquiry[1] into the administrative systems of social

[1] *Methods of Social Welfare Administration*, U.N.O., p. 278–279, New York, 1950.

security in thirty member countries concluded that there were three main 'organisational channels' apart from independent provision of social security by private persons. First, direct administration by the central government as is the case in this country. Second, indirect administration through local government as is the situation in the United States; and third, indirect administration through 'autonomous authorities and agencies' of a wide variety ranging from government ad hoc bodies serving the public to voluntary welfare agencies, trade unions, self-governing insurance funds serving their own members only as in some types of social security provision in Denmark. These three methods are not exclusive of one another. There are many countries today employing all three channels and it is doubtful whether there is any European country which has not used all three at some time or other in its history. The centralised system of this country evolved out of the local authority poor law system and the approved societies' insurance schemes.

The Beveridge Report recommended that the administrative system introduced by the National Insurance Act, 1911, which made approved societies responsible for the collection of contributions and the provision of benefits should be ended for two broad reasons. First, it was 'inconsistent with the policy of a national minimum; second the approved society system has disadvantages for insured persons and involves unnecessary administrative costs'.[1] It provided benefits which varied in amount and in quality from district to district and from society to society. All approved societies provided minimum benefits to all their members but some provided extra benefits because of their favourable financial balance. Invariably this meant that the healthier and the more regularly employed section of the community enjoyed better benefits. It is true that in a capitalist society the wealthier section of the community secures for itself more favourable social security provisions in the private market. It is also true that recent state income-related schemes provide higher benefits for the rich. Nevertheless in the social climate of the last war, variable state benefits were considered unacceptable. Moreover, the small size and the local nature of approved societies hindered the mobility of labour and often caused conflict of interests among societies which sometimes resulted in pushing

[1] Beveridge Report, p. 28.

doubtful cases from society to society. Administrative costs were distinctly higher than those of state administered schemes without always resulting in better services to the people.

The Beveridge Report recommended the creation of a Ministry of Social Security to be responsible for insurance and assistance. Beveridge himself, however, was a great believer in voluntary effort and was not happy to see the work of friendly societies being drastically undermined. The way out of the dilemma was the recommendation that the state might wish to employ friendly societies as its administrative agents. Industrial Life Offices which covered 55% of the insured population in 1938 were not considered suitable for this role because they were profit making enterprises. The recommendation for preferential treatment of friendly societies commanded a fair amount of public support. On the other hand a strong body of opinion, including expert opinion from bodies like the Fabian Society and P.E.P. felt that the age of friendly societies as mutual aid associations with strong ties among their members was over. They had now become indistinguishable from commercial enterprises. 'As an experiment in democracy, Approved Society administration of National Health Insurance cash benefits is an almost complete failure. The only Approved Society which is needed is the Nation itself.'[1]

The first step towards the implementation of the Beveridge proposals was the Ministry of Social Insurance Bill in 1944. Beveridge's suggestion for a Ministry of Social Security had not received much support because of the prevailing emphasis on insurance. The only argument was whether the new Ministry ought to be called Social or National Insurance. Beveridge had used the term social insurance throughout his Report as it implied social solidarity, the pooling of risks and the compulsory element of insurance. During the debates on the second reading of the Bill objections were raised that the word social was too vague and misleading. The word National was considered more explicit and meaningful. The suspicion that the term social might popularly be thought of as an abbreviation for socialist 'was not expressed but was probably intended. And so the "Nationals" won the day.'[2]

The relationship of the new Ministry with the friendly societies was still in the balance. The concession made to them in the

[1] *Planning*, PEP, Vol. IX, No. 190, 14 July, 1942.
[2] *The Economist*, 18 January, 1944.

Beveridge Report was not considered an essential part of the plan and it was eventually ignored by the Conservative and Labour Parties. Friendly societies mounted a vigorous campaign to safeguard their interests during the General Election of 1945. All parliamentary candidates were circularised with a document asking for their support that friendly societies should be 'retained as responsible agents of the Government under the new scheme of National Insurance in the administration of sickness and allied benefits'. Most candidates gave their signature including some members of the new Labour Government. In fact the Labour Party's election manifesto declared that approved societies should be excluded from administering national insurance but not 'bona fide friendly societies and trade unions'. Beveridge himself made a last minute plea for the use of friendly societies for an experimental five-year period.[1] The current, however, was definitely flowing against the friendly societies. It was increasingly being felt that contracting out to friendly societies would deprive the national insurance scheme of its image of comprehensiveness. The state would be responsible for so much of the scheme that it was not worth the trouble to employ the friendly societies as its agents for some of the work. It was not, therefore, unexpected that Mr James Griffiths announced to the House that he 'came to the conclusion that the State, having puts its hand to the plough, must complete the job'.[2] The official Conservative policy was in agreement though a number of Conservatives and indeed Labour members dissented strongly. Only the Liberal Party opposed officially the government's policy using the traditional argument that friendly societies' employees would be more personal than civil servants in their dealings with insured people.

The new Ministry of National Insurance was made responsible for the administration of the insurance schemes under the National Insurance Act and National Insurance (Industrial Injuries) Act, 1946 as well as the family allowances scheme under the Family Allowances Act, 1945. It was not involved in the administration of war pensions or national assistance. The system of war pensions was introduced during the First World War and was administered by the Ministry of Pensions. Several proposals

[1] *The Times,* 5 February, 1946.
[2] 2nd Reading of National Insurance Bill, House of Commons, 6 February, 1946.

made during the inter-war period either to merge the work of the Ministry with that of some other related Ministry or vice-versa to extend its work to other duties proved unsuccessful owing mainly to opposition from war pensioners who feared that either course would lead to a deterioration of the service they received. The Beveridge Report examined the issues involved but made no recommendations. The Labour Government was not anxious either to introduce any administrative changes because on the one hand the number of claims for war pensions was bound to be at its highest during the immediate post-war years which would keep the Ministry of Pensions very busy. On the other hand, the new Ministry of National Insurance had so much preparatory work to do before July 1948 when the National Insurance Acts came into force that it could ill afford to take on extra duties. So the two Ministries were allowed to work parallel to each other until conditions were more favourable for reform. The work of the Ministry of Pensions gradually declined because firstly a great deal of its medical services after 1948 were provided under the National Health Service and secondly because the number of all war pensions payable every year declined from 1,136,000 in 1947 to 948,000 in 1952 and was bound to continue declining further. The Government's intention to amalgamate the two Ministries was announced early in 1953[1] and was implemented later in that year in spite of opposition from ex-servicemen's associations. None of the fears of ex-servicemen proved true and in fact the new Ministry of Pensions and National Insurance was able to report that 'the main effect of this change in relation to war pensions is that war pensioners have benefited from the wider network of local offices provided by the combined Ministry, to which in most cases they have less far to travel, and where their problems can now be considered at the same time from the War Pensions and the National Insurance standpoint'.[2] This merger did not achieve full integration of the work of the two Ministries because a few local war pensions offices were allowed to continue their specialist services. Nevertheless, a reduction of 500 staff was achieved in the first year after the merger and possibly more later.

Traditionally the provision of poor relief was the responsibility

---

[1] The Ministry of Pensions Proposed Transfer of Functions, Cmd. 8842, 1953.
[2] Report of the M.P.N.I. for the Year 1953, Cmd. 9159, p. 4.

of local authorities: The Overseers of about 14,000 parishes were responsible form the Elizabethan Act, 1601 to the Poor Law Amendment Act, 1834; the Boards of Guardians of about 600 unions succeeded the Overseers of the parishes until their functions were transferred to the major local authority Councils under the Local Government Act, 1929, which also changed the name of poor relief to public assistance.

This clear transfer of responsibility from smaller to larger local authorities was the first stage in the centralisation of public assistance. The depression of the early 1930's hastened this process. Insurance unemployment benefits which were payable for fixed periods could not cope with long-term unemployment. The unemployed had to rely increasingly on public assistance with the result that local authorities eventually found the burden beyond their resources. The creation of the Unemployment Assistance Board in 1934 to provide assistance to all the able-bodied unemployed who had exhausted their insurance benefits marked the beginning of the transfer of assistance responsibility from local authorities to central government. The Board's members were appointed by the Crown and its finances came completely from central government funds. Its functions were extended to cover supplementary assistance to old age pensioners in 1941 when it changed its name simply to Assistance Board. The process was completed by the National Assistance Act, 1948, which made all types of assistance the responsibility of the Board which was now renamed the National Assistance Board. Suggestions that the Board should be given a more social work type of name – Social Welfare Board – were rejected by the Minister of National Insurance as 'it might lead to confusion of functions'.[1] Beveridge's proposal that the work of the Assistance Board should be completely merged in the work of the Ministry of Social Security was not accepted firstly because it was felt desirable to distinguish between insurance and assistance benefits and secondly because as the Board had executed its functions satisfactorily it was not felt necessary to make any structural changes. The new National Assistance Board retained its semi-autonomous position: Its members were appointed by the Crown, it administered national assistance through its own network of offices but it was answer-

[1] Mr J. Griffiths, 2nd Reading of National Assistance Bill, House of Commons, 24 November, 1947.

able to Parliament through the Minister of National Insurance.

The transfer of responsibility for assistance from local to central government was important firstly because it made possible the maximum standardisation of services and the liberalisation of conditions necessary to granting assistance. Two important changes in 1943, the abolition of the 'household means test' and of the liability of relatives requirement, paved the way to a more humane application of a personal income test. Secondly, it brought about the separation of social work and national assistance. It was generally thought in the past that the administration of assistance could best be done by people who took a personal interest in those who received assistance. It was feared that the transfer of responsibility from local authorities to central government would damage this personal relationship between the givers and the recipients of assistance. There was a great deal of opposition to the proposal in the Old Age & Widows' Pension Bill to make the officers of the Unemployment Assistance Board responsible for the assessment of need among old people and widows. Among those who opposed this and who wanted this duty entrusted to the local pensions committee was no less a personality than Mr Aneurin Bevan who argued that the 'personal relationship which necessarily must exist between those who are giving assistance to the old people and the old people themselves is so essential a part of the effective and humane administration of the assistance that people are frightened that this is to be revolutionised and that old people are now to be passed under the control of officials over whose conduct there is no effective local check'.[1] As Minister of Health, he was responsible for guiding the National Assistance Bill, 1948 through Parliament which not only entrusted assessment of need to the Board's officers but divorced national assistance from social work completely. Local authority welfare departments and other social work agencies were given the responsibility of providing social work help to families in receipt of assistance in the same way that they help other families. The separation of social work from financial assistance was designed to lessen the popular stigma that was attached to the receipt of assistance. There is no reason, however, why enlightened social work assistance should not accompany financial

[1] 2nd Reading, Old Age & Widows' Pension Bill, House of Commons, 29 February, 1940.

74

assistance where necessary. The Children and Young Persons Act, 1963, enabled Local Authority Children's Departments, as part of their social work programme to assist families financially in an effort to prevent family break-up and to rehabilitate children to their families. Financial assistance in this respect is not an end in itself but 'a component in or an adjuvant to a therapeutic goal'.[1]

There was general relief at the abolition of the last vestiges of the Poor Law system in 1948. 'I think of what we are repealing more than of what we are proposing.'[2] declared one M.P. This was a widely shared sentiment. At the same time there was an equally strong optimism that the new order would eventually wipe out the fear of the means test and the stigma attached to the receipt of assistance. 'This Bill wipes out poverty as we know it and any shame attached to need'.[3] These hopes proved false for a number of pieces of research in the 1950's and 1960's showed that a substantial number of old people in financial need would not apply for assistance even though they were entitled to it.[4] Research conducted by the Ministry of Pensions and National Insurance confirmed this: 700,000 pensioner households representing 800,000 pensioners could have received assistance had they applied for it. There were many reasons for this state of affairs ranging from ignorance to apathy but 'three out of ten of the couples and two out of ten of the single men and women said in effect that their pride would not let them ask for help, or that they disliked "charity" '.[5]

The Government's Ministry of Social Security Act, 1966, was a half-hearted measure which introduced a number of minor procedural and structural improvements but left untouched the traditional administration of social security. The Ministry of Pensions and National Insurance and the National Assistance Board were abolished as separate departments and were replaced by the Ministry of Social Security which included a semi-autono-

[1] G. Hamilton, *Theory and Practice of Social Case Work*, 2nd Edition, p. 87, Columbia, 1961.

[2] Mrs Braddock, 2nd Reading of National Assistance Bill, 24 November, 1947.

[3] Mr Woodburn, Secretary of State for Scotland, 2nd Reading, National Assistance Bill, House of Commons, 24 November, 1947.

[4] P. Townsend and D. Wedderburn, *The Aged in the Welfare State*, Bell, 1965.

[5] *Financial and other Circumstances of Retirement Pensioners*, M.P.N.I., p. 84, 1966.

mous board – the Supplementary Benefits Commission – to do the work of the extinct National Assistance Board. The Supplementary Benefits Commission does not constitute a separate department as the National Assistance Board did but a sub-department of the Ministry of Social Security. Responsibility for the main lines of policy and for the standards of supplementary benefits will be the Minister's. The Commission's role is to ensure that 'the administration is responsive to particular and individual needs and to the variations of changes in social climate' and to act as 'a powerhouse of ideas'.[1] The members of the Commission are still appointed by the Crown and they are selected from among the same circles that provided the members of the National Assistance Board. The Government's decision on the status of the Supplementary Benefits Commission within the Ministry of Social Security was a compromise between those who felt that complete integration of assistance and insurance benefits administration was necessary and those who felt that making supplementary benefits completely the direct responsibility of the Minister might bring them 'within political controversy as to be a disservice'.[2] This notion of keeping assistance out of politics dates back to the creation of the Unemployment Assistance Board. It was felt then that 'by making the Board independent of Parliament an attempt was made to take the dole out of politics'.[3] The operative word is 'attempt' for the allowance scales soon became and remained the centre of political controversy. Miss Herbison, herself, 'was against having a Commission' at first but saw the necessity of it later.

The Government's reasons for creating the new Ministry of Social Security were:[4] First, 'to co-ordinate policy for all social security benefits'. It has been argued that by bringing the Supplementary Benefits Commission within the Ministry rather than leaving it outside as was the case with the National Assistance Board, co-ordination of policy will be more possible.

Second, 'to ensure that people who have claimed contributory

---

[1] Miss Herbison, Minister of Social Security, 2nd Reading M.S.S. Bill' House of Commons, 24 May, 1966.
[2] 2nd Reading, Ministry Social Security Bill, House of Commons, 24 May, 1966.
[3] *British Social Services*, P.E.P., 1937.
[4] Miss Herbison's Speech, 2nd Reading Ministry Social Security Bill, House of Commons, 24 May, 1966.

benefits, retirement pension, sickness benefit and so on, also get any help by way of non-contributory benefit to which they are entitled'. Third, to 'develop a new comprehensive service for the public so that inquiries across the whole range of social security can be dealt with at one point of contact'. This is part of the wider movement towards the reorganisation of social services that has been evident during the last few years. The discussions among social workers for the creation of a family service department or a social service department that will incorporate a number of social work services as well as the appointment of the Seebohm Committee on the reorganisation of the Local Authority personal services are another major part of the movement towards the reorganisation of social services. The Conservative proposal to bring the Ministry of Health under the umbrella of the Ministry of Social Security so that co-ordination of benefits in cash and benefits in kind is achieved is another major part of this trend. According to this view the services needed to deal with social insecurity are not cash benefits only but health and welfare services as well. 'Very often, an hour's help in the house is far more valuable than an extra £2. Very often a visit from the health visitor, the proper type of grouped accommodation with a warden, the proper type of welfare service, such as meals-on-wheels, meets, not only the financial need, but the desperate loneliness and feeling of insecurity and fear which people have. It meets the insecurity which we are trying to conquer.'[1] The Labour Government's reply was that such a Ministry would be too 'unwieldy' for efficient and effective administration.

Fourth, 'to end the sharp distinction we have today in separate offices for the administration of contributory and non-contributory benefits in order to meet the feeling . . . that a non-contributory benefit is inferior in kind and savours of charity'. This is a welcome change in official thinking though it is difficult to see how this can happen so long as the state emphasises the virtues of insurance.

Decentralisation

If centralisation was considered necessary in 1946 to ensure uniformity of service, decentralisation was equally necessary for

[1] Miss Pike, Committee stage of Social Security Bill, 13 June, 1966

efficient and humane administration of the social security services. There was already a greal deal of relevant experience in favour of decentralised administration. The Ministry of Labour and the Assistance Board had been operating successfully through a network of local offices for a number of years. Suggestions for a completely centralised system paying out insurance benefits for the whole country from one large central office were only of academic interest. Such a scheme may have been cheaper to run but it would have involved unavoidable long delays and it would have restricted considerably contact with the public. Both the Beveridge Report and the Labour Government were anxious – perhaps over anxious – to achieve the maximum possible contact between social security administrators and the public. They also wanted to see good co-operation with the other local agencies dealing with other needs – employment, health, housing, etc. – of the people. Mr Griffiths' vision of local social insurance offices was that they would be centres 'where people will not be afraid to go, where they will be welcomed, and where they will not only get benefit but advice. I want to see them become not only security offices but citizens' advice bureaux where everyone can go as of right, to speak to someone who is there not to rob them but to help them'.[1]

The National Insurance Act, 1946, provided for the two-tier system of administration of regional and local offices. Local insurance offices are dealing direct with the public in receiving claims, paying benefits, in assisting, advising and providing the public with general information about the various insurance schemes. Local offices in England were first grouped into twelve regions corresponding with the former Civil Defence regions. Every region is controlled and supervised by a regional office. Scotland and Wales are separate regions under a regional office each. In theory regional offices could be abolished and local offices could all be supervised from one central office. This might be more economical but it is felt that it would be a less efficient system, less flexible and less responsive to local problems of the staff and the public.[2] The number of regional offices in England has now been reduced to 10 while the number of local offices has

[1] 2nd Reading National Insurance Bill, 1946, House of Commons, 6 February, 1946.
[2] Sir Clifford Jarrett, Permanent Secretary to the M.P.N.I., 4th Report from the Estimates Committee, House of Commons, paper 274, Q.619, 1964–65.

declined from about 1,000 in 1948 to about 800 in 1965. The Ministry has been able to close a number of its 'public contact' offices and also to amalgamate a number of the local offices to serve larger areas as the insurance scheme became better known to the public and as the practice of paying benefits by postal draft became almost universal. Though a large part of the work on war pensions is done by the local insurance offices there are still 18 offices for war pensions which deal with specialist cases and advise local offices. These could have been integrated into the national insurance office system but for 'the trouble and antagonism which would be involved'[1] for only marginal economies. The government's policy has instead been to reduce gradually the number of war pensions offices to one in each region.

Beveridge's suggestion for the housing of all social security local offices in the same building with the labour exchanges to provide a better service to the public has not been possible to implement. The siting of social insurance offices has instead been guided largely 'by our ability to get any accommodation in which to have our offices'. It is through accident and not through planning that in 219 cases the local insurance offices were housed with employment exchanges and in 120 cases with the National Assistance Board local offices in 1965. This sharing of premises has proved convenient to the public, though it has not resulted in any administrative economies apart from 'economies on common services such as cleaning and that sort of thing'.[2]

The Ministry of Pensions and National Insurance and the Ministry of Labour ran an interesting experiment in management techniques in 1953 using fifty local insurance offices and fifty employment exchanges which shared premises. They were placed under the same manager and the staff of both offices were made interchangeable. The theoretical advantages of economy and efficiency did not materialise because both offices had always been fully busy before the merger. In addition the scheme created problems of management and efficiency due to the wide range of problems that staff and manager were expected to be able to cope with.[3]

[1] Fourth Report p. xxii.
[2] Q. 329; 330. Mr L. Errington, Director of Establishments & Organisation. M.P.N.I.
[3] H. Woolston, 'The Joint Local Office Experiment', *Public Administration*, Vol. XXIII, 1955.

The optimum size of local insurance offices for maximum efficiency is a matter of conjecture. One expert considers that 'the best and the most economical unit all round is the office with a staff of about 35'. He does not consider very large offices economical 'owing to difficulties of management and the number of senior staff needed for supervision'.[1] Another expert feels that bearing in mind all the various relevant factors, a staff of 100 is the optimum size of a local office.[2] In practice, however, it is not always possible or desirable to arrange local offices according to the optimum size even if this was agreed upon. This is one of the many differences between the organisation of a social or public service and a private business whose only concern is profit. Rural insurance offices are very small with a staff as low as six while some city offices have a staff exceeding one hundred. It would be impossible to group many of these rural offices into a smaller number of larger offices without causing undue hardship to the public.

The Ministry of Pensions and National Insurance has managed to reduce its total staff over the years in spite of these considerations and of the overall increase in its work resulting from increased duties and increased population. At the end of 1948 the Ministry of National Insurance had a total staff of 36,659 and in 1953 it incorporated the Ministry of Pensions with a staff of 5,597. The staff of the Ministry was continually declining until the passage of the National Insurance Act, 1959, which necessitated the employment of an extra 2,800 staff apart from 1,200 it added to the staff of the Inland Revenue. At the end of 1965 the total staff was almost identical to the original number of staff in 1948. They were made up as follows:[3]

	No.	% of total
London Headquarters	1,473	3·7
Blackpool Central Office	2,026	5·1
Newcastle Central Office	8,995	22·6
Regional and Local Offices	27,332	68·6
Total	39,826	100·0

[1] Sir G. King, *The Ministry of Pensions & National Insurance,* p. 104, Allen & Unwin, 1958.
[2] Sir Clifford Jarrett, Q. 619 4th Report.
[3] M.P.N.I., Annual Report for 1965, p. 61.

The work of the Ministry's headquarters in London is the obvious one of looking after matters of general policy concerned with legislation, finance, staffing, public relations and general supervision of the regional and local offices. The Central office in Newcastle is responsible for maintaining a detailed up to date record on every insured person. It is a mammoth task and visitors to this office are amazed at the unbelievable volume of insurance records. So long as the payment of insurance benefits is related to the payment of insurance contributions this is a necessary evil. Even after the death of insured persons, summarised contribution sheets have to be kept indefinitely to deal with eventualities such as this: 'A 80 year old man may marry a 20 year old girl; he dies and she does not re-marry. When she comes to die at 70, her death grant could be based on her former husband's insurance.'[1] In addition, there is a constant two-way flow of insurance cards between Newcastle and the 800 local offices and an emergency system of teleprinters linking it with the Regional Offices. One can only imagine the amount of extra work that is involved every time that contributions and benefits are reviewed or when there is an influenza epidemic for instance, or when both coincide. It is for this reason that the administration strongly recommends to Ministers that reviews should be timed outside the winter months. The Central Office at Blackpool is concerned mainly with the administration of the war pensions scheme in conjunction with the Regional and Local Offices.

The National Assistance Board inherited the administrative structure of its predecessor – Regional and local offices, called area offices. Before July 1948 when the National Assistance Act came into force, local authorities maintained about 1,700 relief offices which paid outdoor relief, often in person, to those in need. The work of these relief offices was incorporated in the work of the Board and the practice of paying allowances over the counter was reduced to the bare minimum. The Board started with ten regional offices in England, one in Wales and one in Scotland and a total of 288 local offices. The number of local offices had to be increased quickly to cope with the extra work but it has remained almost constant – about 430 – during the last few years. The Board also maintains about 800 enquiry points known as Supple-

[1] Mr J. McCarthy, (Q. 238, 4th Report), Controller of Newcastle Central Office.

mentary Stations in local insurance offices or Employment Exchanges in areas where there is sufficient demand for such services but not enough to justify a full-scale local office. Mechanical aids which have proved so useful in reducing the amount of work that falls on the officers of the M.P.N.I. are of limited value to the officers of the N.A.B. who have to rely so much on personal office and home interviews with the public. It is not surprising, therefore, that as the amount of work and the expected standard of service increased, the staff of the Board has also increased from 10,853 at the end of 1948 to 13,946 at the end of 1965. The increase would in fact have been much greater than these figures suggest, had it not been for the fact that one aspect of the work of the Board – provision of Polish Hostels – declined during the same period resulting in a staff reduction of about 2,400 in that sector. The distribution of the Board's staff at the end of 1965 was as follows:

	No.	%
Headquarters	705	5·1
Regional and Area Offices	13,002	93·2
Reception and Re-establishment Centres	191	1·4
Polish Hostels	48	0·3
Total	13,946	100·0

The Ministry of Social Security Act, 1966, has combined the administrative machinery of insurance and assistance benefits at central, regional and local level. As the Minister of Social Security pointed out, however, 'the pace at which integration can proceed must necessarily depend on the practicability as well as on the desirability of making changes'.[1] This is particularly important in the integration of local offices where changes are most necessary. Without the physical integration of the local insurance and assistance offices, there is very little chance that the new Ministry will achieve any of the four aims for which it was created. The staff previously employed by the M.P.N.I. and the N.A.B. are now the employees of the Ministry of Social Security. At the end of 1966 they numbered 58,244, an increase of 4,472 over the 1965 figure, due mainly to the introduction of the earnings-related benefits.

[1] 2nd Reading Ministry of Social Security Bill, 24 May, 1966.

The payment of unemployment benefit is still done outside the Ministry of Social Security. It was felt in 1946 that unemployment benefit could best be paid by the same agency which was responsible for finding employment for the beneficiary. The Ministry of Labour local employment exchanges were carrying out both these duties before 1946 and they were allowed to carry on with the difference that they now act as the agents of the Ministry of Social Security.

The Beveridge Report examined the administrative costs of private insurance and state insurance schemes and came to the conclusion that if 'a risk is of such kind that it can fitly be dealt with by compulsory social insurance, that is as a rule administratively the cheapest way of meeting the risk'.[1] Moreover a comprehensive unified state system is cheaper administratively than a state system composed of individual schemes for individual risks.

Experience since Beveridge has demonstrated the economy of state insurance administration. The proportion of the income of the national insurance and industrial injuries fund spent on administration was jointly 4·2%, 4·7%, 4·4% and 4% for the years 1950, 1955, 1960 and 1965 respectively. If administrative costs are calculated in relation to the annual expenditure of the two Funds, then the proportions for the same years are 5·8%, 5·2%, 4·9% and 3·9% respectively. If to the total expenditure of the Funds is added the cost of family allowances and war pensions which are administered by the Ministry, then the proportions for the years 1955, 1960 and 1965 are 4·0%, 3·9% and 3·4% respectively. Whichever way one looks at the administrative costs of the state insurance scheme, they are about half of those incurred by the state scheme when it was administered by approved societies in 1938. The administration of the graduated retirement pension scheme is so confused that it is difficult to make any reliable calculations of its administrative costs. For 1963–64, its income was £222m., its expenditure £½m., and its administrative costs £5½m. excluding the cost of paying the benefits as this is included in the administrative costs of the Ministry. The other graduated insurance benefits have not been running long enough to provide any estimates of administrative costs.

National assistance has proved more costly to administer than

[1] Beveridge Report, p. 286.

national insurance benefits as it is paid only after investigation of each application. The administrative costs of the National Assistance Board amounted to 4·9%, 5·5%, 5·3% and 7·4% of its total expenditure for the years 1950, 1955, 1960 and 1965 respectively. It is interesting too that the Board's administrative costs increased over the years compared to those of the Ministry of Pensions and National Insurance which have declined. The main reason for this opposing trend is the impossibility of using mechanical aids to facilitate the work of the Board to the same extent as they have been used in the work of the Ministry. Finally, even the administration of the National Assistance Board has proved cheaper than the previous administration of the state insurance scheme by approved societies. A word of caution is, however, necessary for comparisons of different schemes at different periods of time. It is more than likely that had the approved societies been allowed to administer the post-war insurance scheme, they would have made use of mechanical aids as well as rationalisation of their staff due to labour shortages and improved management methods.

The Beveridge Report considered that decentralisation and the 'selection and training of staff with special regard to their functions in serving the public and in understanding the human problems with which they will be concerned'[1] were of outstanding importance in the administration of social security. 'Understanding the human problems' is a very broad term capable of many interpretations. The new Ministry of National Insurance did its utmost to provide some kind of training for its staff and by the appointed day, 5 July, 1948, over 16,000 were trained. The aim of the training, however, was very modest. It intended to give 'the right outlook on insurance matters and on relations with the public, as well as actual knowledge'.[2] This broadly applies to the Ministry's training schemes today which are short and predominantly concentrating on legal and administrative matters. It can be argued that the contact of the Ministry officials with the public is limited and superficial and there is no need for their training to be social work orientated. This cannot be argued, however, with the officers of the Supplementary Benefits Commission. They decide on discretionary allowances and often deal with families and individuals with a host of other problems. Yet

[1] Beveridge Report, p. 146.
[2] H. V. Rhodes, 'Setting Up a New Government Department', p. 44, 1949.

their training 'is clearly – and intentionally – a bread-and-butter programme whose aims are limited. The purpose is to produce in the shortest practicable time an officer who will have an adequate knowledge of the mechanics of the job so that he can safely go on to acquire the fund of local knowledge and experience which alone can make him a first-class officer'.[1] It is a short apprentice-ship course of three months spent mostly at the local office. The last three weeks are spent at the Board's Training Centre in London on a course in the art of interviewing. The Board has considered from time to time the need for some full-time univer-sity training of executive officers in social work and social administration but, so far, only part-time or very short courses have been attempted. The recent advertisement by the Supple-mentary Benefits Commission, however, for a Social Work Adviser indicates that social science and social work training of the Commission's officers is a real possibility.

Adjudication

Claims for insurance benefits and family allowances are dealt with in the first place by the insurance officers of the local offices. In difficult cases they can consult the Regional Insurance Officer or the Chief Insurance Officer at the London Headquarters. They may also refer cases of special interest with no precedent to the local tribunal. In the great majority of cases the decisions of the insurance officers are accepted by the claimants but appeals against the decisions of insurance officers are made in a number of cases to the same local tribunal to which insurance officers are entitled to refer cases. On the available published information, there seems to have been a slight decrease both in the number and proportion of appeals and references made to the tribunals. The number of appeals and references as a proportion of all cases dealt with by insurance officers are as follows:

	Insurance Benefits	Industrial Injuries	Family Allowances
1952	0·5%	0·8%	—
1960	0·25%	0·7%	0·2%
1965	0·2%	0·7%	0·2%

[1] K. R. Stow, 'Staff Training in the N.A.B. Problems and Policies', *Public Administration*, Vol. 39, (N.A.B. Training Officer), Winter Issue, 1961.

About 98% of all cases dealt with by the tribunals are appeals from claimants and the remaining 2% are references from insurance officers. Appeals from claimants are less successful than references from insurance officers. Whether this is due entirely to the fact that insurance officers are more selective in their references than insured persons are in their appeals or whether other factors creep in, it is difficult to know. The same difficulty exists in explaining the opposite trend of the success rate of the two groups of cases over the years. Whereas, on the whole, references have improved their chances of success, appeals stand less chances for success today than they did in 1960 and 1955. The chances of success for both references and appeals vary from benefit to benefit but broadly speaking they are very low in family allowances, increasingly better for national insurance benefits and clearly much better for industrial injuries. It appears that the more involved the rules and regulations the better the chances for success.

TABLE 12

SUCCESS RATE OF APPEALS AND REFERENCES TO TRIBUNALS
GREAT BRITAIN

	1955		*1960*		*1965*	
	% success-ful appeals	% success-ful refer-ences	% success-ful appeals	% success-ful refer-ences	% success-ful appeals	% success-ful refer-ences
All N. Insurance Benefits	23·2	45·3	22·6	48·3	21·1	50·2
Unemployment Benefit	27·8	43·5	25·7	48·8	22·9	52·3
Sickness Benefit	19·3	50·0	19·3	40·0	20·0	29·3
Maternity Benefit	11·3	50·0	8·1	—	7·7	Nil
Widows' Benefit	26·3	25·0	29·2	11·1	22·3	40·0
Guardian's Allowance	18·0	—	17·6	—	14·3	—
Retirement Pension	21·4	59·0	28·7	57·1	20·8	16·6
Death Grant	12·5	50·0	11·3	—	11·4	—
Child's Special Allowance	N.A.	N.A.	—	—	Nil	—
All Ind. Injuries Benefits	N.K.	N.K.	42·1	56·5	39·4	76·9
Family Allowances	N.A.	N.A.	7·4	Nil	5·1	—

— = No appeals or References. N.A. = Not applicable. N.K. = Not Known.

Source: Annual Reports of M.P.N.I.

Until 1959, the adjudication system of family allowances was different and separate from that of the insurance benefits. Claims for family allowances were decided by the Minister and appeals were heard by three independent referees. This system was devised before the National Insurance Act, 1946, was passed and was allowed to exist until the whole system of tribunals was reviewed by the Franks Committee in 1956 which recommended the transference of the functions of the Family Allowance Referees to National Insurance Local Tribunals. The committee also examined the possibility of the amalgamation of all the other tribunals in the field of social security – national insurance tribunals, industrial injury tribunals and national assistance tribunals – but came to the conclusion that the functions of the different tribunals were not 'sufficiently cognate to permit of complete integration'.[1]

Nevertheless the general trend towards the unification of the various branches of social security inevitably led to the amalgamation of the tribunals for national insurance benefits and for industrial injuries benefits under the National Insurance Act, 1966. These two types of tribunals were virtually identical in membership and procedure and their amalgamation legalised what was already existing practice. At the end of 1965 there were 202 local insurance tribunals each covering several local insurance offices. Each tribunal is made up of the Chairman who is appointed by the Minister, after consultation with the Lord Chancellor, for a period of three years. The other two members of the tribunals are again appointed by the Minister, one from among persons who represent the employers and the other to represent work people. The basic idea is that the composition of the tribunal should represent as wide a section of the community as possible. This is an impossibility bearing in mind that there are only two members and that the community no longer consists of two monolithic classes – the proletariat and the bourgeoisie. Both the Chairman's and the two members' term of office is usually extended but it may be terminated if they undertake any work which may influence their independence and impartiality. The Chairman usually has legal qualifications and is paid a fee for each session while the other two members receive reimbursement of their expenses.

The medical adjudication system for industrial injuries was not affected by the changes of the 1966 Act. Medical questions which involve the diagnosis of occupational diseases and the assessment

[1] Report of the Committee on Administrative Tribunals and Enquiries, 1967, p. 3, Cmnd. 218.

of the degree of disablement resulting from accidents at work are decided by independent medical boards. At the end of 1965 there were 110 medical boards in England, Wales and Scotland consisting usually of two doctors. In certain cases, however, one doctor may be sufficient to conduct the medical examination provided the person examined consents to this. Cases of disagreement between the two members of the medical board are referred to a board of three doctors where a majority decision stands. Appeals against the decisions of the medical boards can be made to one of the 12 medical appeal tribunals which can also hear relevant references from the Minister. The decisions of the Medical Appeal Tribunals are final except on points of law where there can be an appeal to the Chief National Insurance Commissioner and to the Courts.

Because of the non-contractual nature of assistance, the proportion of applications which have been rejected by the Board every year has been considerably higher than in the Insurance scheme. It has varied between 12% and 16% since 1948 with no definite upward or downward trend.[1] Appeals against the decisions of the officers of the National Assistance Board were made to National Assistance Appeal Tribunals provided under the National Assistance Act 1948. No attempt has been made by the Social Security Act, 1966 to amalgamate them with the National Insurance Tribunals because of the different nature of cases they deal with. These tribunals were made up of three members of whom the Chairman and one member were appointed by the Minister while the third member was appointed by the Board itself 'from a panel of persons nominated by the Minister to represent work people'.[2] This power of the Board to appoint the work people's representative has now been vested in the Minister. At the end of 1965 there were 152 such tribunals for England, Wales and Scotland.

Appeals from the National Insurance Tribunals can be made to the Chief National Insurance Commissioner and his National Insurance Commissioners. These are full-time appointments made by the Crown on the recommendation of the Lord Chancellor from among Barristers and Advocates of not less than ten years' standing. The decisions of the Commissioner are final under the

[1] See table 61, p. 224.
[2] 5th Schedule, National Assistance Act, 1948.

1946 Act but there can in fact be an appeal to the High Court on errors of law. Such cases, however, are very rare indeed.

Before 1958 appeals against the decisions of the National Insurance Tribunals to the Commissioner could be made by the insurance officer and an association representing the claimant. The claimant, however, could only appeal if the tribunal's decision was not unanimous; otherwise he had to be granted leave from the tribunal or the Commissioner. In industrial injury tribunals, all parties required leave to appeal in every case. The Franks Committee criticised this anomaly and recommended that 'in both national insurance and industrial injuries cases all parties should be given an automatic right of appeal to the Commissioner'.[1] This was adopted in 1958 and it applies to the new combined national insurance tribunals under the National Insurance Act, 1966.

There is no appeal from National Assistance Tribunals. The Franks Reports did not recommend any change to this because 'by their very nature questions of assistance require to be finally determined as quickly as possible'.[2] In cases where the tribunal rejects appeals against the Board's decision not to grant assistance, this objection does not apply. The applicant has nothing to lose by an appeal. It is only in cases where the tribunal rejects appeals against the rate of assistance that the objection raised in the Franks Report is valid. These two types of appeals form 99% of all appeals to the tribunals under the National Assistance Act, 1948. The proportion of appeals which resulted in an increase of the allowance has been rather low as Table 13 shows. It is certainly not impossible to devise a system whereby appeals were allowed in such a way as to satisfy the objection raised in the Franks Report. This would also satisfy the objections of those who consider the finality of the tribunals' decisions as unhealthy to democratic administration. It should be made clear, however, that even under the present system appeals can be made to the High Court in cases where there is an error of law in the tribunal's decision, or where the decision was given in excess of the tribunal's jurisdiction.

Tribunals always run the risk of being over-identified with the Ministry on whose work they adjudicate with the result that their

[1] Franks Report, p. 41.
[2] Franks Report, p. 42.

Administration of Social Security

TABLE 13

APPEALS AGAINST DECISION NOT TO GRANT ASSISTANCE AND THE RATE OF ASSISTANCE – GREAT BRITAIN

Outcome of Appeals	*1955*	*1960*	*1965*
	%	%	%
Decision confirmed or Rate confirmed	83·53	76·4	78·9
Rate increased	16·41	23·5	20·7
Rate reduced	0·06	0·1	0·3

Source: Annual Reports of National Assistance Board.

impartiality, real or apparent, may suffer. Their members are, after all, appointed by the Minister, their Clerk is an official of the Ministry and they often meet in the Ministry's local offices. In 1960, for example, 131 insurance tribunals met in premises of the M.P.N.I. and 93 met elsewhere. Of all national assistance tribunals, 119 met in the offices of the National Assistance Board, 18 met elsewhere and 15 met in both types of premises. Both the Franks Committee and the 1st Report of the Council of Tribunals stated clearly that 'in principle this is not an arrangement which we favour'.[1] Suggestions have also been made for the appointment of independent Clerks.

Before 1958 national insurance tribunals met in private while industrial injury tribunals used to sit in public unless there were exceptional circumstances justifying a private hearing. Since 1958 they have sat in public unless the person concerned asks for a private hearing or matters of security are involved. In the second half of 1959 there were 23,306 appeals to local tribunals and only 633 requests for private hearings, 511 of which were granted. Originally, legal representation was not allowed in national insurance tribunals but it was permitted, with the consent of the Chairman, in industrial injury tribunals. Claimants could, however, be assisted to present their case by a friend or acquaintance. This usually meant that trade union members were represented by union officials while the others presented their case themselves as best they could. Following the recommendation of the Franks Committee, legal representation has been allowed in all social security tribunals but very little use has been made of this in practice.

[1] 1st Report of the Council of Tribunals, p. 19, 1959.

The Donoughmore Committee which examined, among other things, the place of tribunals in government in 1932 regarded them as rather exceptional bodies to be used in special circumstances under strict safeguards.[1] The extension of the public and social services that followed the last war, however, brought about a mushroom growth of tribunals. By the mid-1950's when the Franks Committee examined their work, they were 'a permanent feature of our society and . . . likely to increase rather than decrease'.[2] The function of tribunals is to provide the public with a convenient medium for objections mainly against the decisions of public administrators. They decide on administrative disputes usually between the citizen and the state though in some instances, such as rent tribunals, they adjudicate between individuals on matters relating to the interpretation and administration of the law. Their advantages over ordinary courts are their 'cheapness, accessibility, freedom from technicality, expedition and expert knowledge of their subject'.[3] No comparative study of the work of these two groups of bodies has been made to test the validity of these assertions. A number of letters to *The Times*,[4] for example, after the publication of the Franks Report, including one from a member of the Franks Committee, expressed concern at the mounting complexity of the law and the increasing formality that was creeping into the deliberations of the national insurance tribunals. This state of affairs would have an adverse effect on the outcome of appeals from the public. This was contrary to the general conclusion of the Franks Report that 'the system is generally considered to have operated smoothly for many years, and we are satisfied that no structural changes are called for'.[5]

Appeals to the Minister against the decisions of insurance officers can be made on two main issues: First to determine the insurance class a person belongs to or whether he is insured under the industrial injuries scheme; secondly on questions of contributions usually on whether the contribution conditions for benefit are satisfied. As a rule the Minister orders a local inquiry before giving his decision which is final subject only to appeal on a question of law to the High Court.

[1] Report of the Committee on Ministers' Powers, Cmd. 4060, 1932.
[2] Franks Report, p. 1.
[3] The Franks Report, p. 9.
[4] *The Times,* 6 September, 1962.
[5] The Franks Report, p. 39.

Advisory Committees

All centrally administered public services need some kind of links or bridges between the government departments and the public. 'Social administration', however, 'needs such bridges more perhaps than any other kind of government activity'.[1] The National Insurance Acts, 1946 and National Assistance Act, 1948, provided for the establishment of advisory committees to perform this function of lubricating the lines of communication between the two sides.

Advisory committees exist both at the central and local level of social security. The National Insurance Advisory Committee has two main functions. To advise the Minister on any questions referred to it by the Minister relating to the operation of the National Insurance Acts including changes to the law. It is true to say that the reports which the Committee has made since 1948 have dealt only with administrative points and minor issues and not with major issues of principle. This is not to belittle the work of the Committee for the ironing out of anomalies however small they may be, make for improved administration. The second main function of the Committee is to scrutinise any new regulations made by the Minister. He has a statutory duty, unless there are exceptionally urgent circumstances, to ask the Committee to examine and give advice on any proposed new regulations on social insurance. The Committee is obliged to give public notice and to invite representations from the Ministry's officials and from outside interested bodies and persons on the proposed new regulations. The Committee's reports and recommendations must be laid before Parliament together with the new regulations the Minister may have made. Usually the Minister accepts the recommendations made by the Committee but if he rejects any he must justify his decision to Parliament. This has proved a most useful procedure particularly during the first few years of the new insurance scheme. On the whole the procedure whereby civil servants have to explain to an independent committee the reason and justification of new proposals and regulations 'is a very whole-some discipline to the Department itself'.[2] The Committee con-

[1] E. N. Gladden, 'British Public Service Administration', p. 141, Staples, 1961.
[2] Sir G. King, *The Ministry of Pensions & National Insurance*, p. 120, Allen & Unwin, 1958.

sists of a Chairman appointed by the Minister and four to eight members at least one of whom must be a woman. Four of the members are appointed after consultation with the employers, the trade unions, friendly societies and the government of Northern Ireland. The Minister has power to pay a salary and other expenses to members of the Committee and to reimburse travelling and other expenses to persons who are invited by the Committee to give evidence to it.

The Industrial Injuries Advisory Council performs similar functions in the industrial injuries scheme. It has the additional responsibility of investigating possible occupational diseases and recommending their inclusion in the prescribed list for industrial injury benefits. It does not follow the same formal procedure in preparing or presenting reports as the National Insurance Advisory Committee. Its reports, for example, on draft regulations are not always published and the Minister is not obliged to lay them before Parliament. It would be rash to deduce from this, however, that its reports exercise any less influence on the Minister. It is a larger body consisting of a Chairman and fifteen members all appointed by the Minister. Again the procedure for the appointment of members is not so rigorously laid down in the Act. The only condition the Minister has to meet is that he must appoint an equal number of members representing workers and employers after consultation with the relevant organisations. There are no good reasons, apart from historical accidents, to justify the differences in structure and procedure of the two central advisory committees.

The Central Advisory Committee on War Pensions is very different. It consists of about thirty members with the Minister of Pensions and National Insurance as the Chairman. Its membership includes M.P.s, M.P.N.I. high ranking civil servants, representatives of the local war pensions committees, ex-service men's organisations and relevant welfare organisations. It meets infrequently (it met only once in 1965) and it deals with questions of general policy and administration.

There is no equivalent central committee for supplementary benefits as the functions of such a committee are presumably performed by the Supplementary Benefits Commission.

At the local level, there were until the Ministry of Social Security Act, 1966, 74 separate local national assistance advisory committees with a sub-committee for each local office. About half of the members were appointed on the nominations of local authorities, employers and trade unions. The majority of committees also included one member of the local Old Age Pensioners' Association. Their function was to offer advice to the board's officers on local problems or on individual cases presenting special problems. On the occasions that they see a person on assistance their aim is mainly to assist the Board's officer in his efforts to rehabilitate the person on assistance. The functions of the National Insurance Local Advisory Committees are even more limited because of the statutory determination of insurance benefits. They offer advice on mattersof local interest, i.e., facilities for the public at local insurance offices, opening a new local office, etc. Committee members are appointed by the Minister after consultation with employers' and insured persons' organisations. There were 224 advisory committees for England, Wales and Scotland at the end of 1965 consisting of about 20 members each. The functions of the same committees covered industrial injuries benefits since the Industrial Injuries Act, 1953.

Assistance and Insurance local advisory committees were amalgamated under the Social Security Act, 1966. The function of the new social security advisory committees is not any different from that of their predecessors. It is 'to act as an intermediary between the Ministry and the public, so that on the one hand local opinion may be brought to the notice of the Ministry and on the other the public may be helped to understand what facilities are available at the local offices and under what conditions local administration has to be carried on'.[1] Each committee elects a sub-committee from among its members to deal with supplementary benefits matters. The committees can also advise the Minister on appointments to the local tribunals. They meet at such intervals as they may themselves decide and they sit in private unless they decide to admit members of the public and the Press on special occasions.

When the system of advisory committees in the national insurance and assistance schemes was discussed in Parliament after the war, it was hoped that it would provide the local, personal touch to social security which the officers of the Ministry could

[1] Notes on the Ministry and Advisory Bodies, Ministry of Social Security, 1966.

not provide because of their official status. This has certainly not happened. The scepticism which some M.P.s expressed that these committees were likely to become 'more hidebound than the assistance officers themselves' and possibly 'dumping ground for odd questions'[1] has been proved right. Their functions should be more publicised and they should be extended to enable them to hear complaints from insured persons about all relevant matters affecting them. They have suffered from the fact that their duties were too general and not specific enough. There is always the danger for an advisory committee with too general duties to degenerate 'into a council which receives reports and accepts them – which acts for the most part ex post facto and finds that there is little which it can usefully do'.[2] They should be given more specific functions and they should be made more open to public pressure and criticism.

Finally, there are local War Pensions Committees appointed by the Minister from among persons known for their interest in this branch of social security. Their functions include those of the other committees plus the very important addition that they can hear complaints from individual war pensioners who are not satisfied with decisions of the Ministry, affecting their individual pension.

Prosecution

In a scheme involving on one hand the payment of contributions from a large number of employers employing about 25 million insured persons, and on the other the payment of benefits to an even larger number of persons, it is inevitable that a certain amount of evasion, abuse and fraud will be found. It is indeed difficult to be precise about the real extent of these practices. On the contribution side, about $3\frac{1}{2}$ million 'deficiency' notices are sent every year by the Ministry to contributors whose insurance cards contain fewer stamps than they should do. An unknown number of these contributors have a perfectly good explanation but another unknown number have no such explanation. If there is no reply to the deficiency notice, the Ministry follows up only

[1] Sir H. Webb, 2nd Reading of National Assistance Bill, House of Commons, 24 November, 1947.

[2] R. V. Vernon and N. Mansergh, (Ed.), *Advisory Bodies*, p. 436, Allen & Unwin, 1940.

those cases where the deficiency in stamps is fairly substantial. For small sums, the cost of chasing exceeds the income derived. In fact, from the financial point of view the defaulter may eventually lose more in benefits than what he saved in contributions. There are two reasons for chasing defaulters: The duty to the Insurance Fund and the duty to the contributor. The first is to ensure the collection of all contributions that are payable and the second to protect the contributor from jeopardising futute insurance benefits for himself and his family.

The annual number of prosecutions for failure to pay contributions and allied offences is understandably small. The number of employers against whom legal proceedings were taken has remained constant since 1948. This number, however, does not

TABLE 14

NUMBER OF PROSECUTIONS FOR NON-PAYMENT OF CONTRIBUTIONS

GREAT BRITAIN

	1951	*1954*	*1960*	*1965*
Employers	1182	1163	1602	1158
Self-Employed	1673	4234	6208	2507
Non-Employed	28	52	78	23

Source: Annual Reports of Ministry of Pensions & National Insurance.

tell us the number of employees involved though it is known that it is the small employers who are the defaulters. The number for 1965 does not include those employers prosecuted by the Inland Revenue for non-payment of graduated contributions. The number of self-employed and non-employed defaulters increased steadily up to 1960 when it started declining. Penalties for non-payment of contributions are mostly fines though prison sentences have been applied in serious cases.

Prosecutions against people for offences connected with drawing benefit improperly have not shown any particular trend nor any great variations over the years. The commonest type of offence is undoubtedly drawing benefit while at work. This explains the very sharp decline in prosecutions against widows after the abolition of the earnings rule in 1964. In National Assistance, the increase in prosecutions since 1960 is the result of a change of policy of the Board in 1961 in the prevention and detection of fraud and not so much to any real increase in lawless-

TABLE 15

NUMBER OF BENEFIT FRAUD PROSECUTIONS

GREAT BRITAIN

	1951	*1954*	*1960*	*1965*	*Commonest Type of Offence*
War Pensions		24	16	2	—
Family Allowances	312	165	69	78	Receiving allowance for a child not maintained
Unemployment Benefit	250	370	372	391	Drawing benefit while at work
Sickness Benefit	447	712	520	723	
Maternity Benefit	9	18	10	13	Non-disclosure of earnings whilst in receipt of benefit
Retirement Pension	66	103	45	39	
Widows' Benefit	177	212	123	25	
Guardian's Allowance	1	—	1	—	
Child's Special Allwce.	—	—	—	—	
Death Grant	1	—	—	—	
Industrial Injuries	50	129	83	73	Drawing benefit while at work
Irregular Encashment of postal drafts	—	16	31	49	
National Assistance	978	959	826	2197	Non-disclosure of earnings
Total	2291	2708	2096	3590	

Source: Annual Reports Ministry of Pensions & National Insurance.

ness among assistance recipients. Taking into account the number of existing allowances and the number of new allowances paid in 1965, the number of prosecutions for benefit fraud was only a minute proportion – less than 0·5% – of the Board's cases. The fact that assistance must be granted speedily and on self-supplied information 'is bound to offer temptation to the morally weak as well as to the deliberately unscrupulous'.[1] In order to prevent this and to satisfy the public conscience, the Board has recruited a team of special investigators for difficult fraud cases. On the whole the available evidence shows that the public have shown a remarkable compliance with the rules and regulations of the Social Security system both on its contribution and benefit side.

Time Limits

Insurance schemes must set limits for claiming benefits and for

[1] N.A.B. Report, Cmnd. 1730, p. 41, Year 1961.

cashing orders for payments of benefits. Claims for unemployment benefit should be made on the first day of unemployment at the Employment Exchange, certificates for sickness and injury benefit claims should be sent to the local social security office within six days from the start of incapacity etc. Postal drafts for the payment of unemployment, sickness or injury benefit which are not cashed within three months are not valid and applications for fresh drafts are necessary. Delays in cashing drafts beyond six months from the date of issue may result in loss of benefit. Similar regulations apply to other benefits. These time limits are necessary for efficient and economical administration and for the protection of the Insurance Fund against stale claims or doubtful claims which become increasingly difficult to prove with the passage of time. At the same time, such time limits should not be so excessively strict as to prejudice claims made in reasonably good time bearing in mind the emotional state of the claimant and the non-familiarity of the public particularly first claimants with insurance procedures. The underlying principle of time limits was defined by the National Insurance Advisory Committee as follows: 'While the time limit allowed should not be so long as to encourage laxness on the part of claimants it should be long enough to allow any insured person, able to take a normal interest in his affairs, conveniently to do all that needs to be done in preparing and making his claim'.[1]

The system of time limits seems to have worked well so far and there has been no noticeable public concern about it. This has been made possible through good publicity familiarising the public of the time limit provisions and the use of the escape clause which allows extension of the time limits where there is a good cause for delay.

[1] 'Time Limits', N.I.A.C. Cmnd. 8483, p. 9. 1952.

Chapter Five

UNEMPLOYMENT AND REDUNDANCY BENEFITS

UNEMPLOYMENT creates two main interrelated problems: Finding a new job and providing an income during the period of unemployment. The work of the Ministries attempting to deal with these two problems i.e., the Ministry of Labour and the Ministry of Social Security, must be seen as complementary. It is generally agreed that long-term unemployment demoralises people even when the state provides cash benefits to the unemployed. Vice-versa, even when the unemployed can find a new job without much delay, they need financial support as of right to sustain themselves and their families in good physical and mental health.

I. Unemployment

Who are the Unemployed?

Long-term mass unemployment has been eradicated in this country. The average annual rate of unemployment has been about 2% since 1948. Complete eradication of unemployment, however, is not only impossible but some would say inadvisable. It is impossible in the sense that there is always a minority of the population who for personal reasons find it difficult to keep themselves in permanent employment. There are moreover the young, the newly arrived immigrants or married women returning to work who are in search of a job for the first time. It is inadvisable in the sense that mobility of labour from declining to new industries is vital to the interests of the nation. Some would also argue that an extremely low rate of unemployment forces wages up beyond productivity with detrimental effects on the economy of the country. But if mass unemployment has been abolished, there is still a great deal of the other two types of unemployment – residual unemployment and redundancy. The present Government's measures for the redeployment of labour have focused attention once again on the problems of unemployment which dominated public discussion so much before the last war.

Very little is known about the residually unemployed. An enquiry by the Ministry of Labour in August 1961[1] showed that the Ministry's employment officers considered that 59% of the unemployed men were difficult to place on personal grounds, mostly age and health; another 6% were also considered difficult because of unsatisfactory qualifications; and the remaining 35% were not difficult to place but local opportunities were limited for half of them. Similar observations were made for single women. Married women, however, presented a different picture. Their main problem was the lack of suitable employment opportunities in the locality. 90% of the unemployed men had experienced up to three spells of unemployment in the preceding year and the remaining more than three spells, some exceeding eight or more spells. The situation was better for women, very few of whom had experienced more than three spells of unemployment in the preceding year. Both men and women who had experienced long spells of unemployment were of low educational and occupational standard.

A similar study by the Ministry of Labour in October 1964 confirmed the conclusions reached on the main characteristics of the unemployed.[2] It also provided some interesting results on the relationship between the length of unemployment and the chances of rehabilitation. Most of those with good employment prospects were the short-term unemployed in the process of moving from one job to another. Vice-versa the long-term unemployed were mostly people with personal handicaps. Of the total, about 37·5% were short-term unemployed, i.e. less than nine weeks. This proportion was highest – 77·8% – among those who could get a job without difficulty and lowest among those who would find difficulty in getting employment on personal grounds – 21·5%. Those who would find it difficult to get a job on non-personal grounds occupied a middle position – 37·2%. At the other extreme 12·0% of the total had been unemployed for over two years. The corresponding proportions, however, of

[1] Ministry of Labour Gazette, Vol. LXX, No. 4, April, 1962.
[2] Ministry of Labour Gazette, Vol. LXXIV, No. 4, April, 1966.

those who should get a job without difficulty, of those who would find it difficult to get a job on non-personal grounds and on personal grounds were 1·0%, 7·3% and 18·1% respectively. Further details between the relationship of length of unemployment, personal details of the unemployed and chances of employment are found in Appendix II.

An associated study by the Ministry of Labour in 1961 into the claiming of unemployment benefit of the working population reinforced the general impression that unemployment was mainly concentrated heavily among a small section of the population rather than being spread thinly among the general population.[1] The sample covered persons who were aged 15–53 in 1949 and who drew unemployment benefit for the first time during the period 1949–1961. Table 16 presents the picture of the two extreme age-groups where all the data was available. During the whole twelve-year period covered by the enquiry, less than one-

TABLE 16

FIRST CLAIMS FOR UNEMPLOYMENT BENEFIT ACCORDING TO AGE AND SEX
OF RECIPIENTS FOR THE PERIOD 1949–1961

	Men		Women Single, Divorced Widowed		Married Women	
	16–20 yrs. in 1949 %	41–45 yrs. in 1949 %	16–20 yrs. in 1949 %	41–45 yrs. in 1949 %	16–20 yrs. in 1949 %	41–45 yrs. in 1949 %
July 1949–July 1950	6·6	4·9	4·6	4·5	6·3	8·6
July 1950–July 1951	3·9	2·6	2·7	2·3	2·2	2·8
July 1951–July 1952	4·6	3·9	9·1	5·3	12·0	13·9
July 1952–July 1953	5·0	2·5	3·7	2·8	6·3	3·2
July 1953–July 1954	3·6	1·3	2·2	1·3	2·2	1·2
July 1954–July 1955	2·5	1·2	1·3	1·1	1·7	0·7
July 1955–July 1956	1·9	1·1	1·2	1·5	3·1	2·6
July 1956–July 1957	3·2	1·6	1·6	1·6	3·1	3·4
July 1957–July 1958	2·9	1·8	1·6	2·1	2·2	1·8
July 1958–July 1959	2·7	1·8	2·2	1·2	2·0	1·1
July 1959–July 1960	1·4	0·9	1·8	1·3	1·8	0·9
July 1960–March 1961	1·1	0·6	0·6	0·4	1·7	0·5
Total for all years	39·3	24·3	32·9	25·2	44·6	40·7

Source: Ministry of Labour Gazette, November, 1962. (Vol. LXX, No. 11.)

[1] Ministry of Labour Gazette, Vol. LXX, No. 11, November, 1962.

third of the insured population drew any unemployment benefit. The proportion of younger workers claiming unemployment benefit was constantly higher than that of older workers for both sex and all marital statuses. This might reflect trade union policy of 'last-in, first-out' and the fact that young people are more unsettled in their jobs. Interesting enough, young single women were less likely to claim unemployment benefit than young men. The proportion of married women who drew unemployment benefit for the first time was substantially higher than that of other women or men. This observation, however, should be accepted with a great deal of caution due to the extra limitations of the sample for married women. Moreover the incidence and duration of unemployment benefit do not necessarily go together.

This concentration of unemployment among a section of the population raises policy questions regarding the best methods of dealing with residual unemployment. There is a need of more training facilities, of social work help to some of the unemployed and of better geographical distribution of industry. Raising the overall demand for labour may not be the best method of solving the problem.[1]

Unemployment Benefit Claims

As a result of the low rate of unemployment, the absolute numbers of claims for unemployment benefit have been comparatively low bearing in mind the size of the insured population. The total number of all claims made every year, the overwhelming majority of which are granted, has varied between $2\frac{1}{2}$ million and $3\frac{1}{2}$ million since the scheme came into operation in 1948. Expenditure on unemployment benefits has been low, too, bearing in mind the changes in the amount of benefits.

Not all the unemployed, however, are entitled to unemployment benefit. Table 18 is a summary of the national situation of all persons who registered for work at Employment Exchanges and Youth Employment Offices at four different dates in 1965 – 8 February, 10 May, 9 August and 8 November.

The vast majority of boys and girls under the age of 18 do not qualify for unemployment benefit because they have not yet paid

[1] L. C. Hunter, 'Unemployment in a Full Employment Society', *Scottish Journal of Political Economy*, Vol. 10, 1963.

TABLE 17

CLAIMS AND EXPENDITURE ON UNEMPLOYMENT BENEFIT

GREAT BRITAIN

Year*	Number of Claims	Expenditure
1950	2,795,000	£19,209,000
1951	2,479,000	£17,027,000
1952	3,584,000	£14,795,000
1953	2,849,000	£26,783,000
1954	2,606,000	£22,158,000
1955	2,322,000	£15,662,000
1956	2,611,000	£15,655,000
1957	2,575,000	£20,896,000
1958	3,518,000	£25,374,000
1959	3,002,000	£49,428,000
1960	2,447,000	£41,911,000
1961	2,489,000	£30,177,000
1962	3,451,000	£36,265,000
1963	2,735,000	£64,453,000
1964	2,436,000	£64,640,000
1965	2,364,000	£44,907,000
1966	2,633,000	£49,172,000

* Year ends on 31st December for number of claims but on 31st March for Expenditure.

Source: Annual Reports of M.P.N.I.

TABLE 18

ENTITLEMENT TO UNEMPLOYMENT BENEFIT, 1965

GREAT BRITAIN

	Men	Women, Single, Widowed and Divorced	Married Women	Boys and Girls	Total
	%	%	%	%	%
Receiving Unemployment Benefit Only	44·7	40·8	48·6	16·8	42·4
Receiving Unemployment Benefit and National Assistance	9·4	4·8	—	—	7·3
Receiving National Assistance Only	25·9	27·2	4·9	9·4	22·2
Others Registered for Work	20·0	27·2	46·5	73·8	28·1
Total	100·0	100·0	100·0	100·0	100·0

Source: Ministry of Labour Gazettes 1965–1966.

the necessary number of contributions. The proportion of married women receiving unemployment benefit is comparatively high because married women who do not pay full contributions do not register at Employment Exchanges in the same proportions as women who pay full contributions. The available statistics do not differentiate between these two groups of married women workers. Men and single women show very similar success rates in their claims for unemployment benefit. About half receive unemployment benefit mostly without the addition of national assistance. About one-quarter rely completely on national assistance. This includes those who have drawn all the unemployment benefit they were entitled to, those whose claims were disallowed because they did not satisfy all the qualifying conditions, newly arrived immigrants who have not had time to pay contributions, and those who before registering as unemployed had been self-employed or non-employed. Finally about one-fifth of the men and one-quarter of the single women are receiving no unemployment or assistance benefit. This includes some of the groups just mentioned who do not qualify for national assistance and those who have just claimed benefit and are awaiting a decision on their claims.

Qualifying Conditions for Unemployment Benefit

The National Insurance Act, 1946 did not introduce any innovations in the unemployment insurance scheme apart from extending its scope to cover all employed persons irrespective of their occupation. Similarly no alterations of any substance have been made to the scheme since 1946. The contribution conditions qualifying for benefit introduced by the Act were simple and they still apply today. They are that first, at least twenty-six class I contributions were paid from the date of the person's entry into the insurance scheme and the date of claim for benefit; second, at least fifty class I contributions were paid or credited during the contribution year preceding the beginning of the benefit year. No benefit is paid if the first condition is not satisfied. If it is satisfied but the number of contributions in the second condition is less than fifty, but not below twenty-six, benefit is paid at a reduced rate. An allowance for an adult dependant is also reduced but not an allowance for a dependant child. If both conditions are satisfied, benefit is paid in full. The same contribution conditions apply to sickness benefit.

The Act provided unemployment benefit in normal circumstances for a period of up to 180 days in any one spell. Under special regulations, benefit could be paid up to twelve months for those who were insured for five years or more. The maximum period was extended to 19 months in 1953. The National Insurance Act, 1966 combined the normal and special maximum periods with the result that benefit can now be paid in all cases for a maximum period of 12 months in any one spell of unemployment. Those who have drawn unemployment benefit for the maximum period they are entitled to, can qualify again after they have been at work for 13 weeks and have paid full contributions. The first three days of unemployment are considered 'waiting days' and no benefit is paid unless the person concerned is unemployed or incapacitated for work for a total of 12 days in the subsequent 13 weeks. The 12 days need not be consecutive but they do not include isolated days, i.e., one day of unemployment or incapacity for work per week. The same rules on 'waiting days' apply to sickness benefit as well.

The Beveridge Report recommended unemployment benefit for the whole period of unemployment on two conditions: First, that the recipient should be willing to accept suitable work and second, that after six months' benefit he may be asked to undergo retraining at a training centre as a condition for continued benefit. The Government rejected these proposals as involving undue Government interference in the private life of citizens and it might bring the idea of training into disrepute. Instead it made unemployment benefit completely dependent on the contribution record of the claimant. In many respects this was an unfortunate line of policy because a person's employment record may be completely beyond his control. It may be due to changes in national policy as the recent waves of redundancies have shown.

Payment of unemployment benefit is not automatic even in cases where the contribution conditions are satisfied. The 1946 Act incorporated most of the clauses of previous legislation on unemployment which were intended to minimise the abuse of the scheme and to ensure a speedy return to work. Unemployed persons have to register at the Employment Exchange on the first day of their unemployment and be available for work. Spare-time jobs undertaken during periods of unemployment must not interfere with the availability of the person concerned for full-time employment. For obvious reasons unemployment benefit is not paid if a person is unemployed because of a strike or any other trade dispute unless he can prove that neither he nor any of his fellow workers in the same grade are taking part, financing or directly interested in the dispute. These conditions in effect bar the great majority of workers who are laid off because of a strike. A person may also be disqualified from receiving unemployment benefit for a period up to six weeks if he leaves his employment voluntarily without good reason; if he loses his employment through misconduct for such things as bad time-keeping, non-compliance with work rules, absenteeism without good reason, etc; or if he refuses or neglects to apply for a job or refuses to accept a suitable job. Normally suitable employment means employment in the claimant's usual occupation but if this is not possible other occupations may be considered suitable. The insurance officer has to decide bearing in mind such factors as the period spent searching for employment in the same occupation, the future possibilities of that happening, the man's employment record, etc. In the great majority of cases this is settled with no undue litigation. There has always been, however, a very small number of cases where insurance officers feel, rightly or wrongly, that the unemployed are malingering, i.e., refusing jobs unnecessarily, restricting the kind of work they will accept excessively, etc.[1] These are difficult cases and in the absence of any evidence it is impossible to know whether insurance officers have been able to deal with them satisfactorily. Perhaps it is worth mentioning that refusal to pay unemployment benefit in such cases will almost certainly mean payment of supplementary benefit.

A claimant may also be disqualified for benefit for a period up to six weeks if he refuses, without good cause, to accept training which will enable him to secure a job. The Government's rejection of the Beveridge proposals on training was due not only to matters of principle but to practical considerations, i.e., the lack of training facilities. In fact, until very recently, most government training centres were for disabled workers. It is only during the

[1] 'The Availability Question', *Report of N.I.A. Committee*, Cmd. 8894, 1953.

last three years that training and re-training of physically able, unemployed workers have been taken up seriously by the Government. The Survey of the Ministry of Labour in 1964 mentioned earlier showed that of the 236,500 unemployed men, 80% had been considered for government vocational training. Of these, 65% were judged to be unsuitable for training on account of age, health and similar personal conditions; in 25% of cases training was considered inappropriate as the persons concerned possessed adequate skills; and the remaining 10% were considered suitable for training but refused it on account of travelling, housing difficulties, financial problems, family considerations, etc.

There is an equal lack of enthusiasm for industrial training among employers. Two small surveys in the South of England showed that employers had not suggested industrial training to their employees who returned to work after long-term sickness. The Inter-Departmental Working Party on Industrial Rehabilitation set up by the Minister of Labour in 1964 found that employers treated their workers who returned to work after sickness and particularly industrial injury with consideration. On the other hand, there was 'a tendency towards resettling in simple routine and less responsible work rather than re-training for other skills, and all too frequently downgrading and some loss of expectations, if not reduction in actual earnings was the result'.[1]

Earnings Related Benefits

Since October 1966, earnings related benefits for unemployment, sickness, industrial injury and widowhood are paid in addition to the flat-rate benefits. This automatically excludes all those who do not qualify for flat-rate benefits either because they have not paid enough flat-rate contributions or, as in the case of married women, because they elected not to pay full contributions. The position of married women in the insurance scheme has become very anomalous as a result of the conflicting contribution principles of the National Insurance Acts 1946 and 1966. The first allows them freedom to decide whether to pay full flat-rate contributions or not while the second compels them to pay earnings related contributions. The net result is that a number of

[1] 'Industrial Rehabilitation and the Employed Worker', *Ministry of Labour Gazette*, Vol. LXXV, No. 2, February, 1967.

married employed women pay earnings related contributions which do not entitle them to any benefit.

Earnings related contributions are not paid by employed persons under the age of 18 or by older workers of pensionable age. Consequently they do not qualify for earnings related benefits. Presumably these two groups of the employed population are excluded because they are not considered part of the main stream of the labour force and also because interruption of their earnings does not involve such a drastic fall in their standard of living. This may be true in a number of cases but not in all. It is also difficult to see how the exclusion of the older workers is reconciled with the government policy of encouraging them to continue working beyond pensionable ages.

The rate of earnings related benefit is one-third of that part of the average weekly earnings which falls between £9 and £30. The lower wage limit was necessary because people with such low incomes would not benefit from an earnings related scheme apart from the fact that contributions might weigh too heavily on them. The upper wage limit indicates the degree of social security provision which the state considers itself justified in providing. The combined amount of flat rate and earnings related benefits must not exceed 85% of the recipient's gross earnings. The reason for this wage-stop measure is 'to secure that claimants generally are not better off when sick or unemployed than they would be at work'.[1] There was general agreement between the two main political parties on the necessity of a wages stop during the Parliamentary debates on the National Insurance Bill. What little difference there was between them concerned the level at which the wages stop should be fixed. The Conservative opposition felt that '85% is internationally too high'.[2] The Government considered the figure 85% right because it 'takes into account the fact that gross earnings are subject to deductions for P.A.Y.E., National Insurance contributions and other expenses which do not arise during unemployment or sickness'.[3] In other words when these deductions from earnings are taken into account, a person who is wage-stopped receives as much in benefits as he

[1] Miss Herbison, 2nd Reading, N.I. Bill, House of Commons, 7 February, 1966.
[2] Sir Keith Joseph, 2nd Reading of N.I. Bill, 7 February, 1966.
[3] Miss Herbison, ibid.

would have received in earnings. It is not clear on what evidence the Government reached this conclusion. Low wage earners with large families who suffer from the wages stop do not benefit from P.A.Y.E. savings for obvious reasons. It is also doubtful whether people out of work make any savings from not having to pay fares to work since they may have to spend money on fares to look for a job or, if they are ill, on different diet from the rest of their family. Nevertheless, not having to pay contributions is a saving but it does not amount to 15% of wages. Moreover, it is false saving since a deficient contribution record may eventually lead to loss or reduction in benefits. Taken to its logical conclusion, however, loss or reduction in insurance benefits may only mean payment of supplementary benefits which are borne by the State. This is the kind of circular involvement one gets into when one places excessive emphasis on the effect of social security benefits on people's willingness to work. More will be said about this later.

Table 19 gives a picture of the flat-rate and earnings related benefits for sickness and unemployment. The wages stop affects only the low wage-earner with four or more children. The position, however, is substantially different for those drawing flat-rate

TABLE 19

WEEKLY RATES OF UNEMPLOYMENT AND SICKNESS BENEFIT FOR VARIOUS

LEVELS OF EARNINGS

		Average weekly earnings (gross)					
		£12		£15		£30 and over	
Claimant	*Flat-rate Benefit*[a]	*Earnings-related supplement*	*Total Benefit*	*Earnings-related supplement*	*Total Benefit*	*Earnings-related supplement*	*Total Benefit*
	£ s.	£ s.	£ s.	£ s.	£ s.	£ s.	£ d
Single	4 10	1 1	5 11	2 1	6 11	7 0	11 10
Married	7 6	1 1	8 7	2 1	9 7	7 0	14 6
Married with 2 children	9 8	1 1	10 9	2 1	11 9	7 0	16 8
Married with 4 children	10 17	Nil	10 17[b]	2 1	12 18	7 0	17 17

(a) As from November 1967.
(b) Total benefit amounts to 85 per cent of average weekly earnings.

injury benefit and who also qualify for earnings related benefit. Because injury benefit is higher than sickness and unemployment benefit, the result is that large as well as small families with low incomes are affected.

Earnings related benefits were intended to encourage mobility of labour and to protect families against the hardships and worries which result from a drastic fall in family income. As a measure for labour mobility, they are understandably of short duration. They are paid for a period up to six months after the 12th day of interruption of employment. As a measure to protect the standard of living of a family, however, they should not be of short term duration. The first twelve days were excluded from entitlement to earnings related benefits in order to save time and money in calculating the very large number of very short spells of incapacity and to answer the criticism that benefits at the level of 85% of wages might lead to absenteeism. The Government Actuary has estimated that about 250,000 sick, including 30,000 on injury benefit, about 110,000 unemployed and 70,000 widows will draw earnings related benefits every year.

II. Redundancy

The concept of 'job property' is relatively new in this country. Traditionally it was considered fair for employers to dismiss their employees at will with or without notice. This 'laissez-faire' doctrine was justified on the grounds that employees could also leave their job at will and because trade unions would not stand for arbitrary dismissals. The Contracts of Employment Act, 1963, improved the situation by requiring employers to provide their employees with a document stating their terms of contract of service and secondly, to give their employees minimum notice of one week, rising to two weeks after two years' employment and to a maximum of four weeks after five years' service. This was the first major Government measure towards the establishment of the doctrine of 'job property' for workers. The Redundancy Payments Act was the second such step and in many ways more important than the first.[1]

The Government justified the need for redundancy payments

---

[1] J. Cronin, 'Redundancy and the Law of Employment', *Progress*, Vol. 51, No. 287, January, 1966.

on two grounds: Social and economic. A man has certain rights to his job and these rights gain with years of service. He is therefore entitled to compensation for the loss of these rights. The economic justification is that redundancy payments have 'an important and necessary part to play in allaying fears of redundancy and resistance to new methods and economic change'.[1] The Act is not concerned with such things as the man's family responsibilities or whether he, in fact, suffered a financial loss from being made redundant. He may move into a new job straight away, his new job may be better than the one he lost, and he will still receive a redundancy payment. An employee is dismissed because of redundancy where 'the work on which he was employed has disappeared'[2] irrespective of the reasons which led to the disappearance of the work. If a redundant employee refuses alternative suitable employment offered by his employer in the same firm within four weeks, he may lose his redundancy payment. The Act does not define 'suitable' employment and disputes about this are settled by the industrial tribunals. An employee may also have good reasons for refusing alternative suitable employment and it is again up to the tribunals to arbitrate on this. An employee may also be entitled to a redundancy payment if he has been laid off or kept on short-time, provided this was not caused by an industrial dispute, for any four consecutive weeks or for a broken series of six weeks within a thirteen week period. The reason for allowing redundancy payments for 'lay-off' and short-time is to stop employers evading their responsibilities of paying for redundancy.

The amount of redundancy payment depends on the man's continuous length of service with his employer, his age and his earnings. Service before the employee's eighteenth birthday does not count and service over twenty years, reckoning backwards from the date of redundancy, is not taken into account either. There is also a maximum ceiling for earnings – £40 per week – over which earnings are disregarded. Rates of redundancy allowances are also higher for older workers because they have the most difficulty in finding new employment.

Years of service count for redundancy payment as follows:

[1] Mr R. Gunter, Minister of Labour, 2nd Reading of Redundancy Payments Bill, House of Commons, 24 April, 1965.

[2] Mr R. Gunter, ibid.

(*a*) One and a half weeks' pay for each year of continuous service with the same employer between the ages 41 and 65 for men and 41 and 60 for women.

(*b*) One week's pay for each year of employment between the ages 22 and 41.

(*c*) Half a week's pay for each year of service between the ages 18–22.

One of the few criticisms of the Conservative Opposition was that redundancy payments at this young age was 'rather difficult to justify'.[1] The other main criticism was that rates of payments were too high. This may have been due to the fact that redundancy payments were introduced before the earnings-related benefits.

Employees who have passed retirement age are not entitled to any redundancy payments because they have not 'the same expectation of continued employment as younger workers' and there is not either 'the same case for compensation if they should become redundant'.[2] Dividing lines in social security schemes always cause hardship to borderline groups of beneficiaries. This Act, however, seems to have gone out of its way to increase resentment by stipulating that employees nearing retirement should have their redundancy allowances reduced by one-twelfth for every complete month by which their age exceed 64 for men or 59 on the day of redundancy.

The Government considered the Redundancy Payments Act as part of its 'general programme to push forward the modernisation of British industry as fast as possible, and to enlist the co-operation of workers as well as management in the process'.[2] Earnings-related benefits and an increase in retraining facilities were the other main components of this programme. It is difficult to tell how effective these measures will be in achieving the Government's objective. Certainly, in theory, one can argue that redundancy payments might in fact discourage employers from dismissing excess labour as they have to meet directly part of the cost

---

[1] Mr J. Godber, 2nd Reading of Redundancy Payments Bill, House of Commons, 24 April, 1965.
[2] Mr R. Gunter, ibid.

themselves. Similarly one can argue that by providing a substantial sum they may encourage workers to stay off work and resist moving to another place for new employment.[1] The influence of social security benefits on industrial behaviour is as yet unknown. All that can be said is that the existence of such benefits gives Government plans for labour redeployment a less ruthless image. Certainly the majority of people are loath to move to another area unless they have no choice and even then the things that matter most are housing and pay and promotion prospects. In the Ministry of Labour's Study, 45% of workers would prefer to take a less suitable job locally and only 46% would consider moving rather than take a less suitable job locally if their current employment ceased. Table 20 refers to the replies of this 46% group.

TABLE 20

FACTORS NEEDED TO BE SATISFACTORY BEFORE MOVING

GREAT BRITAIN

Factors	Men %	Women %	Both Sexes %
Pay and promotion prospects	62·5	56·8	61·7
Security of job	39·9	25·5	38·1
Other conditions of work	7·7	12·0	8·2
Housing	81·6	73·0	80·5
Good Schools	16·0	5·4	14·6
Public Transport	5·4	5·8	5·4
Shopping facilities	4·8	3·5	4·6
Social amenities	8·0	11·2	8·4
Other Social characteristics of the area	2·7	6·2	3·1
Amenable surroundings	16·9	18·9	17·2
Contact with friends/family	3·1	6·9	3·6
Consideration of family's wishes	2·4	0·8	2·2
Financial (other than pay)	2·2	0·8	2·0
Miscellaneous answers	0·3	0·4	0·3

Source: 'Labour Mobility in Great Britain', table 40, p. 39.

The theoretical maximum sum of a redundancy allowance is £1,200 (thirty weeks × £40). During the year 1966, 137,208 redundancy payments were made in Great Britain. The industries with the highest figures were construction with 14% of the total number of payments, engineering and electrical goods with 11·8%, distributive trades 10·9%, vehicles 8·7%, transport and

[1] J. A. Torode, 'The Redundant Bill', *New Society*, 10 June, 1965.

communications 6·0%, textiles 5·3%, paper, printing and publishing 4·5% and food, drink and tobacco 4·3%. The total expenditure was £26,488,000 75% of which was paid out of the Redundancy Fund and the remaining 25% was paid directly by employers. The average sum of redundancy payments was £193 though there were wide variations.

Chapter Six

SICKNESS AND MATERNITY BENEFITS

I. Sickness Benefit

LIKE unemployment, sickness creates two main problems: providing an income during the period of incapacity for work and providing medical services for the restoration of health. This country is unique in that its National Health Service is available free to all its citizens irrespective of any insurance considerations. The National Insurance Scheme and the various occupational sick pay schemes attempt to provide an adequate income to the sick and their families.

Sickness and Incapacity for Work

The amount of registered incapacity for work on account of sickness is an underestimate of the real extent since it is based on information provided by the Ministry of Social Security on the number of persons claiming sickness benefit. It excludes two-thirds of married women at work who do not pay full contributions and are not entitled to sickness benefit. It also excludes very short illnesses lasting less than four days for which usually no sickness benefit is paid. Estimates made by the M.P.N.I. in 1951 suggested that the amount of absence from work resulting from very short illnesses was two million one-day spells, two and a half million two-day spells and nearly one and three-quarter million three-day spells, a total of twelve million days.

There are three main indices of the degree of registered incapacity for work owing to sickness: The number of claims for sickness benefit and the number of people involved, the number of spells of incapacity and the amount of working time lost through incapacity.

There has been a distinct rise in the claims for sickness benefit in recent years. Prior to 1958 the average number of claims per year was seven and two-thirds million even taking into account the abnormally high number for 1957 that was due to the influenza epidemic. Since 1958 the average number has been nine and a quarter million.

The number of new claims, however, does not reveal the number of people involved for an insured person may claim more than once during the same year. Column two of Table 21, shows the average number of people incapacitated for work owing to sickness on the third Tuesday of each month. This does not show the same steep rise after 1958 compared with the years before. The combined average monthly number for the eight years preceding 1958 is 912 thousand claimants while the number for the seven year period after 1958 is 949 thousand. This means that the increase in the number of claimants has not been equivalent to the increase in new claims. The explanation for this lies in the fact

TABLE 21.

NEW CLAIMS FOR SICKNESS BENEFIT,

MONTHLY AVERAGE NUMBER OF CLAIMANTS AND EXPENDITURE

GREAT BRITAIN — THOUSANDS

Year.*	New Claims	Claimants	Expenditure £
1950	7,300	—	65,532
1951	7,545	906	68,581
1952	6,857	851	63,301
1953	7,376	934	79,163
1954	7,173	922	84,942
1955	7,919	921	84,456
1956	7,762	911	99,642
1957	9,609	945	96,700
1958	7,887	905	111,351
1959	8,768	948	133,463
1960	8,319	896	130,649
1961	9,152	931	135,000
1962	9,002	942	154,570
1963	9,336	976	161,480
1964	8,998	954	191,360
1965	9,565	995	200,870
1966	10,925	Not available.	248,468

* Year for Expenditure ends on 31st March.

Source: Annual Reports of M.P.N.I.

that there has been an increase in the number of claims made by each claimant since 1958 as Table 22 shows. An equally important point is that about two-thirds of the insured population make no claim for sickness benefit in a year.

TABLE 22

DISTRIBUTION OF INSURED PERSONS ACCORDING TO

NUMBER OF SPELLS OF SICKNESS

GREAT BRITAIN

Number of Spells in Year	*June 1955–May 1956*			*June 1960–May 1961*		
	Men	Single Women	Married Women	Men	Single Women	Married Women
	%	%	%	%	%	%
0	72	68	64	69	64	64
1	21	24	26	22	26	25
2	5	6	7	6	7	8
3 or more	2	2	3	3	3	3

Source: Quinquennial Reviews.

The length of each spell is naturally important in deciding the total amount of incapacity by sickness. In the period 1953–1958, employed men received an average of about two weeks' benefit each year, employed married women about three and a half weeks and other women two and a quarter weeks. In the period 1958–1963 the corresponding figures were 2·1 weeks, 3·1 weeks and 2·25 weeks respectively. On the whole there has been little change in the length of spells of sickness benefit for employed persons. The average number of weeks of sickness benefit for the self-employed persons, however, has increased because a large proportion of them became insured for sickness for the first time in 1948. It was therefore natural that the average length of sickness benefit would rise as a result of the gradual accumulation of long-term sickness.

Taking into account the number of claimants, the number of spells of sickness, the length of spells and the size of the insured population, the total number of weeks of sickness benefit averaged about 28¾ millions per annum for men, 5½ millions for married women and 8 millions for other women in the period 1953–1958. The respective figures for the period 1958–1963 were 30½ millions, 5 millions and 7 millions.

117

Who are the Sick?

It is a well-known fact that there are appreciable regional and social class variations in illness. The Enquiry by the M.P.N.I. in the year June 1961–June 1962[1] showed significant regional variations of incapacity by sickness among the insured population. The proportion of men who were off work sick for four days or more was 28% for Great Britain but it was 27·5% for England, 29% for Scotland and 36% for Wales. There were wide variations within these three sub-divisions: 33% in the Northern Region of England but only 23% in the Southern Region; 33% in East Central Scotland but only 21% in Southern Scotland. Wales had above average rates in all regions.

The relationship between social class and illness is well-known. The Ministry's enquiry provided the most up-to-date national picture. Both the inception rates for men – i.e., the proportion of men who started at least one spell of incapacity during the year – and the number of days of incapacity were inversely related to social class. We are not concerned here with the reasons for social class differences in illness,[2] except to note that some of these differences are more apparent than real. People in heavy occupations or those carried out in difficult circumstances find it more difficult to report to work when not seriously ill than those in light or easy occupations. The regional and social class variations observed for men are also applicable to women workers.

There are also substantial variations in the average number of

TABLE 23

RATES (STANDARDISED FOR AGE) OF INCAPACITY FOR
SICKNESS FOR MEN BY SOCIAL CLASS

Occupational Group	Inception Rates	Days of Incapacity
All Occupations	100	100
Professional and Intermediate Occupations	64	50
Skilled Occupations	100	93
Partly Skilled Occupations	109	117
Unskilled Occupations	124	154
Occupation not known	86	98

Source: Report on an enquiry, table 25, p. xcviii, Part II.

[1] Report on an Enquiry into the Incidence of Incapacity for Work, Part II, H.M.S.O., 1965.
[2] M. W. Susser and W. Watson, *Sociology in Medicine,* Oxford University Press, 1962.

weeks for sickness benefit according to age, sex, marital and occupational status. The number of weeks of sickness benefit increases with age for both sexes, all marital and occupational statuses. Women have higher rates than men though self-employed single women in the lower age-groups have lower rates than employed men. The influence of marital status can be seen for women only, as the available data do not differentiate between single men and married men. Employed married women have substantially higher rates than employed single women. The

TABLE 24
AVERAGE NUMBER OF WEEKS OF SICKNESS BENEFIT PER YEAR, 1958–1963
GREAT BRITAIN

Age Group	Men		Married Women		Other Women	
	Employed	Self-Employed	Employed	Self-Employed	Employed	Self-Employed
15–19	0·79	0·48	1·93	Not Available	1·01	0·29
20–24	0·92	0·63	1·60	,,	1·15	0·63
25–29	0·96	0·57	1·74	,,	1·59	0·83
30–34	1·18	0·67	2·48	,,	2·22	1·34
35–39	1·42	0·66	3·42	,,	2·65	1·73
40–44	1·60	0·80	4·24	,,	3·02	1·98
45–49	1·98	1·07	4·72	,,	3·76	2·79
50–54	2·67	1·54	5·47	,,	4·81	3·48
55–59	4·09	2·57	7·19	,,	5·98	4·12
60–64	7·05	4·64				
Average	2·13	1·63	3·14	,,	2·22	2·82

Source: Government Actuary: Third Quinquennial Review.

number of self-employed married women is so small that there are no separate calculations for them.

Occupational status, too, has a substantial influence on the length of sickness benefit. The rates for self-employed men and women are respectively much lower at all age-groups than those of employed men and women. The fact that the average rate for self-employed men of all age-groups is only 75% of the corresponding figure for employed men is due to the older age distribution of the self-employed men. The same reason explains the fact that the average rate for self-employed single women is slightly higher than that of employed women. If the rates were standarised by age the shorter periods of sickness benefits of the self-employed would have been abundantly clear. The interpretation of these differences is extremely difficult. It is more than likely that the high rates for married women are due to the fact that they are not under the same economic pressures to resume work as the other groups. It is unlikely that married women suffer from more serious illnesses than the rest of the insured population.

The average number of new spells for sickness benefit in a year does not increase with age. In fact some of the younger age groups among the sick have more spells of sickness than the older age-groups. This shows that a substantial part of the longer periods of sickness benefit in the older age-groups is due to longer spells of illness rather than more frequent spells. Whether the longer spells are due to more serious illnesses or to other factors, or to both, is not known. Similarly, the shorter periods of sickness benefit among the self-employed is due more to less frequent illnesses rather than shorter periods of illness. These

TABLE 25

SPELLS OF SICKNESS BEGINNING IN 1962–1963
PER 100 INSURED PERSONS
GREAT BRITAIN

| Age-Group | Employed Persons | | | Self-Employed |
	Men	Married Women	Other Women	Men
15–19	45	51	59	12
20–24	40	47	52	13
25–29	42	41	45	19
30–34	45	49	46	14
35–39	44	58	41	14
40–44	46	61	45	13
45–49	44	67	46	15
50–54	50	68	48	18
55–59	55	57	47	21
60–64	64	—	—	27

Source: Third Quinquennial Review.

conclusions are confirmed by Appendix III. The higher incidence of long spells of sickness with increasing age is quite clear. The proportion of illnesses lasting less than two weeks was 56·3% for employed men, 62% for employed single women, 46·3% for employed married women and only 28·1% for self-employed men. On the other hand the proportion of illnesses lasting more than a year for the four groups were 0·7%, 0·4%, 0·9% and 2·1% respectively.

The proportion of spells of illnesses lasting more than one year is very small indeed. Nevertheless this small proportion contributes substantially to the total amount of illness as Table 26 below shows. The proportion of those who were ill for over one year was about the same in all four groups – 32% of the employed men, 40% of the self-employed men, 37% of the employed married women and 40% of the employed single women. The proportion, however, of those ill for over eight years was double for women than for men in spite of the fact that women retire earlier.

TABLE 26

DURATION OF CURRENT SPELLS OF SICKNESS ON 1 JUNE, 1963

GREAT BRITAIN

	Employed Men	Employed Single Women	Employed Married Women	Self-Employed Men
	%	%	%	%
Not over 6 months	61·0	53·5	57·6	46·9
Over 6 months and not over 1 year	7·3	7·0	5·1	12·5
Over 1 year and not over 2 years	7·3	7·0	6·8	12·5
Over 2 years and not over 4 years	9·8	7·0	8·5	15·7
Over 4 years and not over 6 years	4·9	7·0	5·1	6·2
Over 6 years and not over 8 years	2·4	2·3	3·3	3·1
Over 8 years	7·3	16·2	13·6	3·1
Total	100·0	100·0	100·0	100·0

Source: Third Quinquennial Review.

The clear conclusion of the tables on sickness benefit is that incapacity for work on account of illness has not diminished since the introduction of the National Health Service and the Social Security Schemes. People are healthier today than they were before the last war but they are also able through the social security benefits to stay off work when they are not well. The total number of working days lost through sickness is very substantial though the impact this has on industrial production is not of the same dimension as the absolute numbers may suggest. The long-term sick cause no serious disruption to industrial production as they are discounted from the labour force until their health is restored. National production, however, suffers through the long-term loss of their work. On the other hand, the short-term sick disrupt industrial production though their absence may not result in such a grave loss to national production since employers may be able to rearrange their labour force temporarily to make up for some of the loss. It is impossible to estimate in terms of pounds, shillings and pence the loss to the national economy caused by sickness.

Qualifying Conditions for Sickness Benefit

The contribution conditions for sickness benefit are the same as those for unemployment benefit with one major exception. If 156 Class I or Class II contributions have actually been paid, not credited, sickness benefit can be drawn indefinitely until retirement age. This is a better arrangement than the maximum limit of one year imposed on unemployment benefit. People who have been out of work on account of sickness and unemployment for over a year will need financial assistance from the state irrespective of whether this comes out of the National Insurance Fund or out of supplementary benefits. There may be a small number of self-employed persons who may have resources to manage for a period after the end of the first year of sickness but it is extremely unlikely that there are any employed persons who have enough financial resources to disqualify them for a supplementary benefit after a year of unemployment benefit. It is also far better for the long-term unemployed to draw a benefit as of 'right' than after the necessary investigations of the Supplementary Benefits officers. The two reasons for which the period of unemployment benefit was limited to one year were firstly the fear that if the responsibility for all unemployment was borne by the National Insurance Fund 'it would break this Fund'.[1] The unhappy experiences of the Unemployment Insurance Fund during the mass unemployment of the 1930's were clearly at the back of the minds of the framers of the National Insurance Act, 1946. This, however, no longer applies today. Secondly, a conglomeration of traditional fears and suspicions that the long-term unemployed are more likely to abuse

[1] Mr J. Griffiths, 2nd Reading, National Insurance Bill, House of Commons, 6 February, 1946.

the system than the long-term sick. Understandable though they may be, these fears are not justified because the existing rules of disqualification for benefit, if thoroughly applied, can deal adequately with malingerers. Nor can it be seriously argued that the unemployed are more to blame for their plight than the sick. As the Minister of Social Security said when proposing the extension of the maximum period of unemployment benefit for all to one year 'Unemployment usually arises through social and economic factors over which the individual has little or no control'.[1] For all these, as well as administrative reasons, it would be advisable to extend the maximum period of unemployment benefit to that of sickness benefit.

Claims for sickness benefit are made on medical certificates of incapacity signed by the claimant's doctor. The medical profession has always complained that these certificates have made excessive demands on doctors' time. The rules for issuing certificates have been changed several times since 1948 easing the burden on the medical profession.[2] The extent to which the relaxation of these rules can be taken is limited by the necessity to take adequate precautions against the abuse of the social security scheme. The Ministry of Social Security supervises claims for sickness benefits by means of home visits and references for examination of beneficiaries to the Regional Medical Officers of the Ministry of Health. Persons who fail or refuse to attend these examinations without good cause may be disqualified from further sickness benefit. To avoid misunderstanding and unnecessary hardship the sick person's own doctor is consulted. The same procedure applies to industrial injury benefit and the amount of work involved is quite substantial. The number of home visits has declined from 1,140,000 in 1951 to 476,000 in 1965. The number of references to the Regional Medical Officers for examination, however, has increased from 346,000 to 746,000 for the same two years. The results of these references have not shown any consistent trend or any substantial fluctuations over the years. Since 1948, 36%–40% of persons referred for examination every year terminate their benefit either by sending in final certificates or by failing to attend the examination; another 10%–14% are found fit for work and their benefit ceases; and the

[1] Miss M. Herbison, 2nd Reading N.I. Bill, 7 February, 1966.
[2] N.I.A.C. Amendment Regulations, Cmnd. 2875, 1966.

TABLE 27

OUTCOME OF REFERENCES FOR EXAMINATION OF

INSURED PERSONS, 1965

GREAT BRITAIN

				Result		
	References	*Incapable of work*	*Not incapable of work*	*Incapable of normal occupation but not incapable of alternative work*	*Evidence of recovery submitted before examination*	*Failed to attend examination*
	Thousands			*Per cent*		
Sickness benefit:						
Total	581·0	49	10	2	16	22
Males	400·0	49	10	2	17	22
Females	181·0	51	12	1	15	22
Injury benefit:						
Total	164·9	45	14	—	19	22
Males	129·9	44	13	—	20	23
Females	35·0	49	17	—	15	19

Source: Report of M.P.N.I. for the year 1965, table 37, p. 116.

remaining 46%–54% are found incapable of work and continue to draw benefit.

The basic condition for the receipt of sickness benefit is that the claimant must be incapable of work on account of physical or mental illness. Special conditions, however, apply to those in prison or in hospital. People are disqualified from receiving sickness benefit (as well as unemployment, widows' or retirement benefit) for any period of imprisonment and detention in custody irrespective of the types of offence or the length of the sentence. The justification for this is that insurance benefits are not necessary where another public social service provides maintenance. Hospitalisation, however, does not result in the same automatic withdrawal of benefit. Sickness benefit is paid in full during the first eight weeks of hospitalisation to enable the beneficiary to meet outstanding commitments outside the hospital. The period of eight weeks was chosen because it covers short-term illnesses when 'additional expenditure incurred by patients or their dependants arising from their admission to hospital would off-set any saving in expense on their maintenance'.[1] About nine-tenths of the patients entering hospital are discharged within eight weeks After the end of eight weeks, benefit is reduced substantially if the beneficiary has no dependants and only slightly if he has dependants. At the end of one year, the benefit of persons without dependants is reduced to pocket money level but a small additional amount is saved for them as a 'resettlement benefit' during the second year and it is paid to them on discharge.

Occupational Sick Pay Schemes

The most up-to-date and reliable information on occupational sick pay schemes is the national survey of the M.P.N.I. conducted during June 1961–June 1962.[2] The information contained in this section is from this survey unless otherwise stated. Just over half of men employees and married women employees were covered by sick pay schemes. The proportion of married women may have been an overestimate of the actual coverage of all married women at work because it referred only to those married women paying full contributions. The high proportion of single women covered – almost two-thirds – was a reflection mainly of the fact that proportionately they were more often employed in white collar

TABLE 28

PROPORTION OF EMPLOYEES COVERED BY OCCUPATIONAL

SICK PAY SCHEMES

	All Ages %	Up to 24 %	25–34 %	35–44 %	45–54 %	55–63 men 55–58 women %
Men	56·6	47·2	54·7	58·1	60·7	61·6
All Women	59·5	59·9	63·2	59·1	56·6	55·8
Married Women	52·5	54·1	57·3	49·4	49·6	50·3
Single Women	62·3	61·0	67·0	65·0	62·0	60·0

[1] Report of National Insurance Advisory Committee, Question of Long-Term Hospital Patients, Cmnd. 964, p. 14, 1960.
[2] Report on an Enquiry into the Incidence of Incapacity for Work, Part I: Scope and characteristics of Employers' Sick Pay Schemes, H.M.S.O., 1964.

jobs. With the exception of married women, sick pay cover was lowest among the under-25 age-group but there was no consistent rise with subsequent age-groups.

These overall figures concealed wide industrial and occupational variations. Public services, nationalised industries and private industries employing large numbers of white collar workers provided coverage for 85% to 95% of their employees. On the other hand private industries with large numbers of unskilled workers provided much lower coverage, falling as low as one-quarter of their labour force in the case of agriculture and construction. The social class bias was quite clear in the coverage of all sick pay schemes. The proportion of class I and II covered was double that of class IV and V. The same picture emerged from other studies. An investigation by the British Institute of

TABLE 29

SOCIAL CLASS AND COVERAGE OF SICK PAY SCHEMES

Social Class	Men %	Single Women %	Married Women %
I Professional ⎱ II Intermediate ⎰	88·1	88·8	88·1
III Skilled Occupations	57·3	70·7	59·5
IV Partly Skilled Occupations	52·2	35·6	34·6
V Unskilled Occupations	41·4	50·6	53·2

Management of 64 organisations which were considered among the more go-ahead, established that 24 made no sickness payments to workers but made them to staff.[1]

About 60% of the men and 50% of the women had to serve a qualifying period before they could receive any sick pay. The periods most commonly served were six or twelve months. A

TABLE 30

QUALIFYING PERIODS OF EMPLOYMENT FOR SICK PAY SCHEMES

	None %	6 months or less %	7–12 months %	Over 12 months %	At discretion %	Not Known %
Men	37·1	27·4	27·2	2·7	4·8	0·7
Women	46·1	30·0	13·9	2·4	6·4	1·1

[1] 'Payment for Sickness', *B.I.M.*, 1963.

study of Southampton firms also showed that after six months service most employees were eligible for sick pay.[1]

The period for which sick payment was made varied from industry to industry and particularly according to social class. The proportion of men entitled to benefit for six months or more

TABLE 31

MAXIMUM DURATION OF SICK PAYMENTS

ACCORDING TO SOCIAL CLASS

Social Class	Less than 2 weeks %	2–4 wks. %	5–13 wks. %	14–26 wks. %	27–52 wks. %	Over 52 wks. %	No Limit %	At Employers Discretion %	Not Stated %
Men									
All Social Classes	0·6	5·6	39·3	14·2	11·1	0·7	3·5	23·6	1·4
Class I & II	0·4	3·5	12·3	13·3	28·3	0·7	5·5	34·2	1·8
Class III	0·6	6·4	39·4	13·7	8·7	0·8	4·2	25·0	1·4
Class IV	0·7	6·0	35·5	16·8	6·0	0·6	1·0	16·3	1·1
Class V	0·8	4·3	44·4	12·8	3·4	0·7	0·4	9·8	1·1
Women									
All Social Classes	1·4	9·5	20·1	14·9	19·9	0·4	1·6	28·6	3·7
Class I & II	0·4	2·8	9·3	12·3	58·9	0·2	0·7	13·7	1·9
Class III	1·8	11·6	19·3	12·5	10·5	0·4	2·3	37·0	4·6
Class IV	1·3	11·2	32·5	26·2	5·2	0·6	0·8	18·9	3·2
Class V	0·4	5·7	51·3	21·0	3·2	0·7	—	16·7	1·1

was eight times greater in class I and II than class V. In the case of women the difference was fifteen times greater. Since in the great majority of cases the amount of sick pay was equivalent to full wages, it meant that professional employees not only received sick pay for longer periods but at higher rates as well. It was only in a small minority of cases that sick pay was at a flat rate. White collar workers fared better than unskilled or partly skilled workers in another sense. While there was no 'waiting period' for benefit for 72% of all men, a 'waiting period' was more common among the partly skilled and unskilled employees.

Occupational sick pay schemes usually try to fill in the gaps left by the state scheme. With the introduction of the state earnings-

[1] A. F. Young and J. H. Smith, 'Fringe Benefits', *British Journal of Industrial Relations*, Vol. V, No. 1, March, 1967.

TABLE 32
AMOUNT OF SICK PAY AT BEGINNING OF PAYMENT

	Full Wages Without deduction %	Wages Less N.I. deduction %	50% of wages or more but less than full %	Less than 50% of wages %	£5 or more %	Flat rate of £2 or more but less than £5 %	£1 or more but less than £2 %	Less than £1 %	At employers discretion %	Not stated %
Men	12·4	57·7	3·2	0·6	1·1	7·0	11·5	0·8	3·4	2·4
Women	13·3	75·3	2·4	0·5	—	1·2*	1·3	0·5	4·4	1·0

* denotes £2 or more.

related sickness benefit scheme, the structure of occupational sick pay schemes may change. They may concentrate on supplementing the state benefit to full wage level, they may also provide benefit after the six months period when the state earnings-related benefit lapses, or they may provide full wages during the first two weeks of sickness which are not covered by the earnings-related state scheme. Suggestions have been made from time to time for making short-term sickness the responsibility of the employer and allow the state to concentrate on long-term illness. 'I see no reason why an employer should not be responsible for the first four weeks of payment during an employee's sickness'.[1] Such a change would not only reduce the cost of the national insurance scheme but it might also on balance result in a reduction of administrative costs. On the other hand, even if the bulk of sickness claims falls outside the province of the state, there will still be a need for a government scheme for the self-employed and perhaps for the very small employer. Division of responsibility between state and private schemes creates as many problems as it solves.

II. *Maternity Benefits*

The justification for maternity benefits is twofold: To protect the health of the mother and her child and to alleviate part of the financial hardship caused by the birth of a child. The Factory and Workshops Act, 1891, marked the beginning of social policy for

[1] Mr R. H. Turton, 2nd Reading N.I. Bill, House of Commons, 7 February, 1966. See also *The Economist,* 1 April, 1961.

dealing with the first problem. Employment of women in factories or workshops during the four weeks after confinement was made illegal. The National Insurance Act, 1911, was the beginning of social legislation providing cash benefits during maternity. It provided for the payment of a lump sum to the wife of an insured person, or to a woman who was herself insured, on the birth of a child.

The National Insurance Act, 1946, brought about a drastic reorganisation of the system of maternity benefits to bring it in line with the International Labour Office Maternity Protection Convention, 1919. It provided three types of maternity benefits. A maternity grant and either an attendance allowance or a maternity allowance. The maternity grant was a lump sum of £4 paid before the child was born to help with confinement expenses. Opinion was divided on the flat-rate nature of the grant for all births. It was argued that it ought to be higher for the first child as the confinement expenses involved were also higher than subsequent births. On the other hand, it was felt that families were in a better position to meet the expenses of the first confinement than of subsequent ones when there were other children to maintain. They were similar arguments to those raised with regard to family allowances. The reconciling of these opposing views took a different form in maternity grants and family allowances. In the case of family allowances the second argument gained acceptance while in the case of maternity grants the two arguments were thought to cancel each other out with the result that flat-rate grants for all births were considered to be the best solution. Maternity grants were also criticised as being insufficient in amount to meet the need for which they were devised. This criticism applied to other insurance benefits to some extent but as the National Insurance Advisory Committee observed, the maternity grant was 'by far the least adequate, in relation to the contingency for which it was designed, of all the National Insurance Benefits'.[1] Finally, the system of grants was criticised on the grounds that it did not differentiate, between home confinements and hospital confinements. It was argued that hospital confinements meant less expenses on the family with the result that they encourage an artificial demand for hospital beds. On the other hand, the savings made by a hospital confinement could be

[1] 'Maternity Benefits', N.I.A.C., p. 12, Cmd. 8446, 1952.

cancelled out in cases where the family had to pay someone to look after the children at home. To devise a scheme, however, which would be sensitive to all these refinements would have been administratively complex and expensive. The National Insurance Advisory Committee took the easy way out and recommended a higher grant for home confinements so that 'there should be no financial pressure on a woman either to have her confinement at home or in hospital. Her decision should be taken on other than financial grounds'.[1] This recommendation was implemented by the National Insurance Act, 1953, which introduced a home confinement grant of £3 in addition to the general maternity grant. This arrangement lasted until 1964 when the two grants were merged into one – a situation that prevailed before 1953 with the only difference that the new grant emerged larger in amount out of these amalgamations and de-amalgamations. The reversal to the pre-1953 situation reflected a change in medical practice. Whereas in the 1950's hospital confinements lasted for ten days or more, in the 1960's they often last for two or three days only. The result is that mothers confined in hospital have to meet almost the same expenses as those who are having their babies at home. Moreover the distinction between two grants caused confusion in a number of cases where mothers who had made arrangements to have their babies at home and were paid a home confinement grant had to be admitted to hospital for medical or other reasons.

The original idea for the attendance allowance was to help with the expenditure that was necessary in the brief period of 4 weeks after child-birth when the mother could not look after her family unaided. It was paid as a weekly allowance to differentiate it from the grant which was a lump sum and it was paid as an alternative to the maternity allowance for working mothers. In practice, however, it was found that the attendance allowance was not drawn weekly for weekly expenditure but it was drawn as a lump sum at the end of four weeks. It was considered as another maternity grant and the National Insurance Advisory Committee recommended its abolition and absorption into the maternity grant. This was implemented by the National Insurance Act, 1953, and the idea of an attendance allowance has not been heard since.

The maternity allowance, too, has been modified from its original

[1] ibid., p. 9.

form. Unlike the maternity grant which can be paid on the insurance record of the husband, the maternity allowance is paid to women who have themselves paid the specified number of insurance contributions. The National Insurance Act, 1946, implemented the Beveridge recommendation that the maternity allowance should be paid at a higher rate than sickness or unemployment benefit in order to 'make it easy and attractive for women to give up gainful occupation at the time of maternity'.[1] The inference was that the working mother would soon resume her work. In practice, however, it was soon found that the majority of working mothers did not return to work at all after their confinement or, if they did, after a considerable period of years. Special enquiries by the Ministry of National Insurance showed that out of a large sample of maternity allowance recipients interviewed from two to eight months after confinement 'only one-quarter had gone back to work or had registered for employment; two-fifths had no intention of doing so; and the rest either spoke of going back later or had not made up their minds'.[2] The maternity allowance was not performing its original function and there was no justification for its remaining at a higher rate than other similar benefits. The National Insurance Act, 1953, introduced parity between the amount of maternity allowance on one hand and sickness and unemployment benefit on the other. The same Act made changes to the contribution conditions qualifying for maternity allowance with two ends in mind. First, to restrict maternity allowance to those women who were paying full contributions. It, therefore, abolished the existing favourable concession of special credits for employed married women not paying full contributions. Second, to make it possible for working women to give up work much earlier than previously and still qualify for maternity allowance. The intention was to remedy the existing situation which forced a number of working expectant mothers to remain at work far too late. The Maternity Allowance was therefore extended from thirteen to eighteen weeks covering the week of confinement, eleven weeks prior to it, and six weeks after it. A study by the Ministry of Pensions & National Insurance in 1956 showed that the new contribution conditions may have had the desired effect of not forcing women to work up to

[1] Beveridge Report, p. 132.
[2] 'Maternity Benefits', p. 17, N.I.A.C., Cmd. 8446, 1952.

confinement week. The most favoured week for giving up employment was the twelfth week preceding confinement when 10·5% of the sample gave up work.

TABLE 33

CLAIMS FOR MATERNITY BENEFITS ANALYSED ACCORDING
TO WEEK IN WHICH CLAIMANT CEASED WORK

GREAT BRITAIN

Same week as confine-ment week	*Week preceding confinement claimant ceased work*								
	1st & 2nd	*3rd & 4th*	*5–8th week*	*9–13th week*	*14th–17th week*	*18th–21st week*	*22nd–26th*	*27th or earlier*	*Not Known*
%	%	%	%	%	%	%	%	%	%
0·1	0·5	1·4	9·3	38·1	18·7	10	10	11·6	0·3

Source: Report of M.P.N.I. year 1958, cmnd. 826. Adapted from table 37.

The contribution conditions for a maternity grant have always been easier than those for a maternity allowance. The position today is that the grant is payable to all mothers on their own or their husband's insurance who satisfy these two contribution conditions. First, twenty-six contributions of any class have been paid between the time of entering the insurance scheme and the date of confinement and second that at least 26 contributions of any class have been paid or credited in the last contribution year. In practice the overwhelming majority of expectant mothers qualify for the grant. The three main groups who do not qualify are students married to other students, young parents who are just starting employment and unmarried mothers not at work. It can be argued convincingly that the maternity grant should be paid for all births irrespective of insurance in the same way that family allowances are available for all children. Even if the insurance principle is adhered to, there is no good reason why a maternity grant should not be given for illegitimate children on the putative father's insurance record. The National Insurance Advisory Committee examined this in its report mentioned earlier but felt unable to make any favourable recommendations because it would have involved 'detailed inquiries into the circumstances of the putative father which 'might well be resented'. These arguments do not apply, however, where the putative father

Sickness and Maternity Benefits

TABLE 34
EXPENDITURE AND NUMBER OF MATERNITY BENEFITS
GREAT BRITAIN

Year*	Maternity Grants	Maternity Allowances	Expenditure† £000
1950	757,000	124,000	£8,600
1951	761,000	143,000	£8,400
1952	756,000	153,000	£8,700
1953	not available	—	£10,500
1955	745,000	186,000	£13,000
1956	770,000	164,000	£14,000
1957	782,000	174,000	£14,900
1958	815,000	187,000	£16,000
1959	827,000	188,000	£19,700
1960	843,000	188,000	£20,000
1961	867,000	198,000	£20,600
1962	908,000	211,000	£24,500
1963	918,000	216,000	£25,500
1964	929,000	217,000	£29,500
1965	951,000	235,000	£31,500

Source: Annual Reports of M.P.N.I.

* Up to 1953, year ended 31st December. From 1955 onwards, year ended on 31st March.

† Includes expenditure for attendance allowances and home confinement grants in appropriate years.

accepts paternity before, or after the child's birth or where an affiliation order is issued against him after the child's birth. This may be administratively untidy but administrative convenience should not prevail over people's rights. 'Moral' considerations, too, may have influenced past decisions to exclude the putative father's insurance record for benefit qualification. These considerations, however, are no longer valid when social workers speak of the problem of the unmarried mother as well as the unmarried father and of the need to involve them both in future plans for their child.

The maternity allowance is paid only to employed or self-employed mothers who have been paying full insurance contributions. For the full allowance, fifty contributions must have been paid or credited during the previous contribution year of which at least twenty-six contributions must have been actually paid. A reduced rate of benefit is provided if less than fifty contributions were paid or credited but no benefit is provided at all if the minimum twenty-six contributions were not paid. If the allowance is paid at a reduced rate, then any increase which can be made in special cases for an adult dependant is also reduced. Increases for child dependants, however, are not reduced.

Chapter Seven

DEATH BENEFITS

THE death of an insured person may give rise to one or more of four national insurance benefits: Widows' benefits, guardian's allowance, child's special allowance and death grants.

I. *Widows' Benefits*

The National Insurance Act, 1946, changed drastically the types of widows' benefits, the conditions under which they were paid and the types of widows who received them. Under the previous national insurance scheme, widowhood was considered like old age and as such it attracted benefit.[1] Widows of insured husbands were granted a pension of ten shillings a week for themselves for life and smaller allowances for their children, irrespective of whether they were young or old, whether they had children or not, or whether they were in or out of employment. The only condition was that the widow had not re-married.

The new benefits recommended by the Beveridge Report and introduced by the National Insurance Act, 1946 were designed to meet 'the varying needs of widowhood at different ages and in different circumstances'.[2] There were two underlying principles to the provision of these benefits. First, widowhood inevitably involves financial, emotional and social readjustments. The widow needs time to make new arrangements for her new way of life. During this period, she should receive a rather high weekly allowance for herself and her children, irrespective of any other earnings, to assist her in the process of readjustment. There were no objective criteria to determine the length of this readjustment period but the 1946 Act fixed it to thirteen weeks. A widow's allowance was provided for these thirteen weeks if the widow was

---

[1] See Chapter Eight for a discussion on pre-war and post-war concepts of pensions for the elderly.
[2] Social Insurance, p. 29.

under 60. If she was over 60 and her husband had been drawing a retirement pension she was not considered to have to make any readjustments and she received only a retirement pension which was at a lower rate. The readjustment period of thirteen weeks has been often criticised as being excessively short. Yet there can be no one period which is suited to all widows for all the changes they have to make to their way of life. Emotionally, 'it may take two years or more to become reconciled to bereavement'.[1] Socially, it is impossible to determine any one period during which widows readjust to their new way of life. From the aspect of finding employment, the period varies according to whether the widow was employed or not before the husband's death, family obligations, the impact of bereavement, etc. Marris's findings were that 64% of widows found employment within the 13 weeks and the remaining either took longer or did not return to work. The National Insurance Act, 1966, extended this period to twenty-six weeks which is certainly long enough from the point of view of making the necessary financial and employment readjustments. During this period the widow's allowance will consist of the flat-rate amount and the earnings-related supplement at the weekly rate of one-third of that part of the husband's average weekly earnings which falls between £9 and £30.

Secondly, when the period of readjustment is over, the widow should be expected to go out to work unless she is in one of the excepted groups. The sharp comment of the Beveridge Report that 'There is no reason why a childless widow should get a pension for life; if she is able to work, she should work',[2] was widely supported. This new thinking was influenced mainly by the changed labour market conditions. Whereas, such a requirement would have been harsh in the 1930's, it was considered fair in the 1940's when employment opportunities were ample for all. There are also the obvious psychological reasons for encouraging widows to lead a normal working life: to combat loneliness, to encourage new social contacts, etc. Nevertheless, there were two groups of widows which the Beveridge Report and the National Insurance Act, 1946, considered merited exception to the ruling on account of their special condition. They

[1] P. Marris, *Widows and Their Families*, p. 125, Routledge & Kegan Paul, 1958.
[2] Beveridge Report, p. 64.

136

were the widowed mothers with dependant children and the elderly widows nearing retirement.

Widowed mothers with dependant children may find it difficult to make satisfactory arrangements for their children while they go out to work. There is also the additional consideration that in the case of young children such separation may not be conducive, if not harmful, to their emotional development. Finally, the strain of trying to be a wage-earner and a mother single-handed may prove too much for the widowed mother with detrimental effects on herself and her family. For these reasons, the National Insurance Act, 1946, provided a widowed mother's allowance to those widows with children under school leaving age or up to 16 if the child was receiving full-time education or apprenticeship. Since 1946, two changes have been made to widowed mothers' allowances. The upper age limit for students and apprentices has been raised several times so that it stands at nineteen today. In the case of widows who have to keep house for their adolescent children under 19 at work, a personal widowed mother's allowance was created in 1956. The widow does not receive any benefits for her adolescent children at work but only an allowance for herself for the responsibility she has in looking after them.

The second group of widows who are not expected to support themselves by going out to work are those who have reached a certain age when they 'find it . . . hard to take up paid work again'.[1] The 1946 Act created two such sub-groups who became entitled to a widow's pension. Those widows who, when the thirteen-week period of readjustment came to an end, were between the ages of 50 and 60 and had no qualifying child in their family. Any age limit is to some extent arbitrary and the age of 50 was decided after taking into consideration the capacity to work, especially after a long gap as a housewife, and the possibility of finding employment. The other sub-group of widows entitled to a widow's pension consisted of those who ceased to qualify for a widowed mother's allowance. The age limit for this sub-group was fixed to 40 as an acknowledgement of the services these widows rendered to society as mothers who had brought up their children unaided by a husband. This differential age limit between the two sub-groups created gross inequities in some cases. The rationale behind the sub-division was also questionable and in

[1] Social Insurance, p. 29.

1956 the age limit for both sub-groups was fixed at 50, as it was the original intention in the White Paper on social insurance.

Criticisms of the inflexible nature of the age boundary at 50 have constantly been made since 1946. Examples have been cited of women widowed at the age of 49 years and 11 months, with no children, who lose their pension for the sake of one month. To remedy this situation suggestions have been made to introduce a series of age boundaries which will entitle widows under 50 with no children to portions of the pension.[1] Once, however, the principle of a series of age boundaries is introduced for one insurance benefit, there will be a demand for its extension to other benefits with the result that the administrative complexity of the insurance scheme will increase. It is also doubtful whether more age boundaries will help to reduce public ill-feeling on border-line cases. They may in fact have the opposite effect. The Beveridge Report rejected the idea of a widow's pension altogether because no person of working age who was physically fit for work should be entitled to retirement unless there were special circumstances – i.e., bringing up children. Widows without children who were disabled or unable to find employment would receive disability benefit or assistance. 'Permanent provision for widowhood as such, irrespective of the care of children and of need, is a matter of voluntary insurance by the husband'.[2] The Government's assumption that widows over 50 would find it more difficult to get employment than those under 50 was based on the employment situation of the thirties. What prevents widows today from obtaining employment is mostly the number of young children in their family. It may well be, however, that on humanitarian grounds it would be harsh to expect a woman widowed at 50 who had been a housewife for a number of years to go back to work. But that would not apply if the same widow was in employment at the time of widowhood.

There have been two other major changes to widows' pensions since 1946. Widow's pension was paid only to those widows who had been married to their deceased husband for at least ten years. It was increasingly being felt that ten years was far too long a period to establish the point it was designed for. The need for

[1] Mrs Thatcher, 2nd Reading National Insurance Bill 1964, 25 November, 1964.
[2] Beveridge Report, p. 65.

some length of marriage condition for the widow's pension was regarded essential 'because it provides, together with an age condition, the best available criterion whether a widow can reasonably be expected to rely upon her own earnings and insurance'.[1] In other words women above 50 who gave up work to get married and became widowed soon after can reasonably be expected to return to their work unless of course they have dependant children. The National Insurance Advisory Committee estimated that about 4% of widows were disqualified every year from receiving a widow's pension because of the marriage condition. The Committee considered the ten-year period too long and recommended three years instead. This was introduced by the National Insurance Act, 1957 and it still applies today. The desirability of a marriage condition has been questioned on the grounds that even if a woman had been married for only a few days, the death of her husband creates a new financial situation for her at the advanced age of over 50. It is doubtful, however, whether this is true in the case of a woman who becomes a widow after, let us say, a week's marriage. On the other hand, the period of three years may be excessive. So long as it is accepted that widowhood in itself is not enough to justify a pension, some marriage condition is necessary though the length of the period of marriage is open to question.

The second change to widow's pension was that until 1957 it used to be paid until the age of 60 when it automatically changed into a retirement pension at the same rate. The National Insurance Act of that year made it possible for a widow's pension to be paid up to retirement or the age of 65 to enable widows who work after the age of 60 to earn eventually increments to their retirement pension.[2] In 1963, one-sixth of widows in receipt of a widow's pension who reached the age of 60 transferred to a retirement pension.

Perhaps the main change to widowed mothers' allowances and widows' pensions is the abolition of the earnings rule to which they were subjected under the 1946 Act. Widows who went out to work (as well as retirement pensioners) had their allowance or pension reduced according to the amount of wages they earned. The earnings rule became the centre of very heated arguments and

[1] 'Question of Widows' Benefits', N.I.A.C., p. 16, Cmd. 9684, 1956.
[2] See next chapter for a discussion on pension increments.

it is discussed at length in the next chapter. It was modified several times until it was abolished for widows by the Labour Government under the National Insurance Act, 1964.

The proportion of widows in employment, full-time and part-time, in 1961 was higher than that of married women but lower than that of either single women or divorced women.

TABLE 35

WOMEN IN EMPLOYMENT ACCORDING TO MARITAL STATUS, 1961

ENGLAND AND WALES

Marital Status	under 25 %	25–34 %	35–44 %	45–59 %
Single	75·3	85·9	81·4	75·2
Married	41·6	29·8	36·9	33·0
Widowed	53·1	57·5	66·3	55·4
Divorced	56·3	56·1	72·7	70·5

Source: 1961 Census – Occupation Tables.

In addition to the various types of widows created by the 1946 Act, there is a transitional group of widows married before 1948 to husbands insured under the previous Contributory Pensions Acts. These widows received a basic pension of ten shillings a week, raised to thirty shillings in 1966, until the age of 60 when it automatically becomes a 'contributory old age pension'. The number of these widows is declining and it is estimated that it will disappear altogether by 1990.

Table 36 shows that almost all women who are widowed after the age of 50 qualify for either a widowed mother's allowance or a widow's pension or after the age of 60 a retirement pension. Widowhood below the age of 50 can qualify for a widowed mother's allowance only, with the result that a small proportion of widows receive no widow's benefit at all. This is particularly true of widows under 25 where the possibility of not having any children is greater and of widows in the age-group 45–49 where the proportion of older children getting married or living away from home rises. Widows who do not qualify for a widowed mother's allowance or a widow's pension may, however, be receiving a pre-1948 widow's pension, or they may qualify for sickness or unemployment benefit. Under the 1946 Act when a widow ceased to be entitled to a widow's allowance or a widowed

TABLE 36

PROPORTIONS OF WIDOWS WHO, AT THE END OF THE PERIOD OF
WIDOW'S ALLOWANCE, RECEIVED WIDOWED MOTHER'S ALLOWANCE,
WIDOW'S PENSION OR RETIREMENT PENSION. 1959–62.

GREAT BRITAIN

Age last birthday at widowhood	*Widowed mother's allowance*	*Widow's pension*	*Retirement pension*	*No Benefits*	*Total*
	%	%	%	%	%
Under 25	60	—	—	40	100
25–29	75	—	—	25	100
30–34	83	—	—	17	100
35–39	83	—	—	17	100
40–44	76	—	—	24	100
45–49	58	—	—	42	100
50–54	34	65	—	1	100
55–59	12	87	—	1	100
60–64	3	—	97	—	100
65 and over	—	—	100	—	100

Source: Third Quinquennial Review, 1964.

mother's allowance that she was receiving, she was awarded a
widow's pension until she was able to support herself. This meant
that in some cases, widows found it difficult to get into the
insurance scheme. The National Insurance Advisory Committee
recommended that in such cases widows' contribution records
should be so credited as to enable them to receive sickness or
unemployment benefit. A great deal of importance was attached
to the re-establishment of widows in the insurance scheme 'both
because we think it right in principle, and because, in our opinion,
the advantages it would confer upon widows generally would
enable a fairer line to be drawn than exists at present between those
widows who do and those who do not qualify for widow's
pension'.[1] This was accepted by the Family Allowances Act,
1956.

Widows' benefits cease on remarriage or cohabitation. This
may be just and fair in the case of young widows with one or no
children but it is different for older widows with large families.
Remarriage of widows may be one of the best ways to find social
and financial security but it also involves psychological problems

[1] N.I.A.C., p. 11.

for the widow of forming new bonds of love and loyalties as well as adjustment problems between children and step-father. Remarriage rates of widows are high at young ages but they decrease sharply with advancing age. Also the second and third year after widowhood are preferred to the first year for re-marriage as they allow a fair gap to elapse which enables the widow to get over her bereavement and plan ahead for the future. Young widows tend to marry mostly bachelors but there is a clear tendency for older widows to marry predominantly widowers.

TABLE 37

RATES OF REMARRIAGE OF WIDOWS ACCORDING TO AGE AND THE

YEAR AFTER WIDOWHOOD WHEN REMARRIAGE TOOK PLACE

GREAT BRITAIN

Age at Widowhood	1st year	2nd year	3rd year	4th year	5th year	After 5th	Total re-married
	%	%	%	%	%	%	%
22½	16·0	17·8	17·8	16·2	16·0	14·2	98·0
32½	6·0	9·0	9·4	8·6	7·4	6·0	46·4
42½	3·5	5·8	5·0	3·9	3·0	2·5	23·7
52½	1·3	2·0	1·7	1·5	1·1	0·8	8·4

Source: Third Quinquennial Review.

The tendency of widows to marry widowers is greater at all ages than the tendency of spinsters to marry widowers.

The contribution conditions for widows' benefits are the same as those for retirement pensions and for child's special allowances. They are first, at least 156 contributions must have been paid by the husband since he became insured; second, an average of fifty contributions annually must have been paid or credited for each complete year of insurance. If the first condition is not satisfied no benefit is paid. If it is satisfied but the yearly average of contributions is below fifty, but not below thirteen, benefit is paid at a reduced rate. If it falls below thirteen, no benefit is paid.

Table 38 shows that the total number of widows' benefits has not increased very much since 1950. The number of widows' pensions, however, has doubled due to the cumulative effect of their long-term nature. The increase in widowed mothers'

Death Benefits

allowances is due mainly to the effects of the Family Allowances and National Insurance Act, 1956 which provided a personal widowed mother's allowance. The increases of widows' pensions and widowed mothers' allowances has been counterbalanced by a decrease in the number of widows' basic pensions for the reasons explained earlier.

The discussion in this chapter has not covered war widows or widows whose husbands died of industrial accidents or occupational diseases. These two groups of widows receive pensions on more favourable terms and at higher rates. Their position is discussed in Chapter Nine.

TABLE 38

WIDOWS' BENEFITS IN PAYMENT AT THE END OF THE

YEAR AND TOTAL EXPENDITURE

GREAT BRITAIN

Year *a*	Widows' Pensions	Widowed mothers' allowances	Widows' basic Pensions	Total	Expenditure*b*
	Thousands				£,000.
1950	—	—	—	443	£21,300
1951	—	—	—	437	£21,700
1952*c*	345	97	—	442	£24,000
1953*c*	342	100	—	442	£28,000
1954	182	99	157	439	£30,500
1955	192	102	144	439	£32,000
1956	186	125	130	441	£35,700
1957	201	136	117	454	£38,200
1958	235	143	109	486	£43,800
1959	268	146	101	515	£57,500
1960	302	146	95	543	£61,500
1961	337	146	89	573	£65,500
1962	363	144	85	592	£80,000
1963	373	141	83	597	£84,000
1964	362	157	77	596	£99,000
1965	363	154	76	594	£108,000
1966	361	144	76	580	£136,000

(a) Year ending 31st December for number of benefits, but 31st March for expenditure.

(b) Includes expenditure on widows' allowances which are not shown in the table.

(c) Includes widows' basic pensions.

Source: Reports of Ministry of Pensions & National Insurance.

II. Guardian's Allowance

The guardians' allowances provided by the 1946 Act replaced in effect the old scheme of orphans' pensions that were provided under the Contributory Pensions Acts. They are paid to persons who can satisfy the Ministry of Social Security that they have taken the care and maintenance of an orphan child. In certain circumstances a guardian's allowance can be paid where only one parent died. These are mainly the cases of illegitimate children whose mother died and whose paternity is not known, children of divorced parents where the deceased parent had legal custody and sometimes children whose surviving parent cannot be traced. Guardians' allowances are not paid to an institution or the local authority Children's Departments for children in their care.

It is thought that the majority of guardians' allowances are paid to relatives. It is possible, however, that other persons may receive an orphan child in their family and receive a guardian's allowance. In such cases, the child in effect becomes a protected child under the Children Acts and the local authority Children's Department must be notified. The Ministry advises such guardians to notify the Children's Department but it does not notify the Children's Department itself. In the majority of cases where the guardians are relatives, the Children's Department is not involved unless of course the guardians approach it. This may happen where the guardians apply for the child to be received into care so that they can be paid boarding out allowances which are higher than the guardians' allowances. This is one of the many areas where social security and social work come into contact and undoubtedly the existing arrangements for co-ordination can do with some improving. A number of orphan children are in the care of local authorities though the exact numbers are not known. Similarly, it is possible that some other orphan children are being looked after by relatives without an application for help to the Ministry of Social Security or the Children's Department.

Apart from industrial injuries benefits, guardians' allowances are the only other national insurance benefit for which there are no contribution conditions. All that has to be established is that one of the parents was insured irrespective of how many contributions were paid. The number of new guardians' allowances awarded every year has averaged about 1,400 with no noticeable upward or downward trend. The number in payment, however, at the end of each year declined gradually from 7,300 in 1950 to 5,000 in 1962 as war orphans were reaching the maximum age limit which is the same as that used for family allowances purposes. The present amount of a guardian's allowance of £2 2s. 6d. per week is the same as that for a child's special allowance and for a child allowance paid to widows. The total expenditure of the scheme has changed very little – £700 thousand in 1950 and £480 thousand in 1965. The expenditure in 1950, however, included orphans' pensions and individual children's allowances which were paid for a transitional period to institutions.

III. Child's Special Allowance

This is one of the new benefits introduced by the National Insurance Act, 1957, following a proposal by the Royal Commission on Marriage and Divorce.[1] It is paid to a woman whose marriage has been dissolved and who has not remarried, if her former husband has died and she has a child to whose support he was contributing. The contribution conditions are broadly the same as those for widows' benefits.

Under the initial scheme the allowance was paid only if the child had been living with the mother or maintained by her at the time of the husband's death. This meant that the allowance could not be paid for a child living with the mother who, before the father's death, was living with him. The Family Allowances and National Insurance Act, 1961, removed this limitation. It also removed the stipulation that the amount of the allowance ought not to exceed the amount contributed by the father, or where this was too high, it should not exceed certain other limits. Instead, the new child's special allowances were fixed at the same rate as the allowances for children paid to widows. Illegitimate children are again discriminated against. A child's special allowance is not paid for an illegitimate child where an affiliation order was in existence against the putative father. The order 'lapses on his death'[2] and no contribution is made towards the child's main-

---

[1] Royal Commission on Marriage and Divorce, Report, 1951-55, Cmd 9678, 1956.
[2] V. Wimperis, *The Unmarried Mother and Her Child*, p. 165, Allen & Unwin, 1960.

tenance either from the putative father's estate, if any, or from the state, apart from national assistance.

The number of child's special allowances has been very small – 169 when the scheme started in 1958 and 289 at the end of 1965. Similarly, the expenditure on the scheme has been small – £2 thousand in 1958 and £35 thousand in 1965.

IV. Death Grant

The National Insurance Act, 1946, accepted the Beveridge recommendation and provided for the first time a national insurance benefit for funeral expenses. This need had previously been met mostly by voluntary industrial insurance policies. The new death grant covers the death of the insured person, his wife, and dependant children, as they are defined under the Family Allowances scheme. As part of the insurance scheme, the death grant was not paid to men and women who were aged 65 and 60 respectively in 1948. The qualifying contribution conditions for the others were, and still are, first, at least twenty-six contributions had been paid or credited since 1948 and second, forty-five contributions have been paid or credited during the last complete contribution year or as an average over the whole insured person's contribution period since 1948. No grant is paid if the first condition is not satisfied and a reduced grant is paid if the second condition is not satisfied provided that the number of contributions is not less than thirteen.

The only major change to the scheme since 1946 was introduced by the National Insurance Act, 1957 following the recommendations of the N.I.A.C.[1] The main effect of the change was that the payment of a death grant was no longer linked directly with the incurring of funeral or other related expenses. Instead, it became payable as if it were a benefit that was due to the deceased person at his death. If there are no funeral expenses or they are less than the amount of the grant, the grant will still be paid at the normal rate to the next-of-kin.

The full grant for an adult was £20 in 1948; it was raised in 1958 to £25 and in 1967 to £30. Reduced amounts are paid for dependent children. The amount of the grant was meant to cover the cost of a modest funeral and not anything grand or of any

[1] *Death Grants*, N.I.A.C. Report, Cmd. 33, 1956.

incidental expenses that go with the funeral. Marris' widows, however, found the death grant inadequate even for a modest funeral and 'found the balance from private insurances; gifts from relatives, neighbours, workmates and their husband's employer; and from savings and loans'.[1] It is generally agreed that the value of the grant has been allowed to decline with the result that it no longer fulfils even its modest aim. The total cost of the scheme rose from £2,734,000 in 1953 to nearly £8 million in 1965 mainly because of the increased number of deaths that qualified for a grant. The number of death grants paid in 1953 was 201,000 or 36% of all deaths in Great Britain compared with 399,000 grants in 1965 or 65% of all deaths.

[1] P. Marris, *Widows & Their Families*, p. 105, Routledge & Regan Paul, 1958.

Chapter Eight

RETIREMENT PENSIONS

PROVISION for the elderly occupies a very dominant position in the social policies of all industrialised countries. This is because the problems of old age are many and varied and they extend over many fields of policy – housing, community care services, hospital services, institutionalisation and social security services. At the same time the consequences of old age are not uniform. It may cause severe dependency in any of the fields mentioned and it may cause no dependency at all. This poses not only problems of adequacy of provision but problems of flexibility and co-ordination for the social policy makers. Services provided must not only be adequate but flexible enough to take account of the various sub-groupings within the broad group that is called the elderly. The second reason for which provision for the elderly has taken up such a dominant position in social policy is the increase in the numbers of the elderly. Old age is a natural physiological process and unlike unemployment or sickness it cannot be prevented. A great deal has been said and written before and since the last war about the general trend towards an ageing population in industrialised societies. Though there is some justification for this fear, it is now clear that population projections made by the

TABLE 39

NUMBER OF ELDERLY PERSONS IN GREAT BRITAIN. THOUSANDS

Year	Men aged 65 and over	Women aged 60 and over	Total number of elderly	Proportion of elderly to total population
1911	920	1,830	2,750	6·7%
1921	1,100	2,250	3,350	7·8%
1931	1,420	2,870	4,290	9·5%
1941	1,850	3,680	5,530	11·8%
1951	2,170	4,450	6,620	13·5%
1961	2,318	5,237	7,555	14·7%

Source: Censuses England and Wales, and Scotland.

various Reports in the early 1940's, including the Beveridge Report, exaggerated the rise in the proportion of the elderly among the general population.[1] The dividing age between the elderly and the rest of the population is not universally agreed because of the wide individual differences in physical and mental capacity among persons of any one year of age. The one used in Table 39 and in the discussion that follows is the minimum statutory age for retirement pensions.

Conditions for Retirement Pensions[2]

The Beveridge Report introduced one major change to the existing system of pensions – the retirement condition. Otherwise the new system was very similar to the old. Pensions were to be paid to those who satisfied the necessary qualifying conditions. These conditions were laid down in the National Insurance Act, 1946, and they remain the same today. A retirement pension is paid to every person who has paid the necessary number of insurance contributions, who has reached the age of 60 for a woman or 65 for a man and who has retired from employment, or has reached the age of 65 for a woman or 70 for a man irrespective of whether he or she is still at work.

The contribution conditions for retirement pensions are the same as those for widows' benefits and they need not be discussed again. The great majority of retirement pensioners receive the full pension and only 5% receive reduced pensions. This high percentage has been made possible through the use of credited contributions on account of illness, unemployment, injury benefit, etc.

There are no contribution conditions as such for the graduated retirement pension, apart from the fact that the amount of pension depends on the total amount of graduated contributions paid. For a man, the graduated part of the retirement pension is 6d. for each 'unit' of £7 10s. od. he himself has paid in graduated contributions. For a woman the equivalent unit is £9 because she can retire five years earlier than a man. Since employers pay an equal

[1] For a discussion on population trends see D. C. Marsh, *The Changing Social Structure of England and Wales, 1871–1961*. Routledge & Kegan Paul, 1965.

[2] Unless otherwise stated, retirement pensions mean flat-rate retirement pensions.

amount in contributions, it means that the amount of the 'unit' for 6d. p.w. graduated pension is £15 for a man and £18 for a woman.

Married women who are not at work or who are at work but do not pay full flat-rate contributions can claim a reduced pension on their husbands' insurance. They must, however, be aged 60 or over, they must have retired from work, and their husbands must have retired or reached the age of 70. If, however, a wife is not 60 her retired husband can claim the same amount of pension for her as a dependant provided she is not at work and earning above a certain amount. Reduced pensions for wives are paid depending on the husbands' contribution record. The amount of pension for a married woman on her husband's insurance is just below two-thirds of the retirement pension so it can hardly be said that there is any financial incentive for a married woman at work to pay full contributions. For the graduated part of the pension the position is different. Married women have to pay contributions and they qualify for a graduated pension in the normal way.

Minimum Retirement Age

The second qualifying condition both for flat-rate and graduated retirement pensions is that the claimant must have reached the age of 65, if a man, or 60, if a woman, and must have retired from regular employment.

Social security plans in all countries fix minimum qualifying ages both for administrative and actuarial reasons. Suggestions by sociologists and gerontologists that there should be no set minimum retirement age and that it should be decided after medical and other examinations of each individual case are 'utopian in a century of standardisation and social discipline where, willy-nilly, individualism is no longer possible'.[1] In the same way that flat-rate social insurance benefits are based on average need, so minimum retirement age is based on the average age at which people's physical and mental abilities to continue at full-time employment are presumed to be declining. This 'average' age of declining ability is based on administrative and social decisions and 'medically speaking has been pulled out of a hat'.[2]

[1] E. Lambert, 'Reflections on a Policy of Retirement', *I.L. Review*, Vol. 90, Year 1964.
[2] B. E. Shenfield, *Social Policies for Old Age*, p. 103, Routledge & Kegan Paul, 1957.

Under the 1908 Act, pensions were paid to persons over the age of 70 in order to restrict the financial burden of pensions on the government. The 1925 Act reduced the age to 65 to enable more people to benefit now that the scheme became contributory and the government's share of the expenditure consequently reduced. The Beveridge Report accepted the existing minimum retirement ages of 60 for women and 65 for men, without any discussion. Lord Beveridge later commented that 'the possibility or desirability of changing these (retirement) ages was not discussed in the Report, nor was a change suggested by any responsible organisations giving evidence to my Committee'.[1] The National Insurance Act was hardly in force for a year, however, when the Royal Commission on Population by implication considered the minimum retirement ages low and, looking ahead, commented that 'it is not unreasonable to hope that in the course of years, the average level of fitness now associated with age 65 may come to characterise age 68, or even 70'.[2] Two years later when the country's economic position was not at its best, the same opinion was voiced by the Chancellor of the Exchequer, Mr H. Gaitskell. 'In due course some formal alteration of pension age in pension schemes, both national and occupational, may well be necessary'.[3] The same question was discussed at length by the Phillips Committee three years later. The Committee recommended that the minimum retirement age for men and women should be raised by three years because the available medical evidence backed up by the number of people who continue working beyond the minimum retirement ages 'indicate that over a wide field these do not by any means represent the limit of the working life'.[4] The Committee's recommendations were not only ignored but for political considerations, were contradicted by the Conservative Government in power. The Conservative Party Election Manifesto of the same year stated: 'It is our wish to avoid any change in the present minimum pension age'.[5]

The available evidence on the physical and mental fitness of

[1] Lord Beveridge, 'Social Security Under Review', *The Times*, 10 November, 1953.

[2] Report of Royal Commission on Population, p. 114, Cmd. 7695, June, 1949.

[3] Budget Speech, House of Commons, 10 April, 1951.

[4] Phillips Report, p. 49, Cmd. 9333.

[5] *The Times*, 30 April, 1955.

men and women to continue work after the minimum retirement ages is inconclusive. If one uses as an indicator the health record of the last five-year age-group preceding retirement, i.e., 55–59 for women and 60–64 for men, compared with the health record of preceding age-groups, a slight case can be made for raising the retirement age. The average number of weeks of sickness benefit for employed persons in the age group 60–64 for men and 55–59 for women is higher than that of the 55–59 for men and 50–54 for women by only 3 weeks for men, 1¾ weeks for married women and by 1 week for other employed women. The differences for self-employed persons are even less – 2 weeks for the men and ¾ weeks for single, widowed and divorced women.[1] On the other hand about two-thirds of the men who are sick for eight years or more are in the age group 60–64. Moreover, the Inquiry of M.P.N.I. in 1954 showed that of the men who retired at the age of 65, half did so for health reasons.[2] We do not know either the extent to which the incidence and duration of sickness will rise after the ages of 60 and 65. At present those who elect to continue at work after retirement age are a very selective group and they enjoy extremely good health. The average annual number of weeks of sickness benefit per person for the age group 65–70 for men and 60–65 for women during the period 1958–1962 was 3·88 weeks for employed men, 3·28 for employed married women, 2·50 weeks for other employed women and 3·05 for self-employed men. In the case of employed men this average was lower than those of the age groups 55–59 and 60–64; in the case of employed married and other women, it was lower than for all the five-year age groups after the age of 29; and in the case of self-employed men it was lower than the preceding age group 60–64.[3]

Average figures, however, conceal wide social class and occupational variations. A survey in Birmingham showed that of the men at work aged 70 and over in social class I, 67% were considered fit whereas the corresponding proportion for class V was only 20%.[4] The Government Inquiry also showed that during the year June 1961–June 1962, the average days of incapacity for work

[1] See Table 25, p. 40 and p. 41 table 26, of Third Quinquennial Review.
[2] *Reasons Given for Retiring or Continuing at Work*, M.P.N.I., H.M.S.O., 1954.
[3] Third Quinquennial Review by the Government Actuary, Table 28, p. 43, 1964.
[4] F. Edwards et al. 'Contributions and Demands of Elderly Men' in *British Journal of Preventive Social Medicine*, Vol. 13.

on account of illness per man for all occupations for the age groups 55–59 and 60–63 were 15·23 and 21·63 respectively. For miners and quarrymen, however, the respective averages were 30·21 and 37·56 days; while for administrators and managers the average figures were much lower, i.e., 5·80 and 8·51 days respectively. It can be argued, therefore, that a blanket raising of the minimum retirement age may cause undue hardship in some occupations but none in others.

The different minimum retirement ages between men and women are certainly not based on medical evidence. Had they been, the retirement age for women should have been higher as all the demographic evidence shows that women live longer than men. When contributory pensions for the elderly were first introduced in 1925, the qualifying age was 65 for men and women. The five year differential between the sexes was introduced in 1940 partly to enable wives who were usually five years younger than their husbands to draw their pension at the same time as their husbands. The National Insurance Act 1946, retained this differential but also went a step further to make provisions for the allowance for the under 60 dependent wives of retirement pensioners. In practical terms this has removed one of the original justifications of the five year differential. The other justification was compassion and admiration for spinsters. During the debates on the National Insurance Act, 1946, suggestions were made for the minimum retirement age of spinsters to be lowered to 55.[1] The Phillips Committee rejected the raising of women's retirement age to that of men partly for the same reason. 'Working women, especially single women, who have to run their homes unaided outside working hours may wish to retire as soon as possible'.[2] The other reason was that such a step would not achieve any appreciable saving in national insurance expenditure as it would not affect the large majority of married women not at work, or at work but not paying full contributions. The only reservation to the Committee's recommendation was from the only woman member of the Committee who recommended the restoration of parity between retirement ages of men and women on the grounds that 'If women expect the same opportunities and

[1] Mrs Ridleagh, 2nd Reading of N.I. Bill, House of Commons, 6 February, 1946.
[2] Phillips Report, p. 51.

conditions of work as men, they must also expect to make the same contribution to the productivity of the country through the length of their working life'.[1]

The Retirement Condition, the Earnings Rule and Pension Increments

Before the last war the majority of national pension schemes did not make the payment of pensions conditional on retirement.[2] Today, pension schemes in a number of countries include provisions which restrict the payment of a pension to those whose income is considerably reduced on retirement or who have given up gainful employment. It is a movement away from old age pensions to retirement pensions. This change of policy is shown by the provision of 'old age pensions' by the 1925 Act but of 'retirement pensions' by the 1946 Act in this country. Paying pensions on retirement under the 1946 Act was part of the wider principle which underlay all the main insurance benefits – they were payable when earnings were interrupted or when they ceased.

The arguments for and against the two types of pension schemes are evenly balanced. The advocates of old age pensions argue that in an insurance scheme, a person is presumed to have paid enough in contributions to have earned himself a pension at a certain age irrespective of his financial position or his place in the labour market. This is after all the position in private occupational pension schemes. The counter-argument is that no insured person ever pays enough contributions himself for the amount of state pension he receives at a certain age. This ignores the fact that even though a person may not have paid enough in insurance contributions he may have paid more than enough in direct and indirect taxation. When, however, a person's financial contribution to state pensions is looked at from this wider angle, it ceases to be a financial argument and becomes a social argument for old age pensions. Old age pensions become justified because of 'the contribution the person concerned has made towards the production and development of the society to which he belongs'.[3] On purely financial considerations it is impossible to determine

[1] Phillips Report, p. 93.
[2] 'Compulsory Pension Insurance', I.L.O., Geneva, 1933.
[3] T. Higuchi, 'Old Age Pensions and Retirement', *I.L. Review*, Vol. 90, Year 1964.

whether a person has paid enough or not for his pension. A compromise solution to these opposing arguments is to pay an old age pension, the amount of which is determined actuarially on the recipient's own contributions and to pay the remaining amount of the state pension on retirement. Such a solution, however, will be very involved, administratively expensive and it can only provide very small pensions.

The second group of arguments centre round the amount of the pension and the financial cost to the community. Pre-war old age pensions were so small in amounts that the burden on the government was not so heavy. The very fact that old age pensions were totally inadequate even for subsistence, left no alternative to the pensioners but to continue working. As the International Labour Office study pointed out 'if cessation were made a condition of eligibility for a pension, it would be necessary to pay pensions sufficiently high to provide a livelihood – and this is unfortunately not the case under a large number of cases'.[1] The Beveridge Report, however, recommended pensions which were to be adequate for subsistence without any other means. The Report further argued that if such pensions were paid to all men and women reaching the age of 65 and 60 respectively it 'would impose an unjustifiable and harmful burden on all citizens below that age'.

The third set of arguments revolve round the effects the two types of schemes have on the labour market. Again the arguments are evenly balanced. In countries with high and long-term unemployment, it may be necessary to require older workers to retire on receipt of pension in order to make room for the younger workers. These are the same countries, however, which cannot afford to pay adequate pensions or assistance with the result that continuation of employment is necessary. In countries with a demand for labour there is every reason to encourage workers to remain in employment beyond the minimum retirement age. These countries, however, are precisely those which provide adequate pensions for subsistence and as the Beveridge Report pointed out when 'pensions are adequate for subsistence they will obviously encourage retirement'.[2]

Beveridge's way out of these dilemmas was the creation of an

[1] ibid., p. 16.
[2] Beveridge Report, p. 96.

involved formula which aimed on one hand at reducing the cost of retirement pensions to the community and on the other, at encouraging people to remain at work beyond the minimum retirement ages. The first was to be achieved through the earnings rule and the second through the system of increments to the pensions of those working beyond minimum retirement age. Both these insurance mechanisms were incorporated in the 1946 Act.

The earnings rule applies to all men aged 65–70 and women aged 60–65 who have decided to draw their retirement pension but who also wish to continue working. If their earnings exceed the prescribed limit then their pension is reduced accordingly. After the age of 70 for men and 65 for women, the earnings rule does not apply and people can earn any amount of wages without any deductions to their pension. Savings, life insurance benefits or occupational pensions do not affect the amount of the pension at any age. This was aimed at encouraging people to save or to make private insurance provisions for their old age. It is a worthwhile aim but it still smacks of social class bias when viewed alongside the earnings rule. The earnings limit above which pensions are reduced was fixed at 20s. in 1946 and has been raised seven times since to stand at £6 10s. od. per week at present. The proportional relationship between the earnings limit and the average earnings for men at successive rises of the earnings limit has fluctuated around one-quarter during 1951–1963. The rise in 1963, however, marked the beginning of a more generous consideration of pensioners' earnings. Average earnings conceal occupational variations but on the whole the rise in wages even of the lower paid workers has been in step with the general upward movement of wages. The earnings rule does not apply to graduated pensions. In its original form under the 1946 Act, any pensioner in the earnings rule age group who earned more than 20s. a week had his pension reduced by one shilling for every shilling he earned above 20s. It was a very blunt, insensitive system. The earnings limit was subsequently raised but it was not until after the Report of the N.I.A.C. in 1956 that the present more sensitive system of a sliding scale earnings rule was introduced. At present, pensioners whose earnings are between £6 10s. od. and £8 10s. od. a week lose sixpence off their pension for every shilling in that pound. In other words a pensioner drawing his pension and also earning

TABLE 40

EARNINGS LIMIT AND AVERAGE EARNINGS

Year	Earnings Limit	*Earnings Limit as % of average earnings for men*
1946	£1	16·6
1951	£2	24·5
1956	£2 10 0	21·1
1959	£3	22·8
1960	£3 10 0	24·8
1963	£4 5 0	26·3
1964	£5	28·4
1967	£6 10 0	33·0

Source: Report of N.I.A.C. 'Question of Earnings Limit for Retirement Pensions' Cmd. 3197, Jan. 1967 (Excluding the figures for 1967.)

£8 10s. 0d. per week will lose 20s. from his pension. The situation however, gets worse from the pensioner's point of view if he earns above £8 10s. 0d. He loses the 20s. mentioned plus one shilling off his pension for every shilling earned above £8 10s. 0d. This continues until the pension is extinguished. At present the extinguishment point of the pension is reached when the pensioner earns £12 per week. On the whole both the earnings limit and the extinguishment point have been improved over the years compared with the rise in the earnings for men. The sliding scale applied by the earnings rule is intended to allow pensioners a share of their pension so as to act as an incentive to continue work but not to allow them all their pension, as this would add too much to the cost of the pension bill and it would also mean that a man's total earnings are higher in retirement than before it. In a way the latter possibility may not be a bad thing for it may enable retirement pensioners to save something during their last few years at work for later years. The traditional fear of trade unions that pensioners may be used as cheap labour with detrimental effect on the general wage structure seems to have gradually died out.

The proportion of people whose pensions suffer because of the earnings rule is very small. Those whose pension is extinguished are only 0·8% of all persons in the age group subject to an earnings rule and those whose pension is reduced are again the same proportion. Men suffer more from the earnings rule than women because their wages are higher. The corresponding proportion of men whose pension is extinguished or reduced is

Retirement Pensions

TABLE 41

EFFECT OF THE EARNINGS RULE, JUNE 1965

	Men and Women	Men aged 65–70	Women agep 60–65
Total Number of persons in age-group subject to earnings rule	1,275,000	725,000	550,000
Persons who have retired	685,000	354,000	341,000
Persons who have deferred retirement	370,000	235,000	135,000
Persons working and pension extinguished	10,000	9,000	1,000
Persons working and pension reduced	10,000	7,000	3,000
Persons working and pension not reduced (earnings less than £5 p.w.)	200,000	120,000	80,000
Total value of pensions withheld under earnings rule in a year	£2½ m.	£2¼ m.	£¼ m.

Source: N.I.A.C. Report.

1·2% and 1% respectively. For women the relevant proportions are 0·2% and 0·5% respectively. The picture remains the same if one looks only at the three groups whose pension is either extinguished, reduced or not reduced because their earnings are below the earnings limit. Of the men and women, 4·5% have their pensions extinguished, another 4·5% have their pension reduced and 91% have their pension not reduced. The corresponding proportions for men are 6·6%, 5·1% and 88·3% respectively. For women the proportions are 1·2%, 3·6% and 95·2% respectively. In view of these low figures the National Insurance Advisory Committee felt that the public resentment of the earnings rule sprang partly from 'a widespread public misconception of its effect and impact' and partly from 'the belief that contributions under the national insurance scheme are paid not for a retirement pension but for an unconditional old age pension of the kind that existed at a much lower rate under the pre-1948 insurance schemes'.[1]

On the other hand the Committee agreed that there was some evidence to show that pensioners and employers were restricting the level of the wages in order to fall just below the earnings limit. This was done not only to avoid the financial implications of surpassing the earnings limit but also for psychological reasons stemming from a general unwillingness on the part of pensioners to have their earnings submitted to public scrutiny. This is the general impression of private researchers, too. One writer feels

[1] N.I.A.C. Report Cmd. 3197, p. 9.

Retirement Pensions

TABLE 42
HOURS WORKED BY RETIREMENT PENSIONERS 1964

	Men %	Women %
8 hours but less than 12 hours	6·5	6·3
12 „ „ „ „ 16 „	15·9	16·3
16 „ „ „ „ 24 „	42·6	39·9
24 hours but not more than 30 hours	18·6	26·7
More than 30 hours but less than 40 hours	5·9	6·4
40 hours and over	10·6	4·5

Source: N.I.A.C. Report, Cmd. 3197, p. 36.

that pensioners 'unwillingly and despairingly feel compelled to limit their weekly wages to £5. What a wealth of potential productive power is being wasted'.[1]

The Ministry of Pensions and National Insurance enquiry into the type of work done by retirement pensioners aged 65–69 for men and 60–64 for women, showed that 83·6% worked between 8–30 hours a week, i.e., they were part-timers. The average hourly earnings for part-time work was 4s. 5d. for men and 3s. 9d. for women; full-time work earnings were 4s. 1d. for men and 3s. 1d. for women. In the case of men those working 16 to 24 hours were the group whose earnings were just below the earnings limit. This applied to a certain extent to women but because of their lower hourly earnings even those in the next group, 24 to 30 hours, earned incomes just below the earnings limit. There was a heavy concentration of both men and women in these pre-earnings limit group.

The counterpart to the earnings rule is the system of pension increments. Men and women in the age group 60–65 and 55–60 respectively who defer retirement and remain at work continue paying national insurance contributions in return for higher pensions when they retire or anyhow at the age of 70 for men and 65 for women. Beveridge's opinion which was accepted by the government was that 'the increases for postponement after minimum pensionable age are designed to give to the individual some, though not all, of the saving in pension expenditure resulting through his postponement'.[2] It was felt that these extra

[1] D. R. Snellgrove, *Elderly Employed*, p. 41, White Crescent Press Ltd., Luton, 1965.
[2] Beveridge Report, p. 97.

pension increments should be at such a level as to act as an incentive for people to stay on at work while on the other hand, they should not eventually add an excessive burden on the pension bill. The increments provided by the 1946 Act were unquestionably too low. For every 25 contributions made above retirement age, one shilling was added to the pension for the husband, one shilling for his wife or 1s. 6d. for his widow. In 1951, this was raised to 1s. 6d. for the insured person but increments for dependants were left the same. Since 1959, the pension increment have been one shilling for every twelve contributions plus 6d. for a wife over 60. The National Insurance Act, 1967, has increased further the value of increments: nine contributions will have the same value as the twelve have had so far.

TABLE 43

AWARDS OF RETIREMENT PENSIONS AND INCREMENTS

GREAT BRITAIN

	Retirement Pensioners without increment		Retirement Pensioners with Increments		Average Value of Increments	
	1960 %	1965 %	1960 %	1965 %	1960	1965
Men and Women	61·4	68·8	38·6	31·2	7s. 9d.	9s. 10d.
Men	54·5	63·9	45·5	36·9	8s. 9d.	11s. 3d.
Women on own insurance	67·5	72·6	32·5	27·4	9s. 8d.	12s. 6d.
Wives on husbands' insurance	62·0	69·9	38·0	30·1	4s. 11d.	5s. 0d.
Widows on husbands' insurance	90·4	88·8	9·6	11·2	6s. 0d.	6s. 6d.

Source: Annual Reports of M.P.N.I.

Comparison with the years prior to 1960 on the awards of increments is not possible because of the change in the rate of increments in 1959. From 1960 to 1965, however, there has been a consistent, though slight, fall in the number of pensions awarded every year with increments. The average value of increments is naturally higher in 1965 than 1960 because the more generous increments introduced in 1959 have had time to take effect. Similarly, the total number of pensions with increments in payment in 1965 are higher than in previous years because of the cumulative effect. Of all retirement pensions that were in payment at the end of 1965, 37% included increments for men and 24% for women who qualified on their own insurance. The proportions for 1960 were 32% and 19% respectively and for 1955 they were 19% and 11% respectively.

Increments can also be earned on the graduated pension scheme though it is too early yet for any results. Additional earnings-related contributions above retirement age earn earnings-related pension at the usual rate. In addition, however, half the graduated part of the pension which would have been paid at 65 for men or 60 for women counts as an extra contribution towards higher graduated pension.

It is generally agreed that the financial incentive of pension increments for continuing work after retirement age has been of marginal value, if any at all. In one enquiry in 1950, 11% of persons beyond retirement age at work said they had stayed on in order to accumulate higher pensions.[1] On the other hand, the enquiry of the M.P.N.I. in 1954 showed that only seven in a thousand of the men remaining at work beyond retirement age said that they did so in order to receive a higher pension. 25%, however, said that the knowledge of accumulating increments was a factor which influenced their decision. The Phillips Report discussing the same topic summed up the situation like this: 'A small prospective increase in the pension later on, though welcome when it comes, can seldom affect the decision'.[2]

The reasons for which old people give up or continue work are more fundamental than the incentives and disincentives of pension increments and the earnings rule. Health reasons are obviously more important in dictating retirement than in postponing it. The M.P.N.I. study in 1954 showed that 40% of men reaching the age of 65 retired immediately and over half of these gave up work because of health reasons or the strain of the job. In Townsend's working class sample 'ill health or disability played a part in the retirement of nearly four-fifths of the men and was the main cause for nearly three-fifths'.[3] This exceptionally high disparity in findings is possibly due to the social class bias of Townsend's sample. Good health, however, has not the same direct

[1] G. Thomas, and B. Osborne, 'Older People and their Employment', *Social Survey*, 1950.
[2] Phillips Report, p. 53.
[3] P. Townsend, *The Family Life of Old People*, p. 163. Pelican, 1957.

relationship with postponement of retirement. The general improvement in the health services of the nation, the shortening of working hours, the later start of working life, the improvement in working conditions and the raising of the standard of living must have brought about a corresponding improvement in the health of the nation including those in the older age groups. Yet the proportion of men and women retiring immediately has risen over the years. During the period 1951–54, the proportion of men retiring at the age of 65 was nearly 40%. In 1957 it was 43%, in 1960 49% and in 1963, 54%. A similar trend applies to women also. Reductions in the proportions of people retiring at the initial age are bound to affect the proportions at work in subsequent ages. Under the National Insurance Act, 1957, people who have retired are enabled to go back to work if they wish and qualify for increments. This was an improvement on the 1946 Act which treated retirement as irrevocable. Nevertheless, the number of retirement pensioners who have taken advantage of this provision to 'de-retire' has been small and mostly men, varying between 1,200 and 1,900 a year. The general trend in earlier retirement is also seen from Table 44.

TABLE 44

PERCENTAGE OF ELDERLY OCCUPIED IN GREAT BRITAIN

Year	Men			Women	
	65–69	70 plus	65 plus	65 plus	60 plus
1921	79·8	41·2	58·9	10·0	12·8
1931	65·4	33·4	47·9	8·2	11·0
1951	48·7	20·9	32·0	5·3	8·0
1961	39·0	14·9	24·5	5·5	9·9

Source: Censuses England and Wales, and Scotland.

The decision of a healthy man or woman to continue work after retirement age is influenced by many other factors. Among these the most important perhaps is financial need. Beveridge's observation that adequate pensions were likely to encourage retirement seems to have been proved right. The N.I.A.C. commented recently that it was 'possible that the tendency which has now continued over a number of years for people to give up work earlier than they did may be related for certain groups of the population to this combined availability of occupational and state pension at an improved level'.[1] Conversely, 97·4% of Snellgrove's sample of pensioners gave as one of their reasons for wanting to work the need for more money. The second factor for wanting to continue working after retirement age is social psychological. Townsend's elderly at work 'viewed approaching retirement with uneasiness and ill-concealed fear. . . . Many said they would miss being at work and would have nothing to do'.[2] Similarly, 74·0% of Snellgrove's sample wanted a job in order to be occupied. Other surveys confirm this feeling of frustration and boredom which men face when they retire from work. On the other hand, with the general improvement in educational standards, the greater emphasis that is placed on leisure time activities and in preparing the elderly for retirement may bring about a change in this in the future. Finally, it is not always up to the employee, even if he is healthy, to decide whether to continue at work or not. Employers' retirement policies vary a great deal but generally speaking compulsory retirement age at a fixed age is prevalent in many white collar occupations while the position is more flexible in manual occupations.[3] The Government Survey on Occupational Pension Schemes in 1958 showed that 'for 55% of workers the employer discourages, or does not allow, deferment of retirement; 16% are allowed to choose when to retire, and in the remaining 29% the employer encourages deferment of retirement'.[4] Even when there is no official policy of compulsory retirement, tradition on both the employers' and the employees' side may be equally effective in dictating retirement at a certain age. It is in this respect that the National Insurance Act may have created a general belief that 65 and 60 are the right retirement ages for men and women respectively. What the Act intended to be minimum retirement ages, the public has come to consider as the normal retirement ages.

The system of the earnings rule and the pension increments has failed in its first aim, i.e., to encourage people to remain at work beyond the minimum retirement age. Has it also failed in its second – the reduction in the cost of retirement pensions to the

---

[1] N.I.A.C. Report Cmnd. 3197, p. 11.
[2] ibid., p. 158.
[3] *Employment of Older Men and Women* Cmd. 8963, 1953. *Ministry of Labour Gazette*, April, 1949.
[4] Occupational Pension Schemes, A Survey by the Government Actuary, 1958.

nation? Conservative and Labour governments have so far been in agreement that abolition of the earnings rule would involve immediate additional expenditure estimated at over £100m. a year in 1959 by Mr Boyd-Carpenter[1] and up to £120m. a year in 1964 by Miss Herbison.[2] The emphasis here is on the word 'immediate' for from the long-term point of view it is doubtful whether the Exchequer would be the loser. Abolition of the earnings rule would mean abolition of the increments scheme which would save the government a substantial sum every year. This saving, however, will be gradual for the government will have to honour its obligations towards the existing qualified pensioners. The abolition of the earnings rule will not necessarily encourage a higher proportion of the elderly to continue working. What it will most probably do is to encourage more of the pensioners who remain at work to work more hours. Reviewing the existing evidence the National Insurance Advisory Committee concluded that 'there is a tendency for pensioners' earnings to increase as the earnings limit is raised, and, in so far as this is not merely a reflection of rising earnings levels, it would seem likely that increases in the limit do result in somewhat more work being done by some pensioners'.[3] If the abolition of the earnings rule resulted in more work being done by retirement pensioners then the government and the nation as a whole would gain more than they would lose in the long run from increased productivity and also increased taxation revenue. The final objection to the abolition of the earnings rule is that it would mean paying full pensions to 'many people who are continuing in full-time employment at normal wages'.[4] This objection appears rather lame after the abolition of the earnings rule for widows. An additional gain from the abolition of the earnings rule and the increments is the reduction in the administrative complexity and administrative costs, of the present scheme.

Numbers of Retirement Pensions

The number of new retirement pensions coming into payment

[1] 2nd Reading N.I. Bill, House of Commons, 27 January, 1959.
[2] 2nd Reading, N.I. Bill, House of Commons, 25 November, 1964.
[3] N.I.A.C. Cmd. 3197, p. 13.
[4] Miss M. Herbison, 2nd Reading N.I. Bill, House of Commons, 25 November, 1964.

Retirement Pensions

TABLE 45
No. of Retirement Pensions and Contributory Old Age Pensions in Payment at the end of every Year in Great Britain

Year[a]	Men	Women (own ins.)	Women (Husbands' Ins.)	Widows (Husbands' Ins.)	Total	Expenditure
			THOUSANDS			£000.
1950	1,350	2,508[b]			3,858	£248,944
1951	1,437	2,709[b]			4,146	£248,638
1952	1,410	895	710	1,169	4,184	£275,200
1953	1,433	947	725	1,205	4,309	£315,512
1954	1,456	998	736	1,246	4,435	£334,083
1955	1,472	1,051	754	1,271	4,548	£348,112
1956	1,491	1,095	769	1,289	4,644	£432,504
1957	1,513	1,141	790	1,311	4,755	£447,870
1958	1,756	1,308	944	1,312	5,320	£482,081
1959	1,803	1,357	975	1,312	5,477	£617,397
1960	1,846	1,405	1,004	1,309	5,563	£656,971
1961	1,887	1,450	1,030	1,309	5,676	£676,949
1962	1,935	1,507	1,057	1,315	5,814	£783,904
1963	1,989	1,580	1,091	1,321	5,981	£806,942
1964	2,048	1,654	1,124	1,332	6,158	£958,381
1965	2,121	1,724	1,167	1,345	6,357	£1,013,777
1966	2,190	1,786	1,208	1,349	6,534	£1,235,967

(a) Year ends 31 December for number of benefits but 31 March for expenditure.
(b) Includes all pensions paid to all women.
Source: Annual Reports of M.P.N.I.

every year has shown a continual rise from 220,000 during 1951 to 447,000 in 1960 and to 567,000 in 1965 with increases in all years for wives and children where appropriate. Table 45 gives an outline of the various types of pensions in payment every year. Contributory old age pensions are paid to widows married before July 1948 to men who were insured under the Contributory Pensions Act. They are declining rapidly and there were only 23,000 at the end of 1964. The large increase of retirement pensions in 1958 was due to the fact that about 400,000 late-age entrants to the scheme qualified in that year. They were those who were aged 55–65 for men and 50–60 for women in July 1948 and could not qualify for a pension until the insurance scheme had been in operation for ten years. The higher proportional rise in the number of women pensioners on their own insurance as

165

compared to men is not due to increased numbers of women paying full contributions. It merely reflects the demographic fact that women live longer than men. The Government Actuary has estimated that the total number of pensioners will rise rapidly until about 1980 and then the rise will slow down. The proportion of married women claiming on their husbands' insurance will rise as marriage rates go up and as more married women opt for minimum contributions. The trend will obviously be the reverse for women claiming on their own insurance.

The position with the earnings-related retirement pensions is not clear yet. The number of awards made by the end of the first year after the scheme came into operation, i.e., the end of 1962, were 110,000 costing £15,000. By the end of 1965 the number of awards made were 585,000 costing £970,000. The rise in cost has been greater than the rise in the number of pensions because as the years go by the value of earnings-related pensions rises even though at an extremely slow rate.

Occupational Retirement Pensions

Occupational pension schemes have been growing by an average of about half a million employed persons every year since the mid-1950's. The total number of employees covered by occupational pension schemes was estimated at about 5 million in 1953,[1] 8·1 million in 1956[2] and to 12 million in 1965.[3] The growth of occupational pension schemes was due mainly to the shortage of labour. Employers introduced pension schemes to attract and to keep workers in the competitive period of full employment.

All government and private surveys have shown that the proportion of men covered is higher than that of women, that professional employees are more often covered than workers, that public services and nationalised industries are more comprehensive in coverage than the private sector of industry and that the younger age-groups are more fully covered than the older age-groups. The number of retirement pensioners covered by occupational pensions has naturally reflected this growth of occupational pension schemes during working life. Nevertheless,

[1] 'Employment of Older Men and Women', Cmd. 8963, p. 32.
[2] 'Occupational Pensions', p. 5, Govt. Actuary, 1958.
[3] 'Occupational Pension Schemes', A new Survey by the Government Actuary, p. 7, H.M.S.O. 1966.

a certain amount of wastage of occupational pension rights – estimated to about 15% of total provision – has been taking place due to the lack of official regulations governing the preservation of pension rights when employees change jobs. This loss of pension rights is due both to the rules of some pension schemes which purposely militate against pension rights preservation in order to discourage labour mobility and to the attitude of some employees who prefer to draw the amount of pension due to them when they change jobs rather than elect to have it preserved or transferred to their new job. The Committee of the National Joint Advisory Council were concerned about the ill-effects of this lack of effective policy for pension preservation on labour mobility and on the eventual incidence of occupational retirement pensions and recommended that 'general arrangements for preservation, in as full terms as may be practical, are desirable'.[1]

We are not concerned here so much with the present state of occupational pensions during working life but rather with the occupational pensions which retirement pensioners draw.[2] The number of retirement pensioners who were in receipt of occupational pensions in 1965 was 1,145,900.[3] If to this number is added the number of persons of pensionable age with occupational pensions who had not retired, those who had retired on an occupational pension before the minimum retirement age and some other similar groups, the total number of persons in receipt of occupational pensions was estimated to 2 million. Due to the recent growth of occupational pensions, the proportion of retirement pensioners receiving an occupational pension declines with advancing age. There is also an inverse relationship between age and amount of pension. Advancing age is accompanied for both men and women by reduced amounts of pensions. Previous occupational pensions were not so generous as they are today and they are not always increased to keep up with inflation. This lower incidence and reduced amount of extra sources of income in advanced ages has led some to suggest that the state retirement

[1] 'Preservation of Pension Rights', Report of a Committee of the National Joint Advisory Council, Ministry of Labour, p. 25, H.M.S.O., 1966.
[2] For a full discussion see *New Trends in Pensions*, Pilch and Wood, Hutchinson, 1964. and *Fringe Benefits, Labour Costs and Social Security*. Ed. by G. Reid and D. Robertson, Allen & Unwin, 1965.
[3] 'Financial and other Circumstances of Retirement Pensioners', M.P.N.I., 1966.

pensions should be higher from the age of 70 or 75 onwards. This will certainly help the many in advanced age groups who are in need but it will also waste money on the few not in need. It will not help either those in the younger age group who are in need. The proportion of men receiving occupational pensions is higher than that of women who draw occupational pensions on their own insurance. The proportion of widows is extremely low due to the practice in pension schemes for the husband's pension rights to cease on his death. These general points are shown in the figures of Table 46 below and are representative of the findings of other pieces of research.

TABLE 46

PROPORTION OF OCCUPATIONAL PENSIONERS TO ALL PENSIONERS BY AGE GROUP

Age-group	Men	Women (other than widows) on own insurance	Widows
	%	%	%
60–64		30	14
65–69	58	24	17
70–74	48	27	13
75–79	41	17	8
80–84	33	14	5
85 and over	34	17	4
Total	48	24	11

Source: Financial and Other Circumstances of Retirement Pensions Table A, p. 155.

The social class bias of occupational pensions is as marked as it is in the case of occupational sick pay schemes. In the public sector 90% of male pensioners who were previously in non-manual occupations were in receipt of occupational pensions while among pensioners who were in manual jobs the proportion was 72%. In the private sector of employment the gap was even wider between the two groups – 60% and 31% respectively. This confirmed previous research findings such as Wedderburn's who found that 59% of retired male pensioners who were in white-collar jobs before retirement as compared with 43% who had been in blue-collar jobs were receiving occupational pensions in 1962.[1] The social class bias was equally strong in the amount of pension received by retirement pensioners.

[1] P. Townsend and Dorothy Wedderburn, 'The Aged in the Welfare State', *Occasional Papers in Social Administration*, p. 101, 1965.

Retirement Pensions

The majority of retirement pensioners in the government survey had some other income apart from their retirement pension – 87% married couples, 74% of single men and 67% of single women. The two main sources of income, apart from state benefits were occupational pensions and earnings from employment. The proportion of married couples receiving occupational

TABLE 47

AVERAGE RATES OF OCCUPATIONAL PENSION BY FORMER OCCUPATION

	MEN		WOMEN (except widows)	
Occupation	Non-Manual	Manual	Non-Manual	Manual
Public Sector	140s.	45s.	130s.	40s.
Private Sector	125s.	40s.	70s.	30s.
Self-employed	170s.	—	—	—
All Occupations	135s.	45s.	105s.	35s.

Source: Financial and Other Circumstances of Retirement Pensioners.

pensions or earnings from work was 52% and 26% respectively. The proportions for single men were 40% and 11% respectively, while for single women they were 15% and 13% respectively. Though the proportions of pensioners receiving occupational pensions was higher than the proportion who were in employment, the average amount of income derived from employment was higher than that of occupational pensions as Table 48 shows.

TABLE 48

AMOUNT OF INCOME DERIVED FROM OCCUPATIONAL PENSIONS AND EMPLOYMENT

	MARRIED COUPLES		SINGLE MEN		SINGLE WOMEN	
Amount per week	Occupational Pensions	Earnings	Occupational Pensions	Earnings	Occupational Pensions	Earnings
	%	%	%	%	%	%
Less than £1	19·7	7·3	17·9	8·8	26·6	8·4
£1–£2	26·8	10·3	31·9	13·9	24·1	18·5
£2–£4	23·4	30·7	25·2	32·6	26·3	35·6
£4 plus	30·2	51·7	24·9	44·8	32·8	37·5

Source: Financial and Other Circumstances of Retirement Pensioners.

These findings certainly show that occupational pensions are still very inadequate both as regards persons covered and amount of benefit provided. The state pensions are by far the most important source of income for the great majority of retirement pensioners.

Chapter Nine

INDUSTRIAL INJURY BENEFITS

THE Workmen's Compensation Scheme initiated in 1897 was found wanting in many respects by all who were concerned with its administration. The Beveridge Report summed up the prevailing criticisms under four headings. First, the scheme involved long and complex court litigation between the employee or his trade union and the employer or his insurance company. The result was that it was expensive to administer, it affected adversely industrial relations and, where the employee had no trade union to represent him in court, it meant an unequal court struggle that militated against the employee. This criticism, however, must be seen in the historical context which gave rise to workmen's compensation. It was devised in the paternalistic spirit of the Victorian era when relationships between employer and employee were similar to those between father and child – authoritarian and benevolent. In the same way that the parent-child relationship became gradually freer and more democratic so the employer-employee relations were increasingly turning into industrial partnership. The scheme of workmen's compensation has been outpaced by industrial events and the time was ripe for its reform. Second, the scheme was not comprehensive either as regards risks or persons and it did not afford complete security even to those covered for the employers were not legally compelled to insure with insurance societies against accidents. Third, it permitted payments of compensation in lump sums with the result that where these were mismanaged, they did not provide a permanent source of income. Fourth, the scheme was typical of pre-war planning – or rather lack of planning – in that it made no provision for the medical and industrial rehabilitation of the injured worker. Again the concept of rehabilitation was irrelevant in the realities of the thirties. It became meaningful during World War II with the large number of disabled persons and the acute shortage of labour in war and in peace industries.

Industrial Injury Benefits

The Beveridge Report recommended that the workmen's compensation scheme should be superseded and that industrial disability should become another risk to be covered by the state insurance scheme. Industrial injuries should cease to be a dispute between employer and employee and should become part of the state social services. The Government accepted this new concept of industrial disability. The Minister of National Insurance recommended the National Insurance (Industrial Injuries) Bill to the House 'not only because of its cash benefits but because it is the foundation upon which a great constructive human service can be built, to restore the injured workman to his old job, or, if that is not possible, to train him for a new job, or if that is not possible, to care for him and his dependants'.[1] In spite of all its emphasis on comprehensiveness and streamlined administration, the Beveridge Report recommended the retention of a separate insurance scheme for industrial injuries instead of its complete absorption into the rest of the social insurance scheme. It recognised the force of the argument that 'if a workman loses a leg in an accident, his needs are the same whether the accident occurred in a factory or in the street; if he is killed, the needs of his widow and other dependants are the same, however the death occurred'.[2] Nevertheless, it felt that a separate and superior scheme for industrial injuries was necessary because employees worked 'under orders', certain industries were more dangerous than others and above all there was the long tradition behind a separate scheme for industrial injuries.

The Coalition Government accepted the Beveridge recommendations with the exception of four which it considered contrary to the general principles of social insurance.[3] First, it rejected the recommendation that disability benefits should be higher for long-term than short-term injury. Such a distinction would complicate administration, it might cause resentment between the two groups of the injured and it might encourage the prolongation of incapacity. Second, it did not accept the suggestion for earnings-related pensions for long-term disability as this was against everything that Beveridge argued in other insurance

[1] Mr J. Griffiths, 2nd Reading N.I. (Industrial Injuries) Bill, House of Commons, 10 October, 1945.
[2] Beveridge Report, p. 38.
[3] Social Insurance, Part II, Workmen's Compensation, Cmd. 6551, 1944.

benefits. The Government proposed instead different types of flat-rate benefits for short-term and long-term disability. Third, it considered unacceptable the recommendation for lump sum grants to dependants for fatal accidents as this was one of the drawbacks of the existing scheme. Fourth, the imposition of higher contributions on employers in hazardous industries was rejected as it was contrary to one of the basic principles of insurance, i.e., the pooling of risks. The Labour Government accepted these criticisms and there was wide agreement between the two political parties on the National Insurance (Industrial Injuries) Act, 1946.

Conditions for Industrial Injury Benefits

There are no contribution conditions for entitlement to industrial injury benefits. Broadly speaking, the scheme covers all insured persons in class I irrespective of their contribution record. What has to be proved is that the worker has suffered from one of the prescribed diseases or from an accident 'arising out of and in the course of employment'. This criterion was part of the Workmen's Compensation Act and it was incorporated in the new Act because first, other substitutes had been considered and were found no better; second 'the phrase has been fully examined and interpreted by the courts and its meaning is now reasonably clear and certain'; third, 'it is better to stick to the devil we know than fly to devils that we do not know of'.[1]

The Act, however, introduced a number of changes in the interpretation of this vital clause to the benefit of the injured workman. Whereas in the past, the injured person had to prove both parts of the clause before he won his case, now accidents which arise in the course of employment are deemed to have arisen out of it. The Act also dropped clauses in previous legislation whereby compensation was not paid where an accident was due to the worker's serious and wilful misconduct or disobedience unless the accident had resulted in death or serious and permanent disability. Finally, the new Act improved the arrangements for paying compensation to workers for accidents occurring while travelling to and from work. The new arrangements are

[1] Mr J. Griffiths, 2nd Reading N.I. (Industrial Injuries) Bill, 10 October, 1945.

that compensation is paid if the accident occurs while the worker is travelling to and from work in transport provided by or on behalf of the employer. The suggestion that this should be extended to cover all accidents to and from work irrespective of the transport used was rejected on the grounds that it would be unfair to provide different types of benefits for accidents according to the reason the passenger was using his own or public transport. On the other hand, it can be equally argued that the present arrangements are unfair in providing different benefits to workers depending on whether they use the firm's transport facilities or whether they have to rely on others.

The scope of the National Insurance (Industrial Injuries) Act is not so comprehensive with regard to industrial diseases as it is with industrial accidents. The Act covers a list of diseases prescribed by the Minister as occupational. These diseases are those which are definitely connected with certain occupations and afflict those employed in these occupations and not the general population, i.e., pneumoconiosis for miners, writer's cramp, etc. Persons employed in prescribed occupations who suffer from prescribed diseases are entitled to the various injury benefits in the same way as those who suffer from industrial accidents. There are, however, certain cases where the illness was contracted by accident and not by gradual process which, though not prescribed, give rise to the same benefits. If, for example, fibrositis was contracted by getting wet on a specific occasion at work, it may give rise to injury benefits. Fibrositis, however, which results gradually from working in damp conditions is not covered. The reason for this distinction is that the first is an injury by accident while the second is an injury by an illness which is not prescribed. In other words, the Act does not cover all diseases which 'arise out of and in the course of employment' as it does with accidents. This has made the provisions of the Act look arbitrary and absurd in borderline cases like the one just mentioned.

Government committees which have examined the suggestion of extending the scope of the Act to cover all diseases arising 'out of and in the course of employment' have come to the conclusion that this would be impracticable at the present stage of medical knowledge. A farm labourer may claim that his arthritis is due to the fact that he has to work in all types of weather in the open; a social worker might claim that her depression is due to her dealings with problem families; a manager might claim that his thrombosis is the result of the sedentary nature of his occupation; and so on. The majority of the Beney Committee which examined this question felt that such an extension of the Act would 'create dissatisfaction and multiply hard cases instead of diminishing them. Moreover, a litigious atmosphere would develop . . . and the settling of claims would involve a greatly increased call on the services of specialist doctors in an attempt to solve problems many of which are insoluble in the present state of knowledge'.[1] The minority Report of the same committee, however, recommended the extension of the scheme to provide general cover for long-term diseases where the claimant could 'produce prima-facie evidence of occupational causation'.[2] So far the scheme has remained unaltered since 1946 with the exception of several prescribed diseases being added to the original list.

Though the National Insurance (Industrial Injuries) Act made some improvements in the definition of industrial accidents and occupational diseases, it did not involve a departure in principle from established practice. It was in the assessment and determination of disability and the benefits that flow from it that the Act marked a departure from previous legislation. The assessment of disability is now decided by comparing the condition of the injured person with that of a healthy normal person of the same age and sex. It measures the loss of faculty which the injured person suffered. Loss of faculty is 'the loss of physical or mental capacity to lead a normally occupied life and does not depend on the way in which the disablement affects the particular circumstances of the individual. A normally occupied life includes work as well as household and social activities and leisure pursuits'.[3] Benefits payable as a result of disablement are not therefore related to the loss of earning capacity as before but to the loss of faculty.

The Act made provisions for four types of benefits: Injury benefit, Disablement benefit, Supplementary allowances and Death benefit.

---

[1] Majority Report of the Departmental Committee Appointed to Review the Diseases Provisions of the National Insurance (Industrial Injuries) Act, p. 9, Cmd. 9548, 1955.

[2] ibid., p. 29.

[3] Report of the Committee on the Assessment of Disablement, p. 4, Cmd. 2847, 1965.

Industrial Injury Benefits

Injury Benefit

Injury Benefit is payable during the initial period of incapacity for work but up to a maximum period of six months, after which the injured person may be entitled to disablement benefit.

TABLE 49

MAIN BENEFITS OF THE INDUSTRIAL INJURIES SCHEME

GREAT BRITAIN – THOUSANDS

	INJURY BENEFIT		DISABLEMENT BENEFIT		DEATH BENEFIT	
Year[a]	Number of Claims	Monthly average No. absent from work	Number of Claims	Pensions in Payment	Number of Industrial Deaths[b] Qualifying	Pensions in Payment
1950	818	63	83	59	2,154	4,403
1951	767	58	86	80	2,167	6,196
1952	775	57	96	97	2,097	7,776
1953	783	60	117	109	2,213	9,362
1954	803	59	139	124	2,212	10,873
1955	831	59	156	135	2,424	12,558
1956	822	58	164	143	2,138	13,998
1957	768	55	162	148	2,242	15,521
1958	784	58	164	155	2,160	16,863
1959	826	62	175	163	2,117	18,200
1960	861	61	185	173	2,161	19,486
1961	833	61	182	179	2,157	20,786
1962	810	61	186	185	2,104	21,957
1963	845	64	194	191	2,161	23,239
1964	898	66	207	195	2,044	24,358
1965	957	74	214	199	1,991	25,503
1966	982	—	210	200	1,970	—

(a) Year ends 31st December for benefits.

(b) Number of Industrial Deaths is the actual number and it is not in thousands.

Source: Annual Reports M.P.N.I.

The extent of industrial injuries giving rise to injury benefit can be looked at in the same three ways used for sickness benefit: The number of claims and the number of people involved, the number of spells of incapacity and the amount of working time lost. It is clear from Table 49 that the number of claims for injury benefit has shown the same upward trend since 1959 as the number of claims for sickness benefit. The great majority of these claims – about 95% – have been in respect of industrial accidents and only a small minority were for industrial diseases. For two of the most serious industrial diseases, however, pneumoconiosis and byssinosis, no injury benefit is paid. Disablement benefit is paid instead from the very beginning. The average number of workers who are absent from work every month because of industrial accidents or diseases has shown the same trend as the number of claims – an upward trend since 1959. The average number of claims for the nine year period preceding 1959 is 794·5 thousand while the corresponding number for the eight year period from 1959 onwards is 876 thousand. Similarly, the monthly average absent from work for the same two periods is 58·5 thousand and 64 thousand respectively.

The proportion of men who draw injury benefit is higher than that of women because men are more likely to be employed in dangerous occupations than women. On the other hand, the average number of days of benefit for every new award is greater for women than for men. A similar trend was observed in sickness benefits and it is more than likely that the same explanation applies for both cases even though the figures for injury benefits do not differentiate between single and married women. The explanation

TABLE 50

INJURY BENEFITS: RATES OF AWARD AND AVERAGE DURATION

GREAT BRITAIN

Age-group	Annual Number of New Awards per 1,000 insured population		Average Number of Days of Benefit per new Award	
	Men	Women	Men	Women
15–19	56·2	13·1	16·8	17·7
20–24	56·1	8·0	18·7	23·7
25–29	55·9	7·4	20·9	28·5
30–34	55·0	8·4	22·9	32·2
35–39	53·7	9·6	24·7	34·9
40–44	51·8	10·8	26·3	36·8
45–49	49·2	11·9	27·9	38·3
50–54	46·1	12·7	29·8	40·0
55·59	42·1	12·4	32·4	43·0
60–64	36·8	} 8·8	36·7	} 48·5
65 plus	20·0		43·1	

Source: Table 5, Report of the Government Actuary on the Third Quin-quennial Review National Insurance (Industrial Injuries) Acts.

offered for sickness benefit was that women stay off work longer than men because they are not under the same economic and social pressures to resume work.

Table 50 also shows that age is another important factor affecting the number and the duration of spells for injury benefit. The proportion of men being granted new awards of injury benefits increases with declining age. This is probably due to the fact that younger men tend to do more hazardous jobs and because they are less experienced in handling machines and coping with hazardous operations. The position is not so clear for women. Though the youngest age-group shows the highest proportion of awards of benefits, the rates for the age-group 40–59 are higher than for the age-group 20–39. Both older men and older women stay off work longer than younger persons for every spell of incapacity. The upward trend, however, is steeper and begins earlier for women than for men.

Occupation is another important factor for injury benefits. In the case of men, just over one-third of spells of injury incapacity every year are in coal mining. Construction and transport are the other two hazardous occupations making up between them about one-fifth of the number of spells. For women there is no one trade comparable to coal mining. Distributive trades, food, drink and tobacco industries and textiles make up one-third of all spells of incapacity every year.

About three-quarters of injury benefit spells last less than one month and only about 2% last for the whole six month period for which injury benefit can be paid. Spells for industrial diseases last longer than those for accidents because a large number of accidents are of a very minor nature. Table 51 also confirms the

TABLE 51

DURATION OF INJURY BENEFIT SPELLS, 1952

	Up to 6 days	7–12 days	13–24 days	25–48 days	49–78 days	79–150 days	150–56 days
ACCIDENTS	%	%	%	%	%	%	%
Males	17	25	30	17	6	4	1
Females	12	24	29	19	8	5	3
DISEASES							
Males & Females	9	20	33	23	8	5	2

Source: Annual Report of M.P.N.I.

observation made previously that women's spells of incapacity last longer than those of men.

There have been no changes in the scheme for injury benefits since 1948 apart from some procedural changes in 1953 regarding the injury benefit period. The amount of injury benefit was fixed at a higher rate than sickness or unemployment benefit though the benefits for dependents were the same. Since 1948, however, there has been a slight decrease in the difference between the weekly amounts of the two benefits. For an adult the weekly amount for injury benefit was 45s. in 1948 and it is now 145s., an increase of 322% as compared with an increase of 346% for sickness and unemployment benefit. Injury benefit was 73% higher than sickness or unemployment benefit in 1948 but only 61% higher today. Earnings-related injury benefit is of the same amount as sickness or unemployment and it is only payable if the injured person has satisfied the contribution conditions for sickness benefit.

Disablement Benefit

Disablement benefit is paid usually at the end of the injury benefit period if there is any loss of faculty. In a minority of cases, about 2%, a disablement benefit is paid to persons who suffered a minor accident with a small loss of faculty but who did not receive injury benefit as there was no incapacity for work. In the case of pneumoconiosis and byssinosis disablement benefit is paid from the start because they develop so slowly that the normal period of injury benefit is net sufficient to determine their eventual outcome.

Disablement benefit is of two kinds depending on the degree of loss of faculty: If the extent of disability is assessed at less than 20% a disablement gratuity is paid; if it is assessed at 20% or over a disablement pension is provided. The National Insurance (Industrial Injuries) Act laid down rather stringent qualifying conditions for disablement gratuity. To qualify for disablement benefit, the extent of disability must have been 20% or more or if it were below that there should have been a likelihood that the disability would be permanent to some degree. These conditions for the under 20% disability caused difficulties and anomalies and a certain amount of hardship because it was not always possible for medical boards to predict whether disability would be permanent. They were relaxed by the National Insurance (Industrial Injuries) Act 1953 which made it possible to pay disablement benefit whenever disability was assessed at 1% or more, irrespective of whether it was likely to be permanent or not.

The disablement gratuity is a small lump sum varying according to the degree of disability while disablement pension is a weekly allowance payable as long as the disability lasts. It was felt that to pay small sums in weekly instalments would be administratively costly and of not much use to the beneficiaries either. The degrees of disablement are prescribed in regulations issued by the Ministry from time to time. Loss of a finger was assessed at 14% loss of faculty, loss of thumb at 30%, loss of a leg below knee with stump measuring 3½–5 inches at 50%, absolute deafness or very severe facial disfigurement at 100%, and so on. Assessments up to 20% are expressed in units while assessments between 20% and 100% in multiples of 10%. Suggestions that assessments above 20% should be made in multiples of 5% so as to be more representative of the actual difficulties have not been accepted by the government because in the majority of accidents such exactitude is not possible. Moreover this procedure would work against the injured persons because it would lead more 'to rounding down than to rounding up.[1] At present if the disability is assessed at, let us say, slightly over 30%, the assessment is rounded up to 40% and so on for every multiple of 10%. Other suggestions that the assessment of disability should be weighted in favour of the older age-groups have also been rejected because of conflicting arguments. On the one hand, older people recover more slowly from disability than younger people and they find it more difficult to cope but on the other hand, younger workers' careers suffer more from disablement than those of older workers. Accidents which result in more than one injury qualify for an aggregate of the resulting loss of faculty up to the maximum of 100%.

During the first few years after 1948, there was a marked tendency to award initially more disablement pensions than disablement gratuities. In 1951, one-quarter of the initial awards were gratuities and the remaining three-quarters were disablement pensions. In 1963, however, the position was reversed with

[1] Report of the Committee on the Assessment of Disablement, p. 9, Cmnd. 2847, 1965.

gratuities making up four-fifths of the initial awards and the remaining fifth being disablement pensions. It is difficult to know whether this is due to a rise in minor accidents and a fall in serious accidents or whether this means more stringent assessment of the degree of loss of faculty by the medical boards. Another change that has taken place since 1948 is the increased certainty with which medical boards decide on the temporary or permanent nature of disability. Awards for gratuities are either final or provisional so that in cases where the injured person's condition deteriorates, another gratuity can be awarded or in rare cases the gratuity can be changed into a disablement pension. Similarly, awards for disablement pensions can be either provisional or final and during the first few years of the scheme medical boards tended to make a great deal more provisional than final awards. As they gained in experience, however, the proportion of final awards increased while that of provisional awards decreased. Provisional awards have to be reviewed to decide whether the degree of disability has changed. If the degree of disability has increased a disablement pension is paid at a higher rate; if it has decreased, the pension will be paid at a lower rate or if it falls below 20%, changed into a gratuity; if it has disappeared completely the pension will also cease. The Government Actuary's estimates are that after five years, 80% of disablement pensions are terminated but after that the only cause of cessation is the death of the pensioner. Because of the cumulative process operating in disablement pensions the number in payment at the end of each year since 1948 has increased as Table 49 showed. In 1964, of all disablement pensions in payment, 45% were for a loss of 20% faculty, 26·5% for a loss of 30% faculty, 18% for 40–50% loss of faculty, 7·5% for 60–90% loss of faculty and only 3% were for 100% loss of faculty. This was not very different from the situation in previous years.

Additional Allowances

Both the gratuity and the pension are paid irrespective of other earnings. A man may be earning more after an industrial accident but he will still receive either of the disablement benefits. Similarly, national insurance benefits are paid in addition to the gratuity or the pension. Among retirement pensioners in 1965,

9% of the married couples, 7% of the single men and 3% of single women were receiving war or industrial disablement pensions. As it was mentioned earlier, the reason for this is that the amount of disability benefit depends on the loss of faculty and not on the loss of earnings. The same criterion, however, would have placed the industrially disabled at a clear disadvantage after the National Insurance (Industrial Injuries) Act, 1946 had it not been for the use of the additional allowances. A pilot losing a hand or a violinist a fore-finger would receive a small disability benefit completely out of proportion to the loss of earnings he would suffer. The Act provided a range of additional allowances to deal with such anomalies. The four main allowances are the special hardship allowance, constant attendance allowance, the hospital treatment allowance and the unemployability supplement.

The special hardship allowance is payable in addition to disablement gratuity or pension to injured persons who, as a result of their injury, are unable to follow their regular occupation or to do other similar work of an equivalent standard. The maximum allowance is now £3 1s. od. but when added to the disablement pension they must not together exceed the maximum rate of disablement pension, i.e., the pension paid for a 100% loss of faculty. Within these limits, the amount of the allowance depends on the difference between the man's earnings in his regular occupation and the earnings he is receiving in his occupation after the injury. In 1964, the maximum allowance was paid to 85% of the people receiving a gratuity or pension and the average payment of the allowance was 95% of the maximum amount.

The importance of the allowance has increased over the years. In absolute numbers it has grown from 37,000 in 1950 to 127,000 in 1964. As a proportion of the number of gratuities and pensions it has also risen from 50% in the period 1949–53, to 64% in the following quinquennium and it has remained at that level since. The allowance is more likely to be paid during the initial period of the injured person's return to work than later. With training and experience in the job, a number of injured persons manage to earn wages which are equivalent to their normal occupation earnings, which automatically disqualifies them from the special hardship allowance. The proportion of all hardship allowances that continue in payment for at least five years from the date of award is small and it rises with age from 10% for the age-group

15–19 to 25% for the age-group 60–64. Older persons are less likely to be able to take up their old occupation or another of equivalent standard than younger persons because physical adaptability decreases in older ages and also because of employers' attitudes towards the employment of elderly disabled persons. Of the allowances that remain in payment for five years, three-quarters of them will continue for a further five years. This applies to all age-groups with the exception of those aged over 65 where the proportion is lower due to the great probability of death.

The other three supplementary allowances apply to very small groups of disabled pensioners. Their total cost is only 3·5% of the total cost of disablement pensions while expenditure on special hardship allowances amounts to 55% of the combined cost of disablement gratuities and pensions.[1] The Constant Attendance Allowance is payable to those disabled pensioners who suffer from 100% loss of faculty and who need someone – including a wife – to attend to them regularly. Examples of cases who may qualify are blind or bed-ridden persons. The numbers and proportions of constant attendance allowances have grown due to the fact that as they are very long-term benefits they are cumulative. At the end of 1951, the allowance was paid to 500 disabled pensioners or nearly 20% of all those assessed at 100% disability, while at the end of 1964, the figures were 1944 and 39·5% respectively. The allowance can also be paid to people who, before 1948, were in receipt of compensation under the Workmen's Compensation Acts. The number of these beneficiaries has naturally declined from 500 at the end of 1951 to 330 at the end of 1964.

The Hospital Treatment Allowance is payable to persons receiving a disablement pension at less than the full rate when they are in hospital for treatment of the injury that caused their disablement. The amount of the weekly allowance is the difference between the disablement pension at 100% and the actual disablement pension the person concerned is receiving. At the end of 1951, there were 400 hospital treatment allowances, or 0·5% of all disablement pensions. At the end of 1964, the figures were 535 and 0·3% respectively.

The Unemployability Supplement is an alternative to sickness benefit or retirement pension for those disabled persons who

[1] *Third Quinquennial Review,* table 16, p. 20.

either do not qualify for these benefits or who qualify at reduced rates. It is as rare as the other two benefits since the majority of disabled pensioners qualify for sickness benefit or retirement pension. At the end of 1951 about 300 unemployability supplements were in payment, while at the end of 1964 the number was 900. These numbers include supplements paid to people receiving compensation under the Workmen's Compensation Acts – 90% of all supplements in 1951 and 22% in 1964.

Death Benefit

The number of deaths from industrial accidents and prescribed diseases has remained almost constant since 1950. Coal mining and construction work have accounted for about half of these deaths. The main industrial injuries death benefit is a pension for the deceased's widow and children, though in special cases payments can be made to his parents or other relatives. Not all deaths from industrial accidents and prescribed diseases, however, lead to a death benefit as, for example, the death of single persons with no dependant relatives.

The scheme for industrial widows' benefits is similar to the scheme for ordinary widows' benefits. Widows' allowances for the first twenty-six weeks of widowhood, widowed mothers' allowances, widowed mothers' personal allowances and widows' pensions are the same with the only difference that industrial widows' pensions are paid at a slightly higher rate. There are, however, three main differences between the two schemes for widows' benefits. First, in the case of industrial widows' benefits, there are no qualifying contribution conditions. Second, those industrial widows who do not qualify for any of the benefits mentioned will receive a benefit at a reduced rate – £1 10s. od. per week. It is estimated that 10% of industrial widows receive this benefit. As it was pointed out in Chapter Seven the equivalent group of ordinary widows receive no benefit. Third, while on remarriage ordinary widows lose every benefit for themselves and their children, industrial widows do not lose everything. Their own pension will cease but they will receive one year's pension as a gratuity. Allowances for their children continue to be paid but at less than half the usual rate. Remarriage rates are extremely low. In 1952 only 194 pensions ceased on remarriage of the widow out of a total of 7,235 widow pensioners. In 1964 the numbers were 420 and 23,845 respectively. Comparison between the two years, however, is not possible because of the different age structure of widows, possible differences in size of family, etc.

The number of widows' pensions in payment at the end of each year has increased steadily with very small variation by about 1,450 a year from 4,400 in 1950 to 24,974 in 1965. A very small number of pensions and gratuities are payable to the deceased's relatives, usually his mother or father if he had been contributing at least 5s. towards their maintenance. If the deceased's contribution was over five shillings but not more than half the cost of the claimant's maintenance, a gratuity is paid. If the contribution had been higher than half the maintenance cost, a pension is paid, the rate of which depends on the amount of contribution but at its maximum it is less than a quarter of the widow's pension. The number of these pensions was 180 in 1952 or 6% of the total number of pensions in that year (the other 94% were widows' pensions). The figures for 1964 were 493 and 2% respectively.

Levelling Up

Social policy in this country, unlike that of many other European countries, does not recognise civilian disability. The financial needs of people suffering from very long-term sickness are considered to be the same as those of people suffering from very short illness. In fact the provision of earnings-related sickness benefits results in higher benefits during short-term than long-term illness. On the other hand, the state recognises war and industrial disability and the social security scheme makes special provisions for those disabled in war or at work. There are exceptional risks in war to justify special provisions for war disability but the same can not be said of conditions at work. None of Beveridge's arguments in favour of a separate industrial injuries scheme stands serious examination. The discrepancy between the provisions for the work disabled and the civilian disabled has been criticised constantly since 1948. The general tone of the criticism has been not to remove the advantageous provisions for the work disabled but rather to extend the same provisions to the civilian disabled. Any changes for the integration of the national insurance and industrial injuries schemes should have a levelling up and not a levelling down effect.[1] Reviewing the whole provision for industrial injuries, Young concluded that 'there is ample justification to retain, in the short run, an illogical scheme that under certain circumstances pays more than the minimum in benefits, so that, when the time is ripe, it may be amended and adjusted to meet the full requirements of those incapacitated from whatever cause'.[2]

All the signs indicate that the time is ripe for the recognition of civilian disability. The Labour Party in its pamphlet 'New Frontiers of Social Security' in 1963 and at its annual Conference in 1965 committed itself to the improvement of the benefits and services for the chronic sick. The Disablement Income Group, (D.I.G.), an all-party pressure group has campaigned for the provision of a scheme for a National Disability Income for all the disabled in the country including housewives. The inclusion of housewives is justified by the fact that disability of a housewife can have the same serious effects on the financial standards of the family and on its very survival as disability of the husband. Evidence from small scale research has shown that the civilian disabled are one of the 'pockets of poverty'. A survey of 211 disabled men and women showed that 60% of the households had a total income of less than £10 per week and that nearly half depended wholly or partly on supplementary benefits.[3]

The government's hesitancy in implementing the proposals of D.I.G. is due to the immediate cost involved. It is estimated that there are 750,000 disabled of working age in the country and that the total cost of a scheme for a National Disability Income is £75 million a year. From the long-term point of view the scheme may not be as costly. Provision of adequate cash benefits for the chronic sick will encourage community care which will reduce the number of disabled persons admitted to hospital for non-medical reasons and the possible reception of children into the care of the local authorities. There are no statistics on either of these points but one quoted estimate put the number of hospital beds to be

[1] For examples of differences in the amounts of social security benefits received by the civilian and the industrial disabled see: Jan Elson, 'A National Disability Income', *New Society*, 27 July, 1967.

[2] A. F. Young, *Industrial Injuries Insurance*, p. 172, Routledge & Kegan Paul, 1964.

[3] Research carried out by Miss Sally Sainsbury, University of Essex, reported in *The Guardian*, 6 May, 1967.

emptied by the provision of a National Disability Income to 66,000.[1] It must not be assumed, however, that community care is always cheaper than institutional care. There comes a point of disablement, especially for persons with no dependent children, where the cost of maintaining a person at home exceeds the cost of institutional care. The argument for a national disability income is more ethical than financial but not any less compelling. The inadequacy of social security benefits is only one of the problems of the disabled. Equally important is the unsatisfactory quality of the services provided by the local authority welfare departments. Perhaps even more important is society's abnormal attitude to disability and the way this affects people's relationships with disabled people.[2]

[1] Anthony Cowdy, 'The Forgotten Poor', *The Sunday Times,* 30 July, 1967.
[2] Paul Hunt, (Ed.) *Stigma,* Chapman, 1966.

Chapter Ten

ALLOWANCES FOR CHILDREN

FINANCIAL aid from the state to parents for the maintenance of children takes two forms: Assistance in kind and allowances in cash. Assistance in kind is provided by such services as school meals, welfare food, milk, reduced fares, etc. Assistance in cash is mainly through family allowances, child insurance and assistance allowances and child tax allowances. This chapter is concerned with cash allowances only though occasional references to assistance in kind are made.

Family Allowances

The first attempt for a public scheme of family allowances was made in 1796 when William Pitt as chancellor of the Exchequer introduced a Bill in Parliament for allowances for children. He urged Parliament 'to make relief, in cases where there are a number of children, a matter of right and an honour instead of a ground for opprobrium and contempt. This will make a large family a blessing and not a curse, and this will draw a proper line of distinction between those who are able to provide for themselves by their labour and those who, after having enriched their country with a number of children have a claim upon its assistance for their support.'[1] Pressure of other business prevented further proceedings on Pitt's Bill. The next business of the House was a proposal to change the date of grouse shooting from 1st to 14th September! It was not until the First World War that the idea of family allowances for children was taken up in earnest by the Family Endowment Society with Miss Rathbone as its main champion.

The 25-year long discussion which preceded the Family Allowances Act, 1945, produced two broad reasons for the

[1] Quoted by Sir William Jowitt, Minister of Social Insurance designate), House of Commons debates on Social Insurance, 2 November, 1944.

introduction of a family allowances scheme: Demographic and economic considerations. There were fears that the population of the country was not reproducing itself and that if the decline in birth rates continued the total population of the country would be halved by the end of the century. Family allowances were viewed as a positive social policy measure of arresting and possibly reversing the decline in birth rates. Even the strongest advocates of this policy recognised that economic incentives would not increase the birth rate among those parents who did not want a family because of emotional or strong social reasons. They hoped, however, to induce a higher birth rate among those parents who restricted the size of their family for economic reasons. To achieve this, family allowances needed to be progressive in amount with the size of the family. This was the form that the French system of family allowances took in its attempt to deal with the same problem.

An offshoot of the demographic argument for family allowances was the eugenic viewpoint. The nation's future prosperity was at stake not so much because of the general population decline but because of the decline in birth rates among the middle and upper classes. These were the 'selected classes', superior in stock to the working classes, on whom the progress and prosperity of any nation depended. The state should actively encourage their propagation by a generous system of child allowances equivalent to no less than one-tenth of the earned family income.[1] This proposal was based on the then prevailing view that intelligence is inherited and that it is not affected by environmental factors. Apart from the fact that scientifically the foundation of the proposals was suspect from the start, they were politically unattainable in a country with a democratically elected government.

The economic considerations were based on the findings of social researchers from Booth onwards that one of the two main population groups living in poverty consisted of large families with low incomes. It was held then, and it is still held today, that the wages a man got must depend on the services which he rendered to his employers and they could not take into account the size of his family. The only way to relieve poverty was by

[1] Professor W. McDougall, *National Welfare and National Decay*, Methuen, 1921.

means of a system of family allowances. The need for family allowances was made more imperative since the introduction in 1921 of allowances for children of the insured unemployed. Without a scheme of family allowances it would have meant that total benefits during unemployment and sickness could exceed earnings during work – a situation that was considered both unfair and dangerous. A scheme of universal family allowances could only reduce but it could not eliminate this 'risk'.

By the time the Beveridge Committee was appointed, there was general agreement on the need for a system of family allowances. One of the last converts to the idea of family allowances was the trade unions. Their fear that family allowances might be used – as the Speenhamland System had been – by employers to keep wages down faded gradually with their increased political and industrial power and the reduction in unemployment during the war.

The passage of the Family Allowances Bill through Parliament was a very peaceful affair. Discussion centred mainly on two points: The amount of the allowance and to whom it should be payable. The Bill provided for the payment of the allowance to the father because he was considered the breadwinner of the family. Miss Rathbone complained bitterly that the all-male cabinet were out of touch with women's feelings on this issue. She warned that the payment of the allowance to the father 'will not raise the status of motherhood but will actually lower it'.[1] The Government allowed a free vote and Miss Rathbone's amendment that family allowances should belong to the mother was accepted. They must be claimed by the mother but they can be paid either to the mother or the father. In special circumstances where a court finds the mother not a proper person to receive the allowance, the father can be made the legal recipient of the allowance.

The amount of the allowance depended on two considerations: The amount of the cost for maintaining a child at subsistence level and the proportion of that cost to be met by the state. The Beveridge Report estimated that the entire subsistence cost per child for food, clothing, fuel and light but excluding rent was 7s. a week at 1938 prices. This was an average sum and it naturally varied according to age, social class and geographical area. Allowing for the rise in the cost of living and the provision

[1] 2nd Reading of the Family Allowances Bill, House of Commons, 8 March, 1945.

already made for school meals and milk, the Report considered that an allowance of 8s. a week per child in kind or in cash was necessary. This should not be met completely by the state because 'the principle of social policy should not be to remove all responsibilities from parents, but to help them to understand and to meet their responsibilities'.[1] The state could share the cost with the parents either by paying a reduced allowance for all children or by paying the full allowance for some of the children. The Report preferred the second and recommended an allowance of 8s. a week for the second and subsequent children. It made the important qualification, however, that a lower cash allowance would be justified if provision in kind for children was extended. It was argued then and it is still argued today that the exclusion of the first child was unjust and illogical since the birth of the first child not only involved the family in a number of items of expenditure not necessary for subsequent children but it also meant the reduction of family income since the mother had to give up her employment. The Report felt that most men's wages were sufficient to cover at least two adults and one child and to give a full subsistence allowance for every child could not be described 'as a measure indispensable for the abolition of poverty'.[2] The Coalition Government accepted the Report's recommendations and the Family Allowances Act, 1945 provided an allowance of 5s. a week for every child in the family except the first. The reduced amount of the allowance was defended on the grounds that the provision of free school meals and milk would be extended to all school children. This met with wide support from all sides in the House of Commons partly because of the belief that benefits in kind were certain to be used by the children while cash allowances could be mismanaged by parents. There were a few critics who considered the amount inadequate and some others, including Miss Rathbone, who felt that standard allowances would not encourage large families which was one of the original aims of the family allowances scheme. By this time, however, the importance of demographic factors had declined considerably as the birth rate had risen.

Graded family allowances were introduced through sheer force of circumstances by the Family Allowances Act, 1956. The

[1] Beveridge Report, p. 157.
[2] Beveridge Report, p. 155.

allowance for the third and subsequent children was increased by two shillings a week in order to make up for the abolition of the government subsidy for bread and the reduction of the subsidy for milk. The allowance for the second child was not increased because it was considered that parents could afford to bear the extra cost for the first and second child. It was for this reason that the Labour Opposition argued that graded family allowances were introduced to reduce government expenditure and not because of a desire to help large families as Mr Boyd Carpenter, the Minister of Pensions and National Insurance, insisted. In a curious way, Beveridge's recommendation that family allowances 'should be graduated according to the age of the Child' was implemented.

The Family Allowances Act, 1956, introduced the second change that the scheme has had since its introduction in 1945. Under the original Act the upper age limit for the receipt of the allowance was the compulsory school leaving age or, if the child continued full-time education or was apprenticed, the age limit was the 1st August following the 16th birthday. The 1956 Act raised the upper age limit for apprentices and full-time students to 18. This was raised again in 1964 to 19 where it still stands. Another minor change introduced by the 1956 Act was to pay allowances for children who are too handicapped to go to school or take up employment up to their sixteenth birthday when they become eligible in their own right to national assistance. The effects of the raising of the upper age limit for family allowances have been slight. At the end of 1950, 0·04% of all children in receipt of family allowances were above their 15th birthday; the corresponding proportion at the end of 1964 was 1%.

The measure of scope of protection, i.e.

$$\frac{\text{Children attracting allowances}}{\text{population under normal age limit for payment of allowances}} \times 100$$

afforded by the British scheme is one of the lowest in Europe. It is 48 compared with 100 for Belgium, Denmark, Finland, Ireland and Sweden, 91 for France, 88 for Iceland, 64 for the Netherlands, 51 for Norway, 24 for West Germany, etc.[1] This is, of course, a very rough indicator for the normal age limit for payment of

[1] S. N. Iyer, 'Degree of Protection under Family Allowances Scheme', *I.L. Review*, Vol. 94, No. 5, November, 1966.

allowances varies from one country to another. The majority of family allowances are paid to families with two children as Table 52 shows. It is difficult to draw precise conclusions from the table because of the limited definition of 'children' and the changes in upper age limits discussed above. Nevertheless, the table reflects the increase in family size that has taken place during the last decade.

TABLE 52

FAMILIES RECEIVING ALLOWANCES ANALYSED BY THE NUMBER OF CHILDREN
IN THE FAMILY[a] – GREAT BRITAIN

	31 *December* 1950 %	31 *December* 1960 %	31 *December* 1965 %
2 children	64·1	62·6	59·5
3 children	23·1	23·7	24·8
4 children	8·0	8·5	9·6
5 children	2·9	3·2	3·6
6 or more children	1·8	2·1	2·4

(a) Includes the older or eldest child, for women no allowance is payable, but excludes children over the age limits.

Source: Annual Reports of M.P.N.I.

Family Allowances have been raised three times so far – the lowest number of changes of all social security benefits excepting the death grant. The first rise in September 1952 from 5s. to 8s. per child more than restored the purchasing power of the allowance to its 1946 level. This followed six years of stagnation and was only a short-lived improvement, for by 1956 the retail prices index caught up and surpassed the new allowance. This was the same year when the allowance for the third and subsequent child was raised to ten shillings to make up for the reduction in food subsidies. No change was made for the allowance of the second child until April 1968 when it was raised together with allowances of the other children by seven shillings. Obviously during the whole of this period, family allowances for the second child were well below their 1946 value while allowances for the third and subsequent child were ahead up to 1964 if the reduction in food subsidies is not taken into account. The last rise of family allowances took effect in two stages. All the allowances were raised by seven shillings from April 1968 but in order to cover the preceding winter, a reduced allowance of five shillings for the fourth

and subsequent children was paid from October 1967 to April
1968. The existing allowances of 15s. for the second child and
17s. for the third and subsequent children are well above the 1946
level but it must be remembered that food subsidies have been
reduced and that the price of school meals, which were originally
intended to be free to all school children, was increased at the
same time as the family allowances.*

Apart from financial difficulties, the other main reason for the
neglect of family allowances is the disposal of the demographic
argument for family allowances as a result of the rise in birth
rates. In fact the aim of public policy today is to restrict rather
than encourage the rate of population growth. This, however,
should be achieved through better family planning services and
not through neglect of family allowances which penalises children
already born. Until the recent rise, the value of family allowances
as a proportion of the national income per head of the working
population in this country was one of the lowest in Europe. In
1961, the amount of family allowances for two children was 25%
of the national income per head of working population in France,
27·1% in Italy, 16·2% in Italy, 16·2% in Belgium, 11·1% in the
Netherlands, 6·0% in West Germany and 3·8% in the United
Kingdom.[1]

Occupational schemes for family allowances have been neglected even more. The Royal Commission on Population saw great
advantages in the expansion of occupational family allowances
among professional groups of employees on the lines of the
scheme for university staff. In fact the trend since 1948 has been
the opposite. Not only has there not been any expansion but there
has been a decline of family allowances occupational schemes.
The scheme for family allowances for university staff was abolished
following the recommendations of the National Incomes Commission in 1963. A number of professional bodies have been
opposed to occupational schemes of family allowances because of
the fear that they keep down wages and salaries or on the principle
that remuneration from work should depend on the man's work
and not on his family responsibilities. Government attitude too
has been hostile on the argument that it was the responsibility of
the state to help families with children and that money should not

[1] Mrs M. F. W. Hemming, 'Social Security in Britain and Certain Other
Countries' *National Institute Economic Review*, No. 33, Table 9, August, 1965.

be diverted to this end from other sources. It is difficult to know whether an improvement in occupational family allowances will have any beneficial effects on the state scheme. It will not benefit the low income groups directly because all occupational schemes of social security when not regulated by the state favour the better off sections of the community. On the other hand, an improved occupational family allowances scheme might encourage or even force the state to improve its scheme in the same way that occupational schemes for pensions, sickness and redundancy did.

Income Tax Children's Allowances

Taxation systems in all countries provide a number of reliefs and allowances designed to adjust the burden of taxation with the individual's ability to pay. The main income tax allowances in this country are the earned income allowance equivalent to two-ninths of the first £4,005 and one-ninth of the next £5,940 of a person's net earned income per year; the personal allowance of £220 for a single person or £340 for a married man; allowances for dependent children and relatives; and allowances for payments towards superannuation or other insurance policies and the payment of interest for a bank or a Building Society loan. When these and other minor allowances have been deducted from a person's annual earned income, the remaining amount is taxed on a sliding scale of 4s. in the £ on the first £100; at 6s. in the £ on the subsequent £200; and at the standard rate of 8s. 3d. in the £ on the remaining earned income.[1]

The justification of children's income tax allowances is that a man with children to support has not the same capacity to pay income tax as another man with the same income but with no dependent children. They enable the man with dependent children to keep more of his income than the man with no dependent children. First introduced in 1909, they have been changed several times and today they are £115 for each child not over the age of eleven, £140 for each child over eleven and not over sixteen and £165 for each child over the age of sixteen attending a course of

[1] For a concise discussion on the taxation system see Jebs, 'Personal Taxation' *Fabian Research Series* 255, 1966. For a discussion of the relationship between social security and taxation see Lady Rhys-Williams, *Taxation and Incentive*, Hodge, 1953.

full-time education or apprenticeship lasting not less than two years. Where a child has a separate income of its own exceeding £115 a year, its income tax allowance is reduced by the excess. The present graduated system of children's income tax allowances was introduced in 1957 in response to the recommendations of official reports that the cost of maintaining a child varies according to its age. Yet the same principle was examined and rejected in the case of family allowances. Similarly, while a tax allowance is made for the first child a family allowance is not. On the other hand, a means test was rejected for family allowances but it was accepted in tax allowances since children with personal income over £115 a year benefit less or do not benefit at all. Finally, children's income tax allowances have been upgraded since 1948 while family allowances were comparatively neglected until 1968. The total cost of children's tax allowances to the Exchequer has not only exceeded the cost of family allowances substantially but it has risen at a much faster rate. In 1953–54, the total cost of children's tax allowances was £140 m. while for family allowances, following the rise in 1952, the cost was £103m. By 1965–66 the cost of the tax allowances for children at current prices had almost trebled to £500m. while the cost of family allowances had risen only by 40% to £146m.

The benefit a father receives from the income tax allowances of his children depends on the amount of his annual income. The higher his income the greater the amount of tax benefit he receives because rates of income tax rise with higher income, as Table 53 shows. On the other hand, the value of family allowances

TABLE 53

CHILD TAX ALLOWANCES*

Age of Child	Amount of child tax allowance	Value of Child Tax Allowance according to rate of tax paid by father		
		Tax at 4s. in the £	Tax at 6s. in the £	Tax at 8s.3d. in the £
under 11	£115	£23	£34 10 0	£47 9 0
11 but under 16	£140	£28	£42	£57 15 0
16 or over	£165	£33	£49 10 0	£68 1 0

diminishes with increased income because family allowances are subject to income tax. In 1965, one-sixth of the total cost of family allowances was retrieved in income tax. Taken together, the two types of children's allowances provide more income to the wealthier than the poorer section of the community.

Traditionally, the two types of allowances have been considered to perform different functions and to 'involve different considerations'.[1] None of the Government Reports on social security or Income Tax has recommended their amalgamation. The differences between them have been summed up as follows: 'A vital distinction between a tax allowance and a family allowance is that under the former the taxpayer is permitted to enjoy more of his own income whereas the latter is a state subsidy the financing of which contributes to the present substantial burden of taxation. The raising of tax allowances increases incentive to earn and helps the productive effort and real wealth of the country. Family allowances cannot be said to be of advantage in this respect even by their most ardent advocates'.[2]

Recently, however, it has been increasingly argued that the two allowances do not really involve different considerations and they in fact perform the same role, i.e., they provide state aid to families. Consequently a number of suggestions have been put forward for their integration, the most publicised being those of the Child Poverty Action Group. There are three main proposals. First, people should be able to choose between family allowances and child tax allowances according to their financial circumstances but they should not be able to receive both. The money saved from not paying family allowances to all families should be used to provide increased family allowances, including one for the first child, for those families who opt for them. This is similar in principle to the Option Mortgage Scheme introduced by the Housing Subsidies Act, 1967, which enables mortgage payers to choose between income tax relief and the Government subsidy according to which benefits them most. If decisions are irrevocable, as they are under the Option Mortgage Scheme, they will involve an element of risk since family circumstances change and therefore one scheme that benefits most a family today may not do so ten years later. If on the other hand people are allowed 'to play

---

[1] Beveridge Report, p. 187.
[2] N. D. Vandyk, 'Family Allowances' *British Journal of Sociology*, Vol. 7, 1956. See also G. Howe and N. Lamont, *Policies for Poverty*, Bow Publications, 1967.

hanky-panky' with the scheme, administrative costs and work will be considerable. A compromise solution between these two extreme positions will be necessary. Second, the two schemes should be merged into one to provide one large allowance, free of tax, for every child in the family including the first. This has the advantage of administrative convenience and, to some, it has also an egalitarian appeal. Politically, however, it involves an element of risk to the government that introduces it because of the resentment it will cause among the better off families who will suffer from such a merge of the two allowances. Financially, too, it involves an element of injustice since the benefit which low income families will derive will be at the expense of the better off families with dependent children rather than from single persons or married couples with no dependent children. Third, to allow the two systems of child allowances to continue but to pay child income tax allowances in reverse to those families whose income is too low to qualify them. This will mean that the better off families will not lose anything, the poorer families will gain considerably but the Exchequer will have to meet the considerably increased cost. Because of this, apart from other reasons, this proposal is a non-starter in the present economic situation.

Any of these three proposals will divert more income to those families which at present do not benefit from the child income tax allowance. Those who maintain that the two allowances must be kept separate also agree that low income families must be provided with more income through larger family allowances. They are divided, however, on the means of achieving this. The Labour Government adhered to the policy of universal social benefits and increased all family allowances in April 1968. This, however, meant that 49% of children in families with incomes below supplementary benefits standard before the rise of the allowances were still below that standard after the rise. It also provided extra income to families that did not need it though a larger proportion of this would be paid back to the Exchequer since family allowances are taxable. The Conservative Opposition maintained that had the new rises in family allowances been made on a selective basis, the same expenditure would have sufficed to bring the income of all low income families at least up to supplementary benefits standard.

The desire to help low income families is evidently above party political lines. The decision on how best to achieve this, however, will definitely be taken on political considerations.

Child Insurance and Assistance Allowances

The Beveridge Report did not have to make a special case for allowances for dependent wives and children to supplement the husband's insurance and assistance benefits. That had already been accepted as one of the prerequisites of any social security system. The 1946 and 1948 Acts provided that persons receiving benefits could also receive supplements for one dependent adult (usually the wife) and for all their dependent children. Dependent wives are those who are not earning more than the insurance or assistance supplement for them and are either residing with their husband or, if living apart, are maintained by him at least up to an amount equivalent to the supplement. Dependent children are defined in a similar way provided they are within the age limits for family allowances purposes. Supplements for adult dependents are reduced in proportion to any reduction of the insured person's own benefit if he does not satisfy fully the contribution conditions. Supplements for children, however, are not affected by a deficient contribution record.

For social insurance purposes, Beveridge estimated that, even with the most careful budgeting, 9s. were necessary for a children's allowance to cover the cost of subsistence. Subtracting the value of the services in kind provided for children, he recommended a sum of 8s. a week, the same amount as family allowances. Unlike family allowances, however, this amount could not be shared with the child's parents because the benefit is paid when family earnings are interrupted or cease. The government provided 7s. 6d., which was below Beveridge's recommendation, for the first child that was not entitled to a family allowance and 2s. 6d. for other children. These child insurance allowances were the same for all insurance benefits until 1956 when widows' children were provided with higher allowances as a special consideration for the special difficulties which widows face in bringing up their children single-handed. In fact child allowances for widows are the same in amount as guardians' allowances and child special allowances. This difference has been maintained and today allowances for children of widows are 70% higher than those for the children of other insurance beneficiaries.[1] This difference may be justified in the case of the temporary unemployed or sick but it is hard to justify in the case of the permanently disabled or the long-term unemployed.

Unlike child insurance allowances which are uniform for all the children in the family, child assistance allowances are graded according to age. The Assistance Board felt that as the cost of the maintenance for a child at subsistence level calculated by Beveridge and others varied according to age, assistance allowances for children should continue to be graded as they were before 1948. For a child under 5, the assistance allowance was fixed at 7s. 6d. a week, for a child aged 5–10 at 9s. 10d. and for a child 11–15 at 10s. 6d. a week. These allowances were higher than the child insurance allowances and the differential between them has been maintained. Both child insurance and assistance allowances have been increased several times since 1948 on the same pattern as the increases for adult benefits discussed in the next chapter.

State cash allowances for children have grown up over the years in an unco-ordinated fashion. There is no uniformity of principle behind them and they are badly in need of a thorough reorganisation. First, all child allowances should be payable for all the children in the family, including the first, up to the same age maxima. Second, all child allowances should increase with the child's age on the lines of the supplementary benefits scales rather than those of the child tax allowances. Third, those child allowances payable only when the father's income ceases or is interrupted should be the same in amount irrespective of whether they are paid to parents or other guardians. Fourth, if family allowances and child tax allowances are not integrated into one of the three schemes discussed earlier, family allowances should be paid selectively to ensure that the income of all families from the father's full-time employment does not fall below the supplementary benefits standard. This should be done through the Inland Revenue Department in the same way as the payment of child tax allowances.

[1] See Appendix IV for the amounts of insurance and assistance benefits.
* Family allowances have been increased by 3s, while the total income tax allowances of people receiving family allowances have been reduced by £36 p.a. for each child for whom family allowance is paid.

199

Chapter Eleven

NATIONAL ASSISTANCE

THE National Assistance Act, 1948 (hereafter referred to as the 1948 Act) made it the duty of the National Assistance Board 'to assist persons in Great Britain who are without resources to meet their requirements, or whose resources (including benefits receivable under the National Insurance Acts) must be supplemented in order to meet their requirements'. This general duty of the Board was qualified in three respects. Applications for assistance from persons below the age of sixteen must not be accepted because, as minors, their requirements should be examined as part of the circumstances of the older persons on whom they are dependent or if they have no parent or guardian they should be referred to the Children's Department of the local authority. Second, in ordinary circumstances, assistance cannot be granted to people who are in full-time work or to their dependents. Third, assistance cannot be given to people on strike though it can be given towards the needs of their dependents. To counteract these three restrictions, the Act contains an escape section which gives power to the Board's officers to grant assistance in urgent cases in spite of all other considerations. The Ministry of Social Security Act, 1966, made no changes to these basic principles of national assistance.

This chapter examines first the question of 'resources' of people applying for assistance, second their 'requirements', and third the extent to which national assistance has been used since 1948 and by whom.[1]

Disregard of Resources

The traditional method of determining the amount of assistance to be granted to an applicant has been to set his resources against

[1] This chapter does not examine the responsibilities of the National Assistance Board for the Legal Aid Scheme, Polish Hostels and Reception Centres.

his requirements and, if they are lower, to provide him with an assistance allowance equivalent to the difference between the two. What constitutes a person's resources and requirements is a matter of opinion and the various Acts which have attempted to define them reflect the prevalent public opinion on the nature of poverty. Before the 1930's very few of the applicants' resources were disregarded by the poor law authorities. In addition, the resources of close relatives, whether dependent or not on the applicant, were taken into account in deciding his application. The mass unemployment of the thirties which led to the establishment of the Unemployment Assistance Board in 1934 provided a great impetus to the slow liberalising process that was evident for some time regarding the assessment of the resources of applicants for assistance. Between 1934 and 1948 a number of Acts were passed which changed the method of assessing the resources of an applicant for assistance substantially. The Determination of Needs Act, 1941, modified substantially the household means test. It laid down the important principle that when a person applied for assistance, the only resources apart from his own, which should be taken into account were those of his wife and other persons dependent on him. The resources of persons who were not dependent on him, however closely related to him, were not to be taken into account. There was only one exception to this which was abolished by the 1948 Act: The Board had the power to withhold assistance from a single applicant without dependents if he or she was not a householder but was living in the household of a parent, or a child who had an income above a certain amount. In this way the 1948 Act completed the process of confining the resources to be taken into account to those of the applicant and his dependents.

Side by side with this gradual change from a household means test to a personal means test went another related process, that which led to the abandonment of the destitution test and the adoption of the present system of disregard of resources. In the early days of the Poor Law system, assistance was granted to those who had no resources at all. This was a logical argument if not a humane one. To give assistance to those with resources would mean that public money would be spent where it was not absolutely necessary. It would also mean that people on assistance would have different levels of income depending on whether they lived on assistance only or on assistance and disregarded resources as well. If people's requirements for subsistence were the same, then their resources should be the same. The opposing argument to the destitution test was that a public system which required people to be completely destitute before they could qualify for assistance created more problems than it solved: It discouraged saving, it provided no inducement to people to make private insurance arrangements, charitable societies would see no point in aiding the needy, people on assistance would have no encouragement to do any part-time work, etc. In other words, there would be no point for people to save or to make any attempt to help themselves as this would penalise them when in need and would benefit the Exchequer only. Naturally no public system of assistance could disregard all the resources of an applicant as this would mean giving assistance to those not in need. Some compromise was necessary between the destitution test and the granting of assistance on application without a means test. This compromise solution was the system of 'disregards' whereby certain types of capital and income are wholly or partially disregarded when considering an application for assistance. The first move away from the destitution test towards the system of disregards of resources was introduced by the Outdoor Relief Act, 1894 which authorised Boards of Guardians to disregard sick pay from friendly societies when considering applications for assistance. Once the principle was accepted that resources could be disregarded for assistance purposes, it became a matter of chance and of pressure from interested pressure groups as to which resources were to qualify for official recognition as disregarded resources. It was for this reason that the system of disregarded resources grew in a completely unplanned fashion. The 1948 Act made no attempt to streamline the system; it simply added more resources to the existing list of 'disregards' and liberalised some of the existing disregarded resources. The government took account of the obvious pressure during the debates on the National Assistance Bill that the National Assistance Board should be generous in its determination of need. The dilemma facing the government on disregards was understandable but some thought that its policy was too generous. 'No doubt from the standpoint of encouraging savings it is right that the thrifty should have some advantage over the spendthrift in the determination of need. But the essence of national assistance, as of the poor law which it is superseding is that it is available for the completely destitute. What, after all, are savings for if not to prevent a person from seeking financial help from the state ?"[1]

The disregarded resources can be divided into two groups – Capital Assets and Income. The first capital disregard permitted by the 1948 Act was the full value of a house owned by a person applying for assistance. This was not a new disregarded resource. It was first introduced in the 1930's for certain types of assistance, which were extended later, and it was made general to all types of assistance by the 1948 Act. No change has been made to this by either the National Assistance Act, 1959 or the Ministry of Social Security Act, 1966, the two Acts which have modified the system of disregards introduced in 1948. The preferential treatment given to house capital is partly due to the emphasis which society places on house ownership and partly to practical considerations. If persons applying for assistance were expected to sell their houses and live on the money they received from it not only would they resent it but the problem of homelessness would be aggravated. Present day opinion accepts the impracticability and inhumanity of forcing assistance applicants to sell their houses. Suggestions have been made, however, that in certain circumstances when a house owner dies, the state should be able to retrieve part of or the whole amount of assistance granted to him from the sale of his house. Such a scheme would have to be limited to owner occupiers with no dependents, it would involve the Ministry of Social Security in a great deal of administrative expense, it might discourage people from applying for assistance, it might lead to neglect of houses and it would not at the end yield any considerable revenue. With the present emphasis on giving supplementary benefits a new image, it would be a retrograde step and politically unfeasible.

The second capital disregard under the 1948 Act was war savings up to £375 for each person. They were given preferential treatment over other forms of savings because they were useful to the government in financing the war effort. After the end of the war, any savings in Government securities were considered as war savings and qualified as a disregarded resource. It became

---

[1] *The Economist*, 15 May, 1948.

obvious in the 1950's that the disregard of 'war savings' had outlived its original justification and it was only government fear that public opinion would resent their abolition that kept them in existence until 1966. The Ministry of Social Security Act of that year abolished them as a disregarded resource because they had declined in importance and because it became generally acceptable that government policies should aim at encouraging both private and government savings. There was no good financial or social reason why money invested in government securities should be considered more highly than savings with Building Societies, for example.

Other capital assets owned by a person applying for assistance or by his wife or any other dependents are added together and treated as one sum. Under the 1948 Act, which accepted existing practice, the possession of capital above £400 disqualified a person from receiving assistance. If the amount of disregarded war savings were added to this, it meant that a total capital of £775 for a single person or £1,150 for a married couple disqualified applicants from national assistance. The National Assistance Act, 1959, did not make any changes to the war savings but it increased the maximum amount of other capital to £600. Capital below £50 under the 1948 Act and £100 under the 1959 Act was disregarded while capital between £50–£350 under the 1948 Act or £100–£500 under the 1959 Act was assumed to yield an income of 6d. for every £25. This assumed income was taken into account when a person's application for assistance was considered. It was never enough to disqualify a person from assistance but it meant that the assistance allowance was reduced by an equivalent amount. The assumption that all capital yields income is, of course, erroneous. The alternative, to take into account actual income derived from capital was a fairer method but administratively prohibitive because of the amount of work and cost it would involve.

The Ministry of Social Security Act, 1966, made one important change: It abolished the fixed upper limit of capital which disqualified a person from assistance. The present arrangements are that the first £300 of capital is disregarded, the next £500 are assumed to yield an income of one shilling for each complete £25 and any capital after that is assumed to yield 2s. 6d. for each £25. Assumed income of 20 shillings a week is disregarded if the applicant has no 'other income'. The effect of this is that an applicant with no other income to be disregarded can have a total capital of £800 and still receive the full supplementary benefit allowance.

The proportion of assistance recipients with capital assets rose from 18·7% in 1950 to 40% in 1965 mainly as a result of the general improvement in the financial conditions of the country and to a much lesser extent because of the changes introduced in 1959. The average amount of capital owned by each of the recipients with capital has shown a much smaller rise, from £121 in 1950 to £171 in 1965. It is difficult to draw any conclusions from this as to whether the resources of assistance recipients improved or not bearing in mind the rise in prices and wages, because of many other factors involved. In both years, however, 80% of all capital assets were disregarded. The capital assets of assistance recipients are mostly small amounts as Table 54 shows.

TABLE 54

CAPITAL (INCLUDING WAR SAVINGS) OF ASSISTANCE RECIPIENTS
GREAT BRITAIN

End of year	Less than £100 %	£100– £199 %	£200– £399 %	£400– £599 %	£600– £799 %	£800 and over %
1961	52·9	18·5	18·8	7·4	1·8	0·6
1965	48·9	17·8	20·1	9:6	2·4	1·1

Source: Annual Reports of N.A.B.

Apart from capital disregards, there are income disregards of two kinds: income arising out of earnings from part-time work and income derived from various other sources – private insurance benefits, friendly society benefits, voluntary payments, etc. People on assistance who take up part-time work belong to one of two groups: Those who are required to register for employment as a condition to their receiving assistance, e.g., the unemployed, and those who are under no such requirement, e.g., the retirement pensioner, the wife of a claimant, etc. The 1948 Act provided that the second group should benefit more from their part-time earnings than the first group in order to be induced to take up work where possible. For this reason while part-time earnings of up to ten shillings a week were to be disregarded for assistance purposes for the first group, the corresponding amount for the second group was fixed to 20 shillings. The 1959 and 1966 Acts made further improvements and today the earnings disregards are 20s. for those required to register for work and 40s. for those not so required. The rationale for disregarded earnings from part-time work for those required to register for employ--ment is not very clear. If a person is unemployed, he should be found full-time employment as soon as possible. There is no point in offering him an incentive to get part-time work. On the other hand, there is the small group of unemployed who for social or psychological reasons do not settle in any job long with the result that they are on long-term assistance. To deprive them completely of their part-time earnings will be too harsh, even if it can be argued that it is a logical step.

Other income consists of a multitude of resources which can be grouped under either Income derived from state insurance benefits, or income drived from occupational, charitable, friendly or voluntary sources. The total amount of disregarded income from both groups was fixed to 20s., 30s. and 40s. in 1948, 1959 and 1966 respectively. The main national insurance benefits, i.e., sickness and unemployed benefits, retirement pensions and family allowances are taken fully into account in determining a person's entitlement to assistance. Certain other national insurance benefits e.g., death and maternity grant are completely disregarded. Yet other national insurance benefits, e.g. disablement pensions, the additional amounts payable to war widows and industrial widows over and above the civilian widows' pensions and part of the children's allowances included in national insurance widows' benefits, are disregarded today up to a maximum of 40s. a week. The corresponding amount was 30s. a week under the 1959 Act and 20s. under the 1948 Act. The justification for the complete disregard of income from maternity and death grants is that they are lump sums designed to meet a specific need over and above the daily income needed for subsistence. There has also been general agreement on the desirability of taking fully into account income derived from the four insurance benefits mentioned. It would have been illogical for the state to grant persons insurance benefits and then to disregard them in whole or in part when it comes to supplement these benefits with assistance. Yet, this is precisely what the state does with regard to those national insurance benefits which are partly disregarded. The reason for this illogical policy stems from the fact that insurance benefits for war and industrial disability are higher than civilian disability. It is, however, totally unfair that two persons on assistance with the same circumstances should be provided with different social security incomes simply because they ended up in their present position via different routes.

Other income derived from private sources includes superannuation, occupational sick pay, annuities, payments from charitable societies or individuals, etc. The incomes from these sources that are disregarded under the Acts of 1948, 1959 and 1966 are 20s., 30s. and 20s. respectively. The reasons for these disregards vary. In the case of superannuation, for example, the original justification was that if it were taken completely into account it might discourage occupational and private pension schemes. It is very doubtful, however, whether this will happen today when occupational schemes are so widely used. In the case of voluntary payments from individuals, a ban on disregards could be ineffective as it would be difficult to establish whether a payment was made or not unless it was declared. In the case of income from having boarders, or from sub-letting, it is desirable to encourage it partly to help with the housing problem.

TABLE 55

'UNPROTECTED' INCOME OF NATIONAL ASSISTANCE RECIPIENTS 1965

GREAT BRITAIN

	Super-annuation	Friendly Societies, Industrial Charities, & voluntary	war pensions	Earnings	Others	Total
Number of cases with income	102,200	81,900	31,200	105,900	127,200	484,400
% of cases with income which was taken into account	60·8%	19·9%	59%	48·2%	70·9%	49·1%
Amount of income per week	£107,400	£52,000	£45,600	£211,200	£191,500	£607,700
% of income per week taken into account	39·3%	26·1%	31·6%	63·5%	78·1%	47·2%

Source: *Annual Report* of N.A.B.

Table 55 refers to unprotected income of assistance recipients, i.e., it does not cover income from such sources as retirement pensions, unemployment benefit, etc. which is taken completely into account in determining entitlement to assistance. The various sources of income are not exclusive of each other and therefore the total number of persons with unprotected income is smaller than the total number of cases indicated in the table. The two main sources both in numbers and in amount of income per week are earnings and superannuation, though a far smaller proportion of earnings is disregarded for assistance purposes. On the whole, about half of the total number of cases with income and rather less than half of the weekly income are taken into account for deciding the amount of assistance to be granted. This represents a good saving for the Exchequer and a welcome extra income for the people on assistance.

Determination of Requirements

The national assistance scales provided by the 1948 Act were inadequate in two ways. First, they were deficient in that they provided income designed to meet a minimum number of the recipients' requirements and not the generally accepted requirements for a decent standard of living. Second, they were austere in that they provided income which was not adequate to meet even the minimum requirements they had been designed for. The explanation for these inadequacies was that the allowances were based on Rowntree's physiological concept of poverty and on Beveridge's view that the role of the state was to provide benefits at subsistence level. In turn, these viewpoints on poverty and on the role of the state were the product of the extensive poverty and mass unemployment before the last war and of the hardships and austerity of the war period.

On the other hand, the 1948 assistance scales were an improvement over the existing scales in two ways. First, they were at a slightly higher level than the assistance scales used by local authorities and the two scales administered by the Assistance Board as Table 56 shows. Taking into account the rise in prices, the two administered by the assistance Board were equivalent to the scales introduced in 1936 for the unemployed and in 1940 for the old age pensioners. It is clear from this that scales introduced

TABLE 56

SCALES OF ASSISTANCE ALLOWANCES, 1948

	Before 5th July, 1948				After 5th July, 1948 Ordinary	
	Unemployment Allowances		Supplementary Pensions			
	s.	*d.*	*s.*	*d.*	*s.*	*d.*
Married couple	31	0	35	0	40	0
Single householder	18	0	20	0	24	0
Other persons:						
Ages 21 or over	15	6	17	6	20	0
Ages 18–21	12	6	12	6	17	6
Aged 16–18					15	0
Aged 11–16	10	6	10	6	10	6
Aged 5–11	9	0	9	0	9	0
Aged under 5	7	6	7	6	7	6

Source: *Annual Report*, N.A.B.

by the 1948 Act were only marginally higher than the pre-war scales. Second, the 1948 Act provided only two types of scales – one for the vast majority of the population and a special scale for the blind and the tuberculous – in contrast to the existing two scales administered by the Board and those administered by county and county councils. The idea of nationally enforced uniform scales of assistance allowances was first put into effect by the Unemployment Assistance (Determination of Need and Assessment of Need) Regulations, 1934, for the temporary unemployed who became the responsibility of the newly created Unemployment Assistance Board. Local authorities continued to use their own allowances up to 1948 which varied a great deal on the argument that conditions were different from one authority to another. The cost of living, however, was not very different from one place to another with the exception of rent. For this reason the uniform scales of the 1948 Act did not include an allowance for rent. This was to be met separately to take account of individual variations.

The special scale of allowances provided by the 1948 Act for the blind and for those who suffered a loss of income in order to undergo treatment for tuberculosis of the respiratory system were higher than the ordinary scale of allowances. There was no good reason for the preferential treatment of the blind and the tuberculous apart from historical reasons. They had enjoyed the same treatment before 1948 because of the public sympathy which blindness invoked and because of the fear of the consequences which might result from a spread of tuberculosis. With a free National Health Service, however, and the use of discretionary assistance allowances for special needs provided by the 1948 Act, there was no good economic reason then or today for the existence of special allowances for these two groups. The value of special allowances in relation to the ordinary allowances has declined. In 1948, the special allowance for a single person or for a married couple with both members so disabled was 63% higher than the corresponding ordinary allowance; in 1966 it was only 30% higher.

The comparisons made in Table 57 must be seen in their right perspective. Comparisons between the rise in national insurance and assistance allowances on one hand and the rise in the retail prices index on the other since 1948 will show whether these allowances have kept their value only. Similarly, comparisons between the allowances and the wages index will only show whether the differential between allowances and wages has narrowed or widened over the years. Neither of these comparisons will show whether the existing allowances are adequate for a decent standard of life because they were not designed to provide this in 1948. This point is often missed when comparisons are made among the various indices. To provide allowances adequate for a decent standard of living today will involve new political decisions because what is considered 'adequate' and a 'decent standard of living' is a matter of judgement which changes not only from time to time but varies also at any one period according to the individual's political philosophy. No attempt has been made to re-assess the allowances since 1948. The White Paper in 1959 indicated that national assistance should assume a new role. It should not aim at providing people with allowances for subsistence but with allowances which should give them 'a share in increasing national prosperity'.[1] This implied that relating assistance scales to the retail prices index was not enough. It should be related to the rise in national prosperity. How this was to be done precisely, what criterion or index of the rise in national prosperity was to be used, the White Paper did not say. The Government may have had some criterion in mind but as Lynes

[1] *Improvements in National Assistance,* Cmd. 782, p. 3, June, 1959.

TABLE 57

INDICES[a] FOR N.I. BENEFITS, N.A. ALLOWANCES, PRICES & WAGES,
1948–1967 – GREAT BRITAIN

	N.I. Benefits[b]		N.A. Allowances		Retail Prices	Average weekly earnings for men aged over 20
	Single Person	Married Couple	Single Person	Married Couple		
1948	100	100	100	100	100	100
1949	100	100	100	100	103	105
1950	100	100	108	109	106	109
1951	100	100	125	125	117	119
1952	125	129	146	148	128	130
1953	125	129	146	148	131	139
1954	125	129	146	148	134	148
1955	154	155	156	158	139	162
1956	154	155	167	168	146	175
1957	154	155	167	168	151	180
1958	192	191	188	190	154	189
1959	192	191	208	213	155	196
1960	192	191	208	213	158	211
1961	221	220	223	225	161	225
1962	221	220	240	239	169	234
1963	260	260	265	261	174	241
1964	260	260	265	261	178	263
1965	308	310	317	314	184	282
1966	308	310	338	333	188	302
1967	346	348	358	353	192	304(est)

(*a*) Indices refer to July every year for prices and April for wages.

(*b*) These benefits are unemployment and sickness benefit, widowed mother's allowance and retirement pension.

Source: *Annual Report* of M.P.N.I. and N.A.B. Ministry of Labour Gazettes.

has pointed out, it may have equally meant 'no more than a periodic gesture of paternalist philanthropy, nicely timed to suit the convenience of the Government in power'.[1]

Table 57 shows that assistance allowances have been raised fourteen times since 1948 compared with only seven for insurance benefits. The overall increase over the whole 20-year period has been the same for assistance and insurance benefits but in half the years since 1948 assistance allowances were higher than insurance

[1] T. Lynes, 'National Assistance and National Prosperity', p. 48, *Occasional Papers in Social Administration,* The Codicote Press, 1962.

benefits. With the payment of discretionary allowances and rent, assistance allowances have been substantially higher for every single year since 1948. As a result the number of people drawing assistance allowances has been considerable. This was not the relationship which Beveridge had envisaged. He considered that assistance should be for a small minority of the population who either did not satisfy the contribution conditions or who were in exceptional circumstances. Moreover, it 'must be felt to be something less desirable than insurance benefit; otherwise the insured persons get nothing for their contributions'.[1] It was never envisaged that insurance benefits should be lower than assistance allowances so that recipients of insurance benefits would have to supplement their benefits with assistance allowances. This became part of the wider argument of universal benefits versus means-tested benefits. It was partly a political and partly an economic argument. Lord Beveridge felt that the difference between providing adequate insurance benefits for all and inadequate insurance benefits plus supplementation from national assistance was that 'Insurance benefit as of right without enquiry as to other means puts a floor below inequalities. Assistance subject to means test puts a ceiling above which no one may rise'.[2] The opposite view is that it is wasteful to increase insurance benefits which are payable to all. It makes more economic sense to raise assistance benefits which are directed to the needy. Commenting on the proposed rises in insurance benefits in 1955 the Economist declared that 'the extravagance of the Government's present proposals does not lie in the rates of benefit themselves, but in the fact that they are to be given to so many millions of people who do not need them'.[3] The core of this argument is that there are 'many millions' of pensioners, unemployed, sick and injured who do not need adequate benefits. This has never been established. The existence of a very small minority of people with adequate private incomes when their earnings are interrupted or cease does not justify in principle and in administrative costs holding back rises in insurance benefits and applying assistance allowances on a grand scale.

[1] Beveridge Report, p. 141.
[2] Lord Beveridge, 'Social Security Under Review', *The Times,* 9 November, 1953.
[3] 'Pensions In Perspective', *The Economist,* 11 December, 1954.

The increase in the scales of insurance and assistance allowances between 1948 and 1967 has been real and not due simply to inflation. Both insurance and assistance allowances have risen faster than prices since 1948. While the retail prices index doubled between 1948 and 1967, the indices for insurance and assistance benefits more than trebled. The rise in the assistance allowances index has been consistently higher, year by year, than the rise in retail prices. The position was different, however, for insurance benefits. Between 1949 and 1955, insurance benefits were lagging behind the rise in prices with the exception of 1952 when the rise in benefits brought them temporarily in line with prices. After 1955, however, the insurance benefits index has been consistently higher than the retail prices index. The rises in insurance benefits in 1952 and 1955 were overdue when compared with the retail prices index. The reviews of insurance benefits in 1958 and in subsequent years, however, were not dictated by the rise in the retail prices index. All the five reviews since 1958 were made in spite of the fact that benefits were ahead of the retail prices index. This comparison between the retail prices index may be a good national guide but it is not so good when applied to low income groups which tend to spend a higher proportion of their income on necessities than the general population does. The special low income prices index has risen faster than the retail prices index though not as fast as benefits.[1]

Comparison between insurance and assistance benefits on one hand and the index of average weekly earnings for men reveals a different picture. The overall rise in benefits of both kinds in the period 1948–1967 has been only marginally higher than the overall rise in earnings. Assistance allowances for this period were behind the earnings index for six years and ahead of it for eleven years and about the same in the two other years. They lagged behind the earnings index in the years before 1958 but they have since been ahead of it. If 1959 is the year when assistance allowances outpaced the earnings index once and for all, 1965 is the corresponding year for insurance benefits. Until 1965, insurance benefits trailed behind the earnings index consistently with two temporary exceptions – in 1958 and 1963 when the rise in benefits was slightly

[1] T. Lynes, 'National Assistance and National Prosperity', The Codicote Press, 1962. Prof R. G. D. Allen, 'Movements in Retail Prices since 1953', *Economica,* February, 1958.

ahead of the earnings index. The same picture emerges if one looks at insurance benefits as a proportion of the average weekly earnings for men aged over 20. In July 1948, the insurance benefits (sickness, unemployment, widowed mother's allowances and retirement pension) for a single person and a married couple were 19·4% and 31·3% of the average weekly earnings respectively. With the exception of 1958 and 1963 when these proportions were marginally higher than 1948, benefits formed a smaller proportion of earnings consistently up to 1965 reaching their lowest point in 1951 when they were 16·1% for a single person and 26·1% for a married couple. Even the 1965 review did not alter substantially this relationship between benefits and earnings – the respective proportions were 21·2% and 34·4%. On the whole it can be said that the standard of living of social security beneficiaries today bears the same relationship to the standard of living of the working population as it did in 1948. It may be argued that social security beneficiaries today also enjoy substantial short-term earnings-related sickness and unemployment benefits as well as small earnings-related retirement pensions. On the other hand, the proportion of married women at work has increased since 1948 which has improved the standard of living of many families. The abolition of food subsidies, too, must have been felt more by the low income groups than the population at large.

Payment of Rent

Unlike national insurance benefits which include an amount for rent, national assistance allowances do not cover rent: The Beveridge Report acknowledged that the amount of rent paid varied from region to region and within the same region to such an extent that to provide a uniform rate of benefit covering rent 'must be many shillings a week too high for many cases and many shillings too low for many other cases'.[1] This applied to other necessities such as food, fuel, etc., but to a much lesser extent. Moreover, unlike other necessities, the choice available to individuals is very limited in housing. The amount of rent paid, said the Report, was 'largely a matter of necessity, not of choice'.[2] Finally, when a man is unemployed, sick or injured for brief

[1] Beveridge Report, p. 79.
[2] Beveridge Report, p. 81.

periods, some adjustment or postponement of expenditure on clothing, light or fuel can be made. This is not always possible or so easy to make in the case of rent. In spite of the force of these arguments for a separate allowance for rent to insurance bene-beneficiaries, the Report felt that for administrative convenience and for matters of principle – 'a flat rate of insurance contribution should lead to a flat rate of benefit'[1] – a uniform allowance for rent should be included in the uniform rates of insurance benefits. Beveridge, moreover, looked to the future and hoped that 'the launching of the Plan for Social Security will coincide with a determined and successful effort to deal with urban congestion and shortage of housing. If and so far as this hope is realised, inequalities of rent bearing no relation to the accommodation obtained will disappear; a high rent will then represent a free choice by the householder and it will become indefensible to favour that form of expenditure over other forms of expenditure in fixing scales of benefit'.[1] This sentiment is another reminder of the interrelationship between social security and other social services.

The Assistance Board took a more realistic line than the Beveridge Report. It acknowledged the wide variations in rent and the inability of people with low incomes to make any free choice in the amount of rent they paid. The Determination of Need and Assessment of Needs Regulations in 1943 provided a new assistance scale of allowances which did not include a proportion for rent as it was the previous practice. The scale of assistance allowances provided for all other needs and rent was to be considered and paid for separately. For people on assistance who were not householders, i.e. they lived as members of the household of another person, the Regulations provided that they should be given a rent allowance of not less than 2s. 6d. a week and not more than 7s. depending on the contribution they made to the householder who was responsible for the rent. For the great majority of persons on assistance who were householders the amount to be paid to them for rent by the Board was 'the net rent payable so far as is reasonable in view of the general level of rents in the locality'. In effect, this meant that rent included rates, and in the case of owner-occupied houses an allowance for repairs and insurance and the amount of interest, if any, on mortgages or loans but not capital repayments of the mortgage or loan itself.

[1] Beveridge Report, p. 83.

Any income which the householder derived from sub-letting, less expenses, would be subtracted from the rent allowance he received from the Board. To assist the officers of the Board to decide on what constituted reasonable rents in the locality, the local advisory committees were asked, in accordance with previous practice, to draw up 'local rent rules'. The Board's officers, however, had the power to pay more or less than the amount laid down in the 'local rent rules' where they considered it necessary.

The 1948 Act accepted completely the existing policy for the determination and payment of rent with the slight modification that the maximum allowance for non-householders was raised to 10s. a week. The system of 'local rent rules' suffered from two drawbacks: First, the concept of an average rent in each locality was not very meaningful because of the wide variation of rents paid in any one locality, and the limited choice which people had in finding accommodation. The Board's officers had no alternative but to use their powers and pay rents which were above the average. Second, 'local rent rules' needed constant revision if they were to keep up with the continuing rise of rents since the end of the last war. Local advisory committees, being voluntary and unpaid, could not be expected to do this. Thus, when the 1948 Act came into force, the N.A.B. had to use rent rules drawn up in 1944 and it was not until 1950 that new local advisory committees were reconstituted which were able to draw up new 'local rent rules' by the middle of the same year. These new rules continued in force until the whole idea of local rent rules was abandoned by the National Assistance (Determination of Need) Amending Regulations in 1959. Instead, the amount of rent which may be paid is the net rent payable or such part of it 'as is reasonable in the circumstances' according to the discretion of the Board's officers. This change was bound up with another change which concerned the contribution towards the rent which non-dependent members of a household, mostly earning sons and daughters of people on assistance, should make. Under the 1948 regulations, a single son in full-time employment, for example, living with his parents on assistance was expected to pay only up to 7s. as his share towards the rent of the family. Under the new rules, with certain provisos, the same son would be expected to pay his full share of the rent depending on his wages.

The changes introduced in 1959 brought about a significant reduction in the proportion of rents which were not met fully by the Board. When the new 'local rent rules' were introduced in 1950, the proportion of rents not met fully by the Board dropped to about 7% of the total number of rents paid by householders on assistance. As rents rose and the 'local rent rules' remained unrevised, the proportions rose to 15% in 1954, then dropped slightly and rose after the Rent Act, 1957 to 15% in 1958. Since the introduction of the new rules in 1959 the proportion has varied between 1% and 2% a year. This improvement, however, should be interpreted with caution because of the accompanying changes in 1959 concerning the greater contribution which non-dependent members of households on assistance are expected to make towards the rent as compared with the years before 1959. This has enabled the Board to classify many cases under the heading 'rent paid in full' in spite of the fact that the amount paid by the Board for rent is not different from what it was before 1959. Though the proportion of rents not paid in full is very small, the numbers involved are not insignificant. They have varied since 1959 between 31,000 in 1962 and 18,000 in 1965. A small sample national study conducted by the N.A.B. and reported in its Report for the year 1962 showed that almost all cases where the rent was not paid in full concerned privately rented accommodation particularly furnished accommodation.[1] Nine out of ten of all the cases were in the conurbations of London, Birmingham, Liverpool and Manchester. Less than one-third concerned people above pensionable age; more than half of the recipients were single persons, 10% were married couples without children and the remaining were married couples with children. The amount of rent not paid varied from a few shillings to 40s. or more in some cases. The report is not explicit on the reasons why the Board did not pay the rent in full. It hints, however, at two reasons, the first justified and the second unjustified. Cases where 'satisfactory evidence of the true amount is not forthcoming'; Cases where 'a rent which is not excessive in an absolute sense may nevertheless be considered to be unreasonable in relation to the kind of accommodation provided'. This, however, is inevitable in the large cities where the scarcity of accommodation to let is so acute. What the Board's officers should instead consider is

[1] Report of N.A.B., Cmd. 2078, p. 22–23, Year 1962.

whether there is alternative accommodation available at a lower rent in the locality. People paying exorbitant rents in sub-standard accommodation should not be penalised for being the victims of the policy of a free market in housing. It is equally doubtful, too, whether the new administrative machinery for determining fair rents introduced by the Rent Act, 1965, can be effective so long as the present demand for housing exceeds the supply particularly among certain sections of the urban popula-tion – immigrants, low income groups and large families. Not unnaturally, the proportion of persons in local authority accom-modation whose rent was not paid in full was insignificant. The report does not specify how small the proportion was and why it was necessary for assistance recipients to have to meet part of their rent out of their ordinary assistance allowance simply because two public bodies could not come to an agreement as to what is fair rent. One bone of contention between the Board and Local Authorities has been the treatment of people on assistance under the rent rebate schemes. Local Authorities have maintained that it is the Board's responsibility to meet in full reasonable rents and that it is not fair to expect ratepayers to subsidise the rents of people on assistance whose financial problems are a national and not a local responsibility. The Board, on the other hand, has insisted that all local authority tenants, whose financial circumstances qualify them, should be able to benefit from rent rebate schemes. Having made a plea for an equal treatment of assistance recipients, the Board warned local authorities with rent rebate schemes that if they charged people on assistance the full unabated rent, 'the Board will not be prepared to find the money for the increase and that adherence to the proposal could therefore only cause hardship to the tenants affected'.[1] It is easy to make a good case for both the local authority and the Board. This is a matter of national policy which should be decided at a national level, by the government if necessary, to avoid hardship to local authority tenants on assistance.

The proportion of local authority tenants increased consistently from 21·1% in 1954, when the Board's annual reports first classified people on assistance according to the tenure of their accommodation, to 43·1% in 1965. It is now the largest group and it is bound to increase in the future as more people are re-

[1] Report of the N.A.B. p. 10, Cmd. 8900, Year 1952.

National Assistance

TABLE 58

TENURE OF ACCOMMODATION OF PERSONS RECEIVING NATIONAL ASSISTANCE

GREAT BRITAIN

	Owner-occupiers %	Local authority tenants %	Other rent-paying tenants %	Rent-free and Rates free or paid %
1954	10·5	21·1	66·6	1·8
1960	12·4	33·7	52·2	1·7
1965	13·8	43·1	41·7	1·4

Source: Annual Reports of National Assistance Board.

housed from slum clearance areas to council houses and as more people in council accommodation reach retiring age when the likelihood of applying for assistance rises considerably. On the other hand, the proportion of private tenants has declined from 66·6% in 1954 to 41·7% in 1965. The proportion of owner-occupiers has increased slightly, but at a much slower speed than the increase of the proportion of owner-occupiers in the general population. The Board's policy towards owner-occupiers causes no hardship to those who have paid off their mortgages and no undue hardship to those who have not paid off their mortgage but are on assistance for a brief period since Building Societies will usually make allowances for such cases. The section of owner-occupiers who suffer are those on long-term assistance who have not paid off their mortgages. We know very little about them or how they manage apart from the fact that the Board's report in 1960 stated that about 52,000 (29%) out of the 180,000 owner-occupiers were buying their houses on mortgage or loan. Some may be able to find the amount necessary for capital repayments (for which the Board is not empowered to make any contribution) through sub-letting or through the help of relatives but there must be those who have to find it out of their ordinary assistance allowance. There is a need for new thinking on this point to see whether it will be possible for the new Supplementary Benefits Commission to assist this group of owner-occupiers and, if necessary, retrieve the money in some way.

Discretionary Allowances

Like many other devices of the present supplementary benefits scheme, discretionary allowances have their origin in the creation of the Unemployment Assistance Board in 1935. The aim of discretionary allowances was to enable the Board's officers to grant extra allowances to meet special long-term needs which were not universal to all national assistance recipients and could not therefore justifiably be met by a general increase of the basic assistance allowance. The number of special long-term needs that can be covered by discretionary allowances varies depending on the austerity of the basic assistance allowance and on the generosity of the community towards its necessitous members. The 1948 Act accepted previous practice and created two types of discretionary payments: The discretionary allowance to be paid weekly in addition to the basic assistance allowance for special long-term needs; and the exceptional needs grant which is a single lump sum paid to meet an exceptional need of an applicant.

Table 59 indicates clearly the increasing use made of discretionary allowances since 1948. It refers to discretionary additions because each discretionary allowance made to a person may include payments for more than one special long-term need. The number of persons receiving discretionary allowances is therefore smaller than the number of discretionary additions. The proportion of national assistance recipients at the end of each year since 1948 who were also in receipt of a discretionary allowance has increased from 26% in 1948 to 45% in 1956, and 58% in 1965. Moreover, each discretionary allowance in 1965 included more discretionary additions than in 1948. Thus the ratio between the number of persons in receipt of national assistance and the number of discretionary additions at the end of 1948 and 1965 was about 3:1 and 1:1 respectively. The value of each addition has also

TABLE 59

NUMBER AND TYPE OF DIRECTIONARY ADDITIONS IN PAYMENT AT THE END

OF EACH YEAR – GREAT BRITAIN

Year	Number Total	Type of addition as a percentage of total number				
		Laundry	Domestic Help	Special Diet	Additional Fuel	Other
	000					
1948	341	37·2%	21·4%	32·3%	2·6%	6·5%
1956	1117	31·3%	10·5%	35·5%	13·6%	9·1%
1965	2210	23·5%	12·1%	29·0%	30·3%	5·1%

Source: Annual Reports, N.A.B.

increased. The average amount of the additions was 3s. 3d. in 1948 and 10s. in 1965 at current prices or 5s. at 1948 prices. This rise in the value of discretionary additions has been gradual and consistent over the whole period. On the other hand the relationship between the amount of discretionary addition and the basic assistance allowance has not changed. In 1948 the average amount of discretionary addition was 8·1% of the assistance allowance for a married couple and 13·5% for a single householder. In 1965, it was 8·0% and 13·2% respectively.

Table 59 also shows that though discretionary additions have increased for all four main needs, the increase has been far greater for extra fuel than any other need possibly due to present medical evidence on the ill-effects of colds on the health of the elderly. The rise in the discretionary additions for domestic help would have been higher had it not been for the fact that some local authorities provide this service free to those in financial need. Similarly the number of discretionary additions of all kinds would have been higher had it not been for the fact that persons with disregarded resources are less likely to be granted a discretionary allowance since they have extra means to meet their extra needs.

Table 60 shows that the proportion of the elderly receiving a

TABLE 60

DISCRETIONARY ADDITIONS AND CATEGORIES OF ASSISTANCE RECIPIENTS,
1965 – GREAT BRITAIN

Category of Assistance Recipients	% who received discretionary additions
Assistance paid in supplementation of insurance benefits:	
Retirement Pensions	73·0
Sickness and Industrial Injury Benefits	57·2
Widows' Benefits	49·2
Unemployment Benefit	16·4
Assistance paid in supplementation of non-contributory old age pension	44·4
Assistance to persons not receiving such pensions or benefits:	
Persons registered for employment	13·1
Persons not registered for employment:	
Persons over pension age	45·4
Persons under pension age	20·4
All Categories	57·9

Source: Annual Report N.A.B.

discretionary allowance is higher than that of the other groups presumably because their special needs are greater. The fact that the proportion of the elderly on on-contributory old age pensions who receive a discretionary addition is low is explained by the fact that a great proportion of them are in Homes or hospitals or living as members of someone else's household because of their very advanced ages.

In view of the increased use of discretionary additions, particularly for the elderly, the government felt that a great deal of time and expense was being wasted on detailed investigations for needs which were no longer special. What were considered special needs in the austere times of 1948 came to be viewed as common needs in the more affluent times of the sixties. The Ministry of Social Security Act, 1966, made substantial changes to the scheme of discretionary allowances. A special addition of 9s. a week was authorised for all persons entitled to supplementary pensions, i.e., those over pensionable age and to those persons who have received supplementary allowance for a continuous period of two years excluding those who are required to register at the Employment Exchange. At the end of 1966, 81% of all persons receiving supplementary benefits qualified for the 9s. long-term additional allowance. Officers of the Supplementary Benefits Commission still have the power to grant discretionary allowances but obviously only when special needs exceed the 9s. special addition.

Exceptional needs grants have not been used so much as discretionary allowances. Grants for exceptional needs are usually made to assistance recipients for major replacements of clothing, footwear and bedding articles. The ordinary assistance allowance is supposed, in theory, to cover all these items in ordinary circumstances but in practice people on assistance for long periods find it difficult to budget their allowance in such a way as to save enough to buy, for example, a new overcoat when their old one wears out. Families with growing children are also obliged to buy new clothes or shoes for them before their old ones wear out. The number of these exceptional grants would have been higher had it not been for the fact that applicants for such grants are often referred to the W.V.S. for second-hand articles. The number of grants made in 1949 was 101,500, it increased with ups and downs to 178,000 in 1959 and it has since grown consistently every year to 345,000 in 1965. This is a modest increase compared with the growth of discretionary additions. Moreover, while the value of discretionary additions increased over the years, the value of the exceptional needs grant has declined from an average of £3 10s. od. in 1949 to £4 5s. od. in 1965 at current prices or about half that amount at 1949 prices.

Assistance Allowances

Beveridge's expectation that assistance would be limited in scope and would be temporary in duration has been proved false for two main reasons: First, the superiority of assistance allowances over insurance benefits and second the reduction in the stigma attached to the receipt of assistance that has resulted from general social factors, the publicity given to the right of everyone for assistance and the more enlightened methods used by the National Assistance Board in establishing need.

Applications for national assistance have been dealt with in two ways: Single payments and weekly allowances. Where there has been temporary need only or where there has been sufficient uncertainty about the applicant's immediate financial prospects, single payments have been made. These account for the majority of single payments made every year but a small number has also been made for exceptional needs grants and for National Health Service charges. Single payments are sometimes repeated week after week and some eventually become weekly allowances. The majority of applications during the first six years of the national assistance scheme were dealt with in single payments. Gradually their proportion dropped partly because the Board had gained enough experience to enable it to take definite decisions on new applications without the use of a trial period.

Analyses of single payments for temporary need have shown that slightly less than half were made to unemployed persons either because they were not entitled to unemployment benefit, or because their benefit was inadequate or because they were waiting to receive their unemployment benefit. One-fifth were made to sick persons for very similar reasons. One-sixth were made to employed persons who had just started work but could not manage financially because of the practice among employers not to pay wages during the first week until the new employee had been at work for a fortnight. The remaining payments were made to deserted wives and to other miscellaneous groups. One of these small miscellaneous groups consists of persons without a fixed address for whom the Board cannot obviously make a permanent allowance. Allegations made from time to time that the Board would not grant any assistance to persons without a fixed address have been strongly denied by the Board. After referring to the misunderstandings that have arisen over this issue, the Board declared that it 'would like to make it clear once again that the so-called rule "no address – no assistance" does not exist'.[1]

TABLE 61

APPLICATIONS FOR NATIONAL ASSISTANCE

GREAT BRITAIN

Year	Number of applications during the year	Rejected	Outcome of Applications		Weekly allowances in Payement at the end of the year	
			Single Payment Granted	Weekly Allowance Granted	Number	Per cent over previous year
	Thousands	%	%	%	*Thousands*	%
1949	2750	12·0	60·4	27·6	1157	14·4
1950	2770	12·6	56·0	31·4	1349	16·6
1951	2690	11·9	56·9	31·2	1462	8·4
1952	2890	11·8	54·7	33·5	1667	14·0
1953	2500	14·4	47·2	38·4	1761	5·6
1954	2100	14·3	42·4	43·3	1796	2·0
1955	1830	14·7	45·3	40·0	1612	−10·3
1956	1827	14·8	42·4	42·8	1656	2·3
1957	2079	15·1	42·9	42·0	1712	3·4
1958	2161	15·8	41·5	42·7	1649	−3·7
1959	2346	14·9	39·1	46·0	1766	7·1
1960	2247	13·2	40·6	46·2	1857	5·1
1961	2430	14·3	44·2	41·5	1884	−0·7
1962	2801	14·9	41·0	44·1	2007	8·8
1963	2990	14·5	40·8	44·7	1971	−1·8
1964	2706	14·4	44·2	41·4	1961	−0·5
1965	2847	13·9	49·3	36·8	1997	1·8
1966	3491	14·1	51·6	34·3	2396	20·0

Source: Annual Reports of N.A.B.

A national assistance book entitling a person to draw weekly allowances has been granted where it has been considered that the need is of long-term duration. The number of weekly allowances

[1] *Annual Report*, 1964, Cmd. 2674, p. 32.

in payment at the end of each year has increased from 760,000 in 1949 to 1,096,000 in 1966. This increase was greater during the first few years after 1948 and generally in years when insurance benefits lagged behind assistance allowances. The sharp rise in 1966 was due to the introduction of the Supplementary Benefits and the government's efforts to reach all those who were entitled to assistance but would not apply for various reasons. The number of people covered by weekly allowances is naturally greater than the number of allowances. In 1965, for example, about one allowance in five provided for the needs of a wife and one in ten for dependent children. The allowances in payment at the end of 1949 provided for the needs, wholly or partly, of 1¾ million persons or about one person in thirty of the total population in the country. This was about half the proportion of persons dependent on outdoor relief in the middle of the nineteenth century but it was more than the proportion at the beginning of

TABLE 62

DURATION OF ALLOWANCES WHICH CEASED DURING THE 12 MONTHS
ENDING IN OCTOBER 1964 – GREAT BRITAIN

	Proportion of allowances which lasted:			
	Three months or less	*Four months to one year*	*One to three years*	*More than three years*
	%	%	%	%
Assistance paid in supplementation of insurance benefits:				
Retirement pensions	11	12	22	55
Sickness or industrial injury benefit	59	23	11	7
Widow's benefit	25	26	28	21
Unemployment benefit	48	35	15	2
Assistance paid in supplementation of non-contributory old age pensions	—	4	—	96
Assistance to persons not receiving such pensions or benefits:				
Persons registered for employment	59	20	17	4
Persons not registered for employment:				
Persons over pension age	7	11	16	66
Persons under pension age	40	30	17	13
Total	40	22	17	21

Source: Table 7, p. 20, N.A.B. Report 1964.

this century. At the end of 1965, current allowances covered just over 2¾ million persons or one in eighteen in the country.

The life expectancy of weekly allowances can be considered in two ways: The duration of allowances which cease during a certain period and the duration of allowances which are in payment at any one date. Table 62 shows that four out of ten of all allowances ending in the year had lasted for three months or less, five out of ten for six months or less, six out of ten for one year or less, eight out of ten for three years or less and only two out of ten for over three years. The proportion of allowances, however, that had lasted for over three years was very high among the elderly – 55% for the retirement pensioners and 96% of the non-contributory old age pensioners. With the meagre amount of the non-contributory old age pensions, it is only to be expected that the vast majority have to be supplemented with assistance. On the other hand the proportion of allowances for the sick and the unemployed that had lasted for over three years was small. The great majority of allowances for these two groups lasted for less than six months. Allowances for widows occupied a middle position between these two extremes since the length for which they are paid is determined by so many factors – age of children, age of widow, remarriage, etc.

Allowances, however, which last for three years or more have a cumulative effect with the result that if one looks at the length of allowances in any one time, the proportion which have been paid for three years or more is far higher. This applies to all groups, as Table 63 shows, though the rise for the elderly is not so great simply because they die.

About two-thirds of the people receiving weekly allowances at any one time have been on assistance for three years or more. This does not, however, take into account the large number of people who receive assistance in single payments. Obviously if the two groups are considered together the picture will be very different – the proportion of people who have been on assistance for short periods will be vastly greater.

Women account for the majority of assistance allowances because there are more of them over the pensionable age when the incidence of assistance rises, particularly for women who are widowed. In 1965 of all women assistance recipients, 69% were widows, of whom 9 out of ten were over the age of 60. Women

National Assistance

TABLE 63

DURATION OF ALLOWANCES CURRENT AT DECEMBER 1964

GREAT BRITAIN

	Proportion of allowances which have been in payment			
	Three months or less	Four months to one year	One to three years	More than three years
	%	%	%	%
Assistance paid in supplementation of insurance benefits:				
Retirement pensions	3	8	20	69
Sickness or industrial injury benefits	16	19	29	36
Widow's benefit	5	13	29	53
Unemployment benefit	39	37	20	4
Assistance paid in supplementation of non-contributory old age pensions	—	2	4	94
Assistance to persons not receiving such pensions or benefits:				
Persons registered for employment	17	15	32	36
Persons not registered for employment:				
Persons over pension age	1	5	11	83
Persons under pension age	6	14	22	58
Total	6	11	20	63

Source: Table 8, p. 22 N.A.B. Report, 1964

also predominate for assistance allowances below retirement age, though not to the same extent, because they attract assistance as widows, deserted wives and unmarried mothers. In 1965, women accounted for 68% of all assistance allowances (excluding those paid to wives as part of their husbands' allowance), for 71·5% of allowances paid to persons over the age of 65 and for 61% of those to persons below the age of 65. It is evident from what has been said so far, that the largest proportion of assistance allowances goes to persons above retirement ages. This is clear from Table 64 which also shows that the incidence of assistance allowances rises with age for both men and women.

The greatest proportion of assistance allowances is granted to those in receipt of insurance benefits. This applied from the very beginning of the scheme in 1948 but the proportion increased consistently particularly after the improvements in assistance

National Assistance

TABLE 64

ALLOWANCES IN PAYMENT IN DECEMBER 1965 ACCORDING TO AGE AND
SEX OF RECIPIENTS – GREAT BRITAIN

Age-Group	Men %	Women %
16–20	2·2	1·8
21–29	4·2	3·7
30–39	5·9	3·8
40–49	7·3	4·8
50–59	12·3	8·0
60–64	10·9	9·7
65–69	16·8	15·1
70–79	27·5	34·8
80 plus	12·9	18·3

Source: Report of N.A.B., 1965.

allowances in 1959. As Table 65 shows, however, this increase is
due almost solely to the rise in the number of retirement pensions
that are supplemented by assistance. In turn, this growth in the
assistance supplemented retirement pensions is absolute and not
relative. The proportion of all retirement pensions that were
supplemented by assistance in 1951 was the same as that in 1965,
i.e., 23%. The proportions of sickness, unemployment and
widows' benefits that were supplemented by assistance declined

TABLE 65

WEEKLY ASSISTANCE ALLOWANCES ACCORDING TO CATEGORY OF RECIPIENT
GREAT BRITAIN

Category of Recipient	Dec. 1949 %	Dec. 1965 %
Assistance paid in supplementation of insurance benefits:		
Retirement Pensions	48·2	59·9
Sickness or industrial injury benefits	7·9	7·5
Widows' benefits	7·5	4·9
Unemployment benefit	2·6	1·7
Assistance paid in supplementation of non-contributory old age pensions	8·5	2·6
Assistance to persons not receiving pensions or benefits:		
Persons registered for employment	3·1	3·9
Persons not registered for employment:		
Persons over pension age	5·4	6·4
Persons under pension age	16·7	13·1

Source: Reports of N.A.B.

between 1951 and 1965. The respective proportions for the two years were 15% and 12% for sickness benefit, 16% and 13% for unemployment benefit and 23% and 17% for widows' benefits. Similarly, the decline in the proportion of non-contributory old age pensions is not due to any less need for supplementation but simply to the numerical decline of this type of pensions. Though insurance beneficiaries account for the majority of assistance allowances – 74% in 1965 – they account for less than half of the expenditure on assistance allowances – 48% in 1965 – simply because the assistance supplements consist of small amounts. On the other hand, the amount of assistance granted to persons not in receipt of insurance benefits is normally the full assistance allowance. Consequently though this group accounts for the minority of assistance allowances, they make up over half of the assistance expenditure.

The number of persons in receipt of assistance who were not entitled to any insurance benefit or the old age contributory pension numbered 467,000. Of these between one-third and one-quarter were old people mostly over the age of seventy who were too old to qualify for retirement pension under the National Insurance Act, 1946. A group of 138,000 under retirement age were unfit for work but were not receiving sickness benefit because they were mostly persons who had been incapacitated since childhood. The size of this group does not vary greatly from year to year and they are likely to be on assistance for life. A survey of the group in 1959[1] showed that 61% had been disabled since birth or childhood. The proportion was 96% for mental defectives, 87% for epileptics and 82% for those with paralysis. The great majority (78%) were considered to have no chance of becoming even partly self-supporting, 10% could become partly self-supporting and the remaining 12% had some chance of becoming wholly self-supporting.

A third group which received assistance but did not qualify for insurance benefits consisted of 108,000 women with dependent children, mostly separated wives, divorced women and mothers of illegitimate children. They were only part of the total number of 154,000 such women on assistance. Their numbers declined from 110,000 in 1953 to 93,000 in 1957 and then rose consistently to their present size. There is no official estimate of the number of

[1] N.A.B. Report 1959 Cmd. 1085 App. X.

separated wives but using Wynn's estimate that they numbered 365,000 with divorced and unmarried mothers in 1961, about one-third of the group were drawing assistance in that year.[1] The size of the group that draws assistance depends partly on the size of the family, for the larger the number of children in a family the greater the possibility that the family will draw assistance. It also depends on whether there is a maintenance or affiliation court order in force, the amount of the order and to what extent it is complied with. The proportion of separated wives and of mothers of illegitimate children on assistance with a maintenance or affiliation order or with an out of court agreement for maintenance has improved from 38% in 1957 to 50% in 1965. Part of this improvement is due to the extension in 1961 of the Legal Aid Scheme to maintenance and affiliation proceedings in Magistrates Courts which made it easier financially for women to prosecute deserting husbands or putative fathers. The proportion of maintenance and affiliation orders and out of court agreements of women on assistance which are complied with has shown little change in spite of the Maintenance Orders Act, 1958 which authorised Courts to make attachment orders so that employers could deduct the amount of a maintenance or affiliation order from a man's earnings if he failed to comply with the order. In 1957, no payments were made in 23·5% of maintenance and affiliation orders and out of court agreements; in 18·5% irregular payments were made; and in 58% payments were made regularly. In 1965 the proportions were 29%, 11% and 60% respectively.

The 1948 Act enabled the National Assistance Board to apply to courts for maintenance and affiliation orders against men who neglected to maintain their dependents on assistance. The Board's policy, however, has been to encourage women to make their own applications for court orders and in only a very small minority of cases, when they are unable or unwilling to take court proceedings, the Board has itself applied for court orders. The Board has taken a more active interest in tracing and prosecuting men who fail to maintain their dependents. In 1965, the Board prosecuted 594 such men of whom 244 were sent to prison. From the financial point of view it is clear that this aspect of the Board's work is a liability. The time and money spent to trace and prosecute men and maintain those sent to prison far exceeds the

[1] Margaret Wynn, *Fatherless Families*, p. 24, Michael Joseph, 1964.

amount of money gained in maintenance contributions. Nevertheless, the Board has considered this necessary 'not only to bring home to the man his liability to maintain his dependents but also to deter other would-be offenders'.[1]

The existing system of making and enforcing maintenance and affiliation orders places far too much responsibility and work on the women who have enough worries in caring alone for their families. Several suggestions have been made for transferring a great deal more of this responsibility to the state, i.e., the Ministry of Social Security or the Inland Revenue. It is also becoming increasingly clear that the present social security system which makes different provisions for families according to whether they became fatherless through widowhood on one hand or desertion, divorce and similar circumstances on the other needs revising. Beveridge's suggestion for an end of marriage allowance has so far been ignored because 'Something about the proposal conveys a sense of hedonism – "Leave your husband and get a payment'."[2]

The last main group of those receiving assistance but not qualifying for insurance benefits are the unemployed. Together with the smaller group of unemployed who are receiving unemployment benefit, as well as assistance, they make up about 6% of the total number of persons drawing assistance allowances. In spite of their small numbers, the 1948 Act, following the precedent of previous legislation, provided two extra conditions for granting assistance to them as compared with other applicants. First, assistance is granted to them subject to their registering for employment at the Employment Exchange. The great majority remain on assistance for short periods but there is a small proportion who remain unemployed for long-term periods. Surveys conducted by the N.A.B. confirmed the conclusion drawn in Chapter Five on the problems and characteristics of the long-term unemployed. In conditions of full employment 'the hard core of the unemployed as represented by those who have been maintained for lengthy periods by national assistance consists to a very large extent of unskilled men and women who are under some bodily or mental disability, and that wilful idleness, unconnected with any such disability, accounts for lengthy unemployment in

[1] N.A.B. Report 1965, p. 28.
[2] Alvin L. Schorr, *Alternative in Income Maintenance*, Social Work, Vol. 11, No. 3, July, 1966.

only a small minority of cases'.[1] The large majority of the long-term unemployed are not 'workshy or layabouts sponging on the Welfare State'[2] but people who are anxious to get a job but are prevented by lack of skills or by personal handicaps of a psychological or physical nature or a combination of all. The Board has tried various methods to deal with the problems of the long-term unemployed. First, since 1961 a number are referred for medical examinations every year. This has had the double effect of providing useful information to the Board's officers and of forcing some of the unemployed, who have no good reason to be out of work, to find employment. Second, the Board has allocated a number of officers to specialise in the problems of the long-term unemployed and to try and help them. This is one of the many instances where there is an obvious need for trained social workers in the Ministry of Social Security. Third, the Board has provided a small number of re-establishment centres, two residential and six non-residential in 1966, whose aim is 'not to teach a man a trade but simply to reintroduce him to the habits, routine and demands of a normal working life'.[3] The great majority attend these centres voluntarily though a minority are directed to attend by National Assistance Tribunals.

For the very small minority who are unemployed without good reason and who refuse offers of jobs, the Board can refuse assistance. This may be effective in the case of single persons but it is not practicable in the case of married men because they would live on the assistance granted to their families. The 1948 Act provided two sanctions against those refusing work without good cause: They could be directed to attend a re-establishment centre or they could be prosecuted for failing to maintain themselves and their families by working. The first may be effective for the single but not for the married for refusal to attend a re-establishment centre would mean non-payment of assistance which is not a practicable proposition. Though prosecution is used very sparingly, the number of prosecutions every year has risen from about 50 in the early 1950's to 178 in 1965. The great majority are convicted and one-half to two-thirds are sent to prison.

The second special condition attached to assistance granted to

---

[1] Report 1956, p. 15.
[2] N.A.B. Report Year 1965, Cmd. 3042, p. vii.
[3] Report 1965, p. 33.

an unemployed person is the wages stop, i.e., that the amount of assistance granted must not, unless there are exceptional circumstances, exceed the income he would receive if he were in full-time employment. The annual Reports of the N.A.B. and the Supplementary Benefits Commission have not referred to any cases where the presence of exceptional cricumstances made the use of the wages stop inadvisable. One can only assume from this that the wages stop has been used automatically. Between one-seventh and one-eighth of all unemployed persons receiving assistance have been wage-stopped. The number tends to be higher during years of high unemployment and improvements in assistance scales. The wage stop may also be applied to persons drawing assistance who are suffering from a temporary sickness. In practice this is used for a minority of cases for the first six months of temporary sickness and permission from Headquarters is necessary to extend the wages stop beyond this period. The N.A.B. Reports make no reference to the permissive use of the wages stop for the sick. The first Report of the Ministry of Social Security, however, gives the number of the sick wage stopped as 3,000 out of a total of 25,000 wage-stopped. Obviously the wage-stop affects mostly large families with low incomes with the result that the number of children involved is substantial, 60,000–80,000.

Successive governments have accepted the application of the wages stop as a necessary evil. It follows naturally from the official policy that a man's income while in full-time work need not necessarily be adequate for the maintenance of his family even by national assistance standards. The 1948 Act and the Ministry of Social Security Act, 1966, forbid the payment of assistance to people in full-time work. The result is that official policy has been in a quandary. On the one hand it fears, rightly or wrongly, that if it provides people with social security benefits which are higher than their earnings from full-time work, it might encourage people to remain idle. On the other hand, applying the wages stop means that it forces a number of families to live below subsistence level which is contrary to the very existence of a social security system. The way out to this dilemma must be found on the employment side. Abolishing the wages stop will solve part but not the whole problem. The Government's study showed that in addition to the 15,000 families on assistance who were wage-stopped, there were 70,000 families with 255,000 children with the father in full-time

work whose income was below national assistance standards.[1]
Suggestions put forward from Government members for a system
of 'family endowment' and from the Conservative Opposition for
a 'supplementary family allowance to those whose income is
below a certain figure'[2] are very similar and can both deal satisfactorily with the problem. This is also one of the alternative
suggestions put forward at the end of Chapter Ten.

Apart from the wage-stopped and those with low earnings from
full-time employment, there is also another population group
whose income is below the supplementary benefits level – those
who qualify for supplementary benefits but who do not apply for
them. This is only one aspect of the wider problem of the under-
utilisation of social services in general. Private research first and
government research later established that this group consisted
of about ¾ million retirement pensioners[3] and 75,000 families with
two or more children.[4] The recent publicity of the Supplementary
Benefits Commission has achieved good results but there is still
room for improvement. The suggestion from the Conservative
Opposition that the officers of the Ministry of Social Security
should have a positive duty to seek out and assist those in need
merits favourable consideration. Co-operation with the local
authority personal services as well as with voluntary organisations
needs to be much closer than it is at present. Finally, the public
must be encouraged to question intelligently the decisions of the
officers of the Supplementary Benefits Commission. At present
this is difficult because the Commission's detailed instructions to
its officers in the form of a Code on how to decide various types
of applications for benefit are a departmental secret. This not only
makes it difficult for people to know whether it is worth ques-
tioning the officers' decisions but it also makes it impossible for
the Commission itself to know whether 'its instructions are being
carried out at the local level, since the secrecy of the Code deprives
it of the necessary feed-back from dissatisfied customers and
others acting on their behalf'.[5]

[1] 'Circumstances of Families', Ministry of Social Security, H.M.S.O., 1967.
[2] Miss Mervyn Pike, 2nd Reading Ministry of Social Security Bill, House
of Commons debates, 24 May, 1966.
[3] D. Cole with J. Utting, 'The Economic Circumstances of Old People',
Occasional Papers in Social Administration, No. 4, 1962. 'Financial and Other
Circumstances of Retirement Pensioners'.
[4] 'Circumstances of Families'.
[5] T. Lynes, 'Entitled to Benefit', *The Guardian*, 12 September, 1967.

Chapter Twelve

SOCIAL SECURITY, THE ECONOMY
AND THE STATE

THE nature of the social security scheme depends a great deal on the character of the national economy in which it operates. One of the main reasons for the present government's difficulties in implementing all its pre-election pledges on social security is the failure of the economy to grow at the rate it was envisaged in the National Plan. A growing economy is necessary to provide the wealth to meet the cost of social security as well as of the other government services. It is not only as a financier that the nature of the economy is important to social security. It also affects people's expectations of the standards of social security benefits. The rise in incomes which has been evident for some years will continue in the future though the rate of growth is much in doubt. As incomes rise, people's expectations of the standards of social security benefits will also rise. There is an automatic in-built interrelationship between rising standards of life and rising expectations. Improved standards do not satisfy expectations for ever; they merely prod them on to demand even better standards.

The recent failure of the economy to grow at a rate parallel to the growth of rising expectations and public expenditure has highlighted once again the role of the state in social provision. The Institute of Economic Affairs has recently been the severest critic of the role of the state as a vast Friendly Society providing for all the needs of all its members in adversity. It maintains that government universal social services were necessary when the working classes had neither the economic nor the political power to fend for themselves. Government services were then needed to reduce social suffering and industrial conflict. The liberal economists of the nineteenth century who opposed the intervention of the state in social and economic affairs were wrong because they misread the times. Government intervention on a grand scale was a necessary evil that has outlived its function. Today with the growth of personal incomes, the role of the state must be limited to the bare minimum of helping those who cannot help themselves. The majority of the people can afford to and should be allowed to buy welfare services in the open market in the same way that they buy consumer goods. There is nothing intrinsically different between buying a policy for a retirement pension and a car on hire-purchase.

Though the arguments of the neo-liberal economists apply to all social services we shall restrict our discussion here on social security. Seldon has suggested that national insurance should be wound up and be replaced by a more generous scheme of national assistance for those in need. Retired persons should make income returns and those who are found to be in need should receive assistance payment as of right.[1] Government fiscal and tax policies should encourage people to make private arrangements for retirement pensions and other social security benefits. The decision whether a person should make provision for retirement 'is an intimate, elemental, personal decision, and a free society will not lightly tamper with it'. A more recent statement of the position, however, concedes that it 'may be desirable for the state (a) to require saving of minimum amounts sufficient to enable the saver to avoid dependence on society in retirement and possibly (b) to provide "saving power" for people with low incomes'.[2] These two approaches coming from the same school of thought are substantially different. They illustrate the problems involved in trying to devise a private retirement pension scheme for the entire population. Seldon's approach would mean that the state may be left with the job of providing assistance to considerable numbers of retirement pensioners since there will be no obligation on the working population to insure against old age. The second approach would mean state compulsion for insurance and a state subsidy towards it which is very similar to the position today. The only difference being that instead of a state scheme for all retirement pensioners there will be a multiplicity of retirement pension schemes provided by private insurance companies. Will the insurance companies and their schemes be subjected to govern-

[1] 'Pensions for Prosperity', *Institute of Economic Affairs*, 1960.
[2] 'Towards a Welfare State'. The report of an I.E.A. study group, *Occasional Paper 13*, p. 30, 1957.

ment inspection and control? If they are, state intervention will be just as extensive as it is today but it will assume a different form. If they are not, the state will be subsidising pension schemes over which it has no control.

All the suggestions for dismantling the state social security system have assumed uncritically that real incomes have risen so considerably since the war that the number of people who need 'saving power' from the state must be very small. The limited available evidence, however, shows that there has been very little vertical redistribution of income during the last twenty-five years.[1] Routh's study of the occupational and pay structure during the last fifty years led him to the conclusion that 'the most impressive finding was the rigidity of the inter-class and inter-occupational relationships'.[2] Professor Titmuss's examination of the available statistics on income redistribution exposed their inadequacies. 'Ancient inequalities have assumed new and more subtle forms; conventional categories are no longer adequate for the task of measuring them'.[3] The recent government survey also exploded the prevalent notion that poverty among wage-earners is restricted to large families. Of the 70,000 families with the father in full-time work earning wages below the supplementary benefits level for his family, 25,000 had two children, 20,000 three children and the remaining four or more children.[4]

The real cost of private pension schemes to the community will be higher than the state scheme because of the higher administrative costs involved in running a variety of schemes by numerous insurance societies. The advantages claimed for private schemes are first that they will divert funds into social security from expenditure on consumer goods with the result that they will make more generous provisions. It is true that at present more of the gross national product goes into expenditure on consumer goods than public services but there is no guarantee that young people will decide voluntarily to curtail their immediate expenditure on personal and household goods and spend more on

---

[1] J. L. Nicholson, *Redistribution of income in the United Kingdom in 1959, 1957 and 1953*, Bowes and Bowes, 1965.

[2] G. Routh, *Occupation and Pay in Great Britain*, Cambridge University Press, 1965.

[3] Prof. R. M. Titmuss, *Income Distribution and Social Change*, Allen & Unwin, 3rd impression, p. 199, 1965.

[4] 'Circumstances of Families'.

retirement, an eventuality long ahead in their lives. If retirement
pensions, and other social services need improving why not
finance them through direct and indirect taxation? It has been
argued that increases in direct taxation act as a disincentive to
hard work. There is no evidence for this. The Royal Commission
on Taxation concluded that very few workers 'have sufficient
knowledge of the way they are affected by the tax to be able to
take that factor accurately into account in deciding upon behaviour to work'.[1] They based their conclusion on the evidence
of a survey conducted on their behalf by the Government Social
Survey. The argument of tax incentives to greater work effort is
based on the assumption that workers are in a position to influence
the amount of their earnings either by more overtime or higher
productivity. In fact as the Royal Commission pointed out 'a large
proportion of the body of manual wage-earners is unable to
achieve any direct increase of earnings by working harder or
faster'.[2] There are also those who are not so much concerned with
the effects of the taxation system on the millions of wage-earners
and salaried persons but with the effects on the small minority of
wealth creators.[3] This elite minority is held back from taking
financial and business risks and from opposing conventional
business methods by the financial insecurity imposed upon them
by the taxation system. These are the people with incomes of
£5,000 a year or more. All concepts are relative, but even then it is
difficult to understand how people earning such sums can be said
to be financially insecure. Apart from this there is no real evidence
that business men's performance is in fact affected by the taxation
system or that it is motivated solely by economic considerations.
The effects of the taxation system on the will to work are not
known. They are overestimated or underestimated according to
the political and moral beliefs of the writer. In the last resort, the
amount of revenue collected through direct and indirect taxation
rests on political and not economic considerations.

Second, private social security schemes will encourage personal
choice and do away with the stigma attached to the receipt of
state benefits. This sounds plausible but it is false because it is

[1] Royal Commission on The Taxation of Profits and Income, 2nd Report,
Cmd. 9105, p. 14, 1954.
[2] ibid., p. 15.
[3] R. H. Grierson, 'The Case for Incentives Now', *The Times*, 11 October,
1967.

based on the premise that all citizens have equal purchasing power
to enable them to buy the type of social security that they prefer
best. In fact the result will be that people's choice of social
security scheme will be limited by the amount of income they
have and by whether they constitute 'bad risks' for the insurance
societies. The stigma attached to the receipt of benefits from
certain schemes will increase and vice-versa the social esteem of
of other exclusive schemes for the wealthy will rise. There is
enough evidence of this happening in the States and in Canada.[1]

Third, it will encourage private enterprise and it will restrain
the growth of state influence in social and economic policy. This
is a matter of political philosophy but even the Economist
warned that it is 'a mistake to suggest that a peculiar moral
splendour automatically attaches to any act conceived in individual economic independence and a peculiar moral obloquy to
the use of any public services'.[2]

None of the three main political parties has accepted the
arguments of the choice in welfare school. As Professor Marsh
has said, however, they have 'contributed most to the thinking
about the ways in which citizens ought and could be provided
with a choice in welfare'.[3] There was remarkable agreement
between the Labour and the Conservative parties on almost all
issues of social security for a number of years after the Beveridge
Report. In the 1960's, however, they have showed some important differences. They are still agreed on the desirability of the
existing social security benefits. They disagree, however, on the
administration of the graduated retirement pension scheme and
on the level and scope of the flat-rate benefits. They both intend
to abolish the present graduated retirement pension scheme which
is an uneasy compromise between the state and private enterprise.
The Conservatives will replace it with a more generous earnings
related scheme run by the employers, financed by the employers
and employees and supervised by the state. It will have to meet
minimum standards set by the state and it will ensure preservation
of pension rights for those changing jobs.[4] It is not clear, how-

---

[1] Prof. R. M. Titmuss, 'Choice and the Welfare State', *Fabian tract* 370, 1967.
[2] *The Economist*, 25 June, 1960 commenting on Seldon's 'Pensions for
Prosperity'.
[3] Prof D. C. Marsh, 'The Welfare State and Choice in Welfare', *Social
Service Quarterly*, Summer, 1966.
[4] Sir Keith Joseph, *The Times*, 17 November, 1965.

ever, what level of earnings-related benefit the new scheme will provide. The Labour government is still committed to the state, universal, half-pay on retirement scheme put forward in 1957 and hopes to have it on the statute book 'before the end of the present Parliament'.[1] Both the Conservative and the Labour plans hope to encourage employers to make additional pension provisions for their workers over and above the required state minimum.

Comparison between the two plans on economic considerations shows the Conservative to be superior to the Labour plan on one count and inferior on two. It is superior in the fact that contributions to the fund are likely to be invested more profitably by employers and insurance companies than by the state. This has been the case so far but there is no reason why the state should not be able to invest just as profitably as insurance companies. It is inferior because first, it will involve higher administrative costs as it will depend on so many firms and insurance companies and as retirement pensioners will be drawing pensions from the state and from other sources. Second, it will involve an element of risk in that some firms may go bankrupt or they may be unable to pay pensions indefinitely at a level which will keep their real value against inflation. How many firms can guarantee that they will be able to meet unspecified amounts for retirement pensions either because of post retirement inflation or because of real improvements in the standard of pensions? If they are to provide real security, retirement pensions have to be increased to keep up with the rise in prices and also to keep up with the rise in the economic prosperity of the country. There is also the additional fear that firms might tend to avoid employing workers who are considered bad insurance risks. Legislation can easily force employers to make pension provisions for all their employees but it will find it difficult to compel employers to employ people whom they do not consider satisfactory workers.

The choice between the Labour and Conservative plans, however, is fundamentally a matter of political beliefs concerning the role of the state in social policy. If the state is left to administer the flat-rate scheme only, the impression which exists among some

[1] Letter from Mrs Hart, Minister of Social Security, to Mr Woodcock, General Secretary of the T.U.C., published in *The Guardian,* 1 September, 1967.

sections of the middle and upper classes that state social security is something for the poor will be made even stronger. Vice-versa the impression of the supposed superiority of private over state provision will be strengthened. To those who believe that the state has a duty to make adequate provisions for all its citizens, social security schemes are best provided and administered by the state. Also, those who consider vertical redistribution of income as one of the aims of state social security would 'like to see the lower paid getting somewhat more than their money's worth and the better paid somewhat less'.[1]

The second main disagreement between the two political parties is the level and scope of the flat-rate benefits. It is the argument of universal versus selective benefits. The position of the universalists is clear: Social security benefits must be provided at the same level to all who qualify. Recently, however, there has been a slight change of opinion. Some within the Labour Party have been forced to concede that for economic reasons it is necessary for rises in family allowances to be granted on a selective basis in order to solve the problem of poverty among families of low wage-earners. Lord Collison, Chairman of the Social Insurance and Industrial Welfare Committee of the T.U.C., acknowledged that there is 'no likelihood whatever that any Government could provide money needed to increase the level (of family allowances) if the income of every other family regardless of need has to be increased by the same amount. There is thus a strong case for selective increases which will concentrate available resources where they are needed'.[2]

The selectivists fall into two main groups. Those who hold the extreme view that social security benefits should be paid to those in need only and those who believe that rises in social security benefits should be granted selectively to those in need. Let us look at the two schools of thought separately. The extreme view will result in the abolition of social insurance benefits paid as of right and the extension of national assistance paid after proof of need. Will this, however, mean that national assistance benefits will be financed out of taxation or will the present system of contributions

[1] Brian Abel-Smith, 'Beveridge II: Another Viewpoint', *New Society*, 28 February, 1963.
[2] Lord Collison addressing the T.U.C. Conference as reported in *The Guardian* 6 September, 1967.

continue? From the actuarial point of view both systems of finance are possible though it is illogical to ask people to pay specific contributions which do not carry an automatic qualification to benefits. What will a scheme of national assistance benefits for all in need achieve? It will not achieve any economies in national expenditure for the great majority of people whose incomes are interrupted or cease will need national assistance from the state. There may be a small minority who will not need assistance but the savings made from this group will be more than outweighed by the higher administrative costs of assistance schemes compared with insurance schemes. This will be particularly true if need will be established by the traditional means test. It will also involve the very real danger that it will deter some of those who are in need from applying for assistance. Even if some form of computerised income test is used the administrative costs will still be higher than the present system bearing in mind the complexities of such a system. All in all, abolition of insurance benefits as of right is a totally retrograde step; it involves serious risks to social progress and it has no advantages whatsoever over the existing system of insurance and supplementary benefits.

The second group of selectivists maintain that social insurance benefits should continue to be provided by the state but future increases should be granted on a selective basis to those who need them and not to everybody.[1] At first sight, it appears to be an extension of Lord Collison's view on family allowances. There is, however, one basic difference: Unlike all the other social security benefits, family allowances are paid when there is no interruption or cessation of earnings from work. This means that a large number of families receiving family allowances do not need them at all or do not need them at a higher rate than the present level. The same can not be said, however, of the flat-rate insurance benefits. They were set at a very low level in 1948 and in spite of subsequent improvements, they are by no means generous. Though they have risen faster than prices, they have not risen as fast as earnings. The great majority of people in receipt of insurance benefits have no other incomes of any consequence to enable them to live on reduced rates of benefits. There are also

[1] G. Howe & N. Lamont, 'Policies for Poverty', *Bow Group Memorandum,* 1967.

other objections to paying different rates of benefits according to need. Administratively the scheme will be more involved and more expensive. It is difficult to know whether the rise in administrative costs will be more or less than the savings made by paying differential rates of benefits. It is also difficult to see how it is possible to keep an up to date account of the incomes of all families to enable insurance benefits to be paid promptly and accurately. Income tax returns made annually and income returns from employers made weekly or monthly are not sufficient. The first are out of date and the second do not always cover all the income of a family. Second, what income will be taken into account when deciding what rate of benefit should be paid to an applicant? Will the earnings of his wife or single children living with him be taken into account? Will such a scheme also take into account all the applicant's savings or will it disregard some in the same way as the present scheme of supplementary benefits? Third, how many grades of benefit rates will there be? What effect will this have on personal savings? These and other similar problems and difficulties make it abundantly clear that any attempt to pay different rates of social insurance benefits according to the recipients' needs will result in administrative chaos without any apparent savings to the Exchequer.

Social insurance benefits are best provided universally on economic grounds, on administrative convenience and on principles of social cohesion. This does not mean that selectivity has no place in social provision. A number of social service benefits are already provided on a selective basis – rate rebates, home help service, school meals, grants for University students, etc. In a complex and comprehensive system of social services there is a place for both universal and selective benefits. The current public discussion on universal versus selective social service benefits must be conducted on a pragmatic basis to ascertain which services are best provided universally and which should be provided on a selective basis without deterring or offending the dignity of the groups who are entitled to them. As Professor Titmuss has said the real question that society has to decide is 'what particular infrastructure of universalist services is needed in order to provide a framework of values and opportunity bases within and around which can be developed acceptable selective services, provided, as social rights, on criteria of the needs of specific categories, groups and territorial areas and not dependent on individual tests of means?'[1]

The social security system must be examined not only in relation to the other social services but to the economic system of the country. It was pointed out earlier that very little vertical redistribution of income has taken place since the last war. We need to know in a detailed manner the ways in which the economic system opens or closes doors of opportunity to people of different social classes. If it is established that the children of the poor today have no option but to become the impoverished parents of tomorrow, then state intervention is needed to make the social services more vertically redistributive and to break down the rigid barriers that have become institutionalised in the country's economic system.

[1] Prof. R. M. Titmuss, 'Universal or Selective', *New Statesman,* 15 September, 1967.

APPENDICES

Analysis of Public Expenditure

United Kingdom – £ Million

Type of Service	1955 Amount	1955 % of Public Expenditure	1965 Amount	1965 % of Public Expenditure
1. Military Service	1537	24·8	2095	16·6
2. Civil Service	30	0·5	26	0·2
3. External Relations	135	2·2	301	2·4
4. Roads & Public Lighting	135	2·2	428	3·4
5. Transport & Communication	217	3·5	577	4·6
6. Employment Services	25	0·4	43	0·3
7. Other Industry & Trade	483	7·8	1012	8·0
8. Research	34	0·5	154	1·2
9. Agriculture, Forestry & Food	188	3·0	336	2·7
10. Housing	532	8·6	934	7·4
11. Water, Sewage & Refuse	117	1·9	255	2·0
12. Public Health Services	14	0·2	34	0·3
13. Land Drainage & Coast Protection	15	0·2	26	0·2
14. Parks, Pleasure Grounds, etc.	27	0·4	68	0·5
15. Miscellaneous environmental	67	1·1	173	1·4
16. Libraries, Museums & Arts	17	0·3	50	0·4
17. Police	91	1·5	211	1·7
18. Prisons	10	0·2	36	0·3
19. Parliament & Law Courts	17	0·3	48	0·4
20. Fire Service	23	0·4	53	0·4
21. Education	549	8·9	1567	12·4
22. National Health Service	579	9·4	1269	10·0
23. Local Welfare Services	19	0·3	57	0·5
24. Child Care	21	0·3	43	0·3
25. School Meals, Milk & Welfare Food	82	1·3	130	1·0
26. Social Security	993	16·1	2413	19·1
27. Finance & Tax Collection	99	1·6	155	1·2
28. Other Services	125	2·0	104	0·8
TOTAL PUBLIC EXPENDITURE	6183	100·0	12598	100·0

N.B. Items 21–26 inclusive are officially classified as Social Services.

PROSPECTS OF FINDING EMPLOYMENT ACCORDING TO SEX AND MARITAL STATUS

	Should get work without difficulty	Will find difficulty in getting work because of:						Total
		Lack of local opportunities	Inadequate Qualifications	Age	Physical and Mental Condition	Attitude to Work	Other[a] Personal Reasons	
Men	52,920	37,110	3,280	54,790	47,960	24,380	16,080	236,520
Married Women	9,900	11,190	1,030	3,280	4,020	2,750	9,280	41,450
Single Women	9,690	5,660	800	5,110	8,060	2,170	3,470	34,960
Men and Women	72,510	53,960	5,110	63,180	60,040	29,300	28,830	312,930

PROSPECTS OF SECURING EMPLOYMENT AND DURATION OF CURRENT SPELL SINCE LAST EMPLOYMENT

No. of weeks since last employment	%	%	%	%	%	%	%	%
Up to 8 weeks	77.8	37.5	33.3	20.6	19.8	17.5	30.6	37.5
9–26 weeks	14.9	24.2	25.2	19.3	15.3	20.2	22.2	18.8
27–52 weeks	4.0	14.2	12.9	17.4	13.6	14.8	15.9	12.6
53–104 weeks	1.7	12.5	11.5	18.3	15.7	18.6	13.6	12.5
105–199 weeks	0.7	6.4	8.2	15.6	16.4	15.0	8.9	9.9
200 and over	0.8	5.1	8.8	8.7	19.1	13.9	8.8	8.7

Source: Ministry of Labour Gazette, April 1966, Adapted from Tables 1 and 3.

(a) The main reasons included in this heading are: Prison Record, Colour, Lack of English, Restriction on Availability for Work and Lack of Financial Incentive.

Appendix III

SPELLS OF SICKNESS TERMINATING IN THE YEAR MAY 1962–MAY 1963 PER
100 INSURED PERSONS IN THE AGE-GROUP – GREAT BRITAIN

Age-Group	Not over 2	Duration of Spells in Weeks Over 2 and less than 13	Over 13 and less than 26	Over 26 and less than 52	Over 52	All Durations
Employed Men						
15–29	28·7	10·9	0·5	0·2	0·1	40·4
30–44	25·5	15·3	0·8	0·3	0·1	42·0
45–59	20·4	21·1	1·6	0·6	0·4	44·1
60–64	17·5	29·0	2·6	1·0	1·1	51·2
15–64	24·2	17·0	1·1	0·4	0·3	43·0
Employed Single Women						
15–29	36·7	14·9	0·5	0·2	0·1	52·4
30–44	19·6	17·3	1·1	0·6	0·3	38·9
45–59	14·8	20·0	1·6	0·6	0·5	37·5
15–59	29·2	16·4	0·9	0·3	0·2	47·0
Employed Married Women						
15–29	22·2	18·1	1·3	0·4	0·2	42·2
30–44	22·7	23·0	1·9	0·6	0·6	48·8
45–59	18·0	29·6	2·1	0·8	0·8	51·3
15–59	21·2	22·0	1·6	0·6	0·4	45·8
Self-Employed Men						
15–29	7·1	8·3	0·5	0·1	0·1	16·1
30–44	4·5	7·2	0·6	0·2	0·1	12·6
45–59	3·7	9·1	1·2	0·6	0·3	13·9
60–64	2·4	11·5	2·0	0·9	0·6	17·4
15–64	4·1	8·8	1·0	0·4	0·3	14·6

Source: *Third Quinquennial Review*, Table 32.

Appendix IV

	£	s.	d.
Unemployment or sickness benefit:			
Adults	4	10	0
Married women (normal rate)	3	2	0
Persons under 18	2	10	0
Retirement pension:			
Insured person or widow	4	10	0
Uninsured wife of retirement pensioner	2	16	0
Increases for dependants (where payable):			
Wife or other dependent adult	2	16	0
First or only dependent child	1	5	0
Second or third dependent child		17	0
Each other child		12	0
Widow's benefit:			
Widow's allowance (first 26 weeks of widowhood)	6	7	0
Increase for first or only dependent child	2	2	6
Increase for second dependent child	1	14	6
Increase for third dependent child	1	12	6
Increase for each other child	1	7	6
Widowed mother's allowance	4	10	0
Increase for first or only dependent child	2	2	6
Increase for second dependent child	1	14	6
Increase for third dependent child	1	12	6
Increase for each other dependent child	1	7	6
Widow's pension	4	10	0
Maternity benefit:			
Maternity allowance	4	10	0
Child's special allowance:			
First dependent child	2	2	6
Second dependent child	1	14	6
Third dependent child	1	12	6
Each other dependent child	1	7	6
Guardian's allowance	2	2	6
Death Grant (lump sum) Persons over 18	30	0	0
Persons under 3	9	0	0
Injury benefit	7	5	0

Appendix IV

	£	s.	d.
Disablement benefit (100% assessment)	7	12	0
Unemployability supplement	4	10	0
Special hardship allowance (maximum)	3	1	0
Constant attendance allowance (normal maximum)	3	0	0

Increases for dependants payable at the same rates as for unemployment and sickness benefit.

Industrial death benefit:

	£	s.	d.
Widow's pension during first 26 weeks of widowhood	6	7	0
Widow's pension	5	1	0
Allowance for first or only dependent child	2	2	6
Allowance for second dependent child	1	14	6
Allowance for third dependent child	1	12	6
Allowance for each other dependent child	1	7	6

SCALES OF SUPPLEMENTARY BENEFITS, NOVEMBER 1967

	£	s.	d.
For a husband and wife	7	1	0
For a single householder	4	6	0

For other persons:

	£	s.	d.
aged 21 or over	3	11	0
aged 18–20	2	18	0
aged 16–17	2	10	0
aged 11–15	1	17	0
aged 5–10	1	10	0
aged under 5	1	5	0

MAIN WEEKLY RATES OF FLAT-RATE CONTRIBUTIONS

1. Employed Persons (Other than those contracted out of the Graduated Scheme).

	National Insurance		Industrial Injuries Insurance		National Health Service		Redundancy Fund (Employer only)	Combined Contributions		
	Employed Person	Employer	Employed Person	Employer	Employed Person	Employer		Employed Person	Employer	Total
	s. d.	s. d.	s. d.	s. d.	s. d.	s. d.	s. d.	s. d.	s. d.	s. d.
Men over 18	12 1½	13 7½	10	11	2 8½	7½	10	15 8	16 0	31 8
Women over 18	10 6½	11 10½	7	8	2 0½	7½	5	13 2	13 7	26 9
Boys under 18	8 3½	9 2½	5	5	1 4½	7½	—	10 1	10 3	20 4
Girls under 18	6 9½	7 7½	3	4	1 4½	7½	—	8 5	8 7	17 0

2. Employed Persons Contracted Out of the Graduated Scheme

	National Insurance		Industrial Injuries Insurance		National Health Service		Redundancy Fund (Employer only)	Combined Contributions		
	Employed Person	Employer	Employed Person	Employer	Employed Person	Employer		Employed Person	Employer	Total
	s. d.	s. d.	s. d.	s. d.	s. d.	s. d.	s. d.	s. d.	s. d.	s. d.
Men contracted out	14 6½	16 0½	10	11	2 8½	7½	10	18 1	18 5	36 6
Women contracted out	12 0½	13 4½	7	8	2 0½	7½	5	14 8	15 1	29 9

3. Self-Employed Persons

	National Insurance	National Health Service	Total Combined Contribution
	s. d.	s. d.	s. d.
Men over 18	18 2	2 10	21 0
Women over 18	15 1	2 2	17 3
Boys under 18	10 4	1 6	11 10
Girls under 18	8 7	1 6	10 1

4. Non-Employed Persons

	National Insurance	National Health Service	Total Combined Contribution
	s. d.	s. d.	s. d.
Men over 18	13 9	2 10	16 7
Women over 18	10 9	2 2	12 11
Boys under 18	7 10	1 6	9 4
Girls under 18	6 1	1 6	7 7

In addition to the above flat-rate contributions, there are the earnings-related contributions paid by Employed Persons and their Employers. These were explained in Chapter Three, pages 53–56.

INDEX

251

INDEX OF PERSONS

For Product Safety Concerns and Information please contact our EU
representative GPSR@taylorandfrancis.com
Taylor & Francis Verlag GmbH, Kaufingerstraße 24, 80331 München, Germany

www.ingramcontent.com/pod-product-compliance
Lightning Source LLC
Chambersburg PA
CBHW070352270326
41926CB00014B/2515